Later in the day Lieutenant Greengold was stunned to hear reports of the massive Arab attack. . . . Soon he was put in charge of a makeshift platoon of two hastily repaired tanks and told to head south along the Tapline Road to join up with the Barak Brigade at the front. His tiny command was dubbed "Zwicka Force."

Over the next twenty-four hours, Lieutenant Greengold fought against an advancing Syrian armored brigade, at times with nothing more than his own tank. During the night, he maneuvered deftly between advancing enemy units, using the terrain to mask his sudden appearances in the midst of Syrian tank columns. Surviving the destruction of his own tank, he leaped out, wounded and burning, rolled in the dirt to put out the flames, and commandeered another tank to continue the fight. Outnumbered fifty to one during most of the night, Zwicka succeeded in destroying at least twenty enemy tanks himself while he disrupted and defeated several advancing columns. Zwicka's obstinate defense convinced the Syrians that they were up against a formidable Israeli tank force, delaying their advance during the critical hours of that first night. In the early hours of the war, when the fate of Israel hung in the balance, Zwicka and many others like him battled with a determination and skill that bought the time so desperately needed to bring up reinforcements and save the front.

—From "Soldiers of Gideon: The Defense of the Golan, October 1973" by Lt. Col. Robert R. Leonhard in *By Their Deeds Alone*

BY THEIR DEEDS
ALONE

America's Combat Commanders
on the Art of War

Edited by
Richard D. Hooker Jr.

PRESIDIO
PRESS

BALLANTINE BOOKS • NEW YORK

A Presidio Press Book
Published by The Random House Publishing Group
Compilation copyright © 2003 by Richard D. Hooker Jr.
Foreword copyright © 2003 by Rick Atkinson

" 'I Order You to Die': Kemal at Gallipoli" © 2003 by Michael R. Fenzel
"Epic at Narvik: The 3d Mountain Division in Norway"
© 2003 by Richard D. Hooker Jr.
"The Ghost Division: The 7th Panzer Division in France" © 2003 by Dana J. H. Pittard
" 'A Most Daring Enterprise': The Conquest of Fortress Singapore"
© 2003 by John F. Antal
" 'Flashing Sword of Vengeance': The Kharkov Counteroffensive"
© 2003 by H. R. McMaster
" 'By Their Deeds Alone': The 4th Armored Division at Nancy-Arracourt"
© 2003 by Peter R. Mansoor
"Soldiers of Gideon: The Defense of the Golan, October 1973"
© 2003 by Robert R. Leonhard
" 'Action Front': The 2d Dragoons at 73 Easting" © 2003 by John K. Tien
"African Holocaust: The Rwandan Civil War" © 2003 by James R. McDonough
"Face of the Future: The Russian Assault on Grozny" © 2003 by John F. Antal
"In and Out of Africa: Noncombatant Evacuation Operations in Liberia"
© 2003 by Daniel P. Bolger

Presidio Press and colophon are trademarks of Random House, Inc.

www.ballantinebooks.com

Library of Congress Control Number: 2003107223

ISBN 0-89141-807-5

Cover image © Getty Images

Manufactured in the United States of America

First Edition: December 2003

10 9 8 7 6 5 4 3 2 1

Contents

Foreword

No less an authority than George S. Patton Jr. believed every officer "must be so soaked in military lore that he does the military thing automatically." For Patton that meant studying the past, not to prepare for the last war or to refight old battles, but rather to draw both tactical lessons and inspiration from history. The past is a torch with the power to illuminate the future, making events, if not quite foreseeable, at least more comprehensible as they unfold.

The eleven battles recounted in this volume are unified by neither time nor space. Although all occurred in the twentieth century, they span more than eight decades, from 1915 to 1996. The action unfolds on three continents, on battlefields as disparate as Singapore is from Norway and Turkey is from Rwanda. Three of the tales—and each chapter is first and foremost a good yarn—focus on the German military; three involve the Americans; and the others recount exploits of the British, Japanese, Israelis, Russians, and Rwandans. The battles range from company actions to the clash of army groups. Most but not all show outnumbered forces overcoming steep odds to win. Action ranges from conventional tank shoot-outs to a "noncombatant evacuation operation," the sort of quasi-battle that has become so commonplace in the wake of the Cold War.

What *does* unify the chapters is the common denominator of capable leadership making the difference between victory and defeat. And what leaders! Here we see the young Erwin Rommel, commanding from the front, as usual, ushering his 7th Panzer Division across the Meuse River to unhinge French defenses in 1940; or Tomoyuki Yamashita, another first-echelon commander, conquering impregnable Singapore with a force half that of his British adversaries; or Paul Kagame, a willowy, introverted Tutsi colonel who masters both guerrilla and conventional warfare in central Africa. It is this depiction of leaders leading well that gives the eleven episodes a powerful coherence, allowing each to surmount its particulars in showing us something universal and timeless.

What's more, the authors have provided many fine brush-strokes of detail that bring their stories and characters to life. We see Gen. Ian Hamilton in pajamas on his flagship at Gallipoli, a worthless travelogue and obsolete treatise on the Turkish army in his briefcase. We see British soldiers struggling ashore at Narvik with thirty-five pieces of winter gear apiece, perplexed when office furniture lands before artillery shells. We see: Japanese infantrymen bicycling through Malaya to forestall traffic congestion; Israeli tank crews chalking "Damascus" on their hulls; Rommel firing houses along the Meuse as an improvised smoke screen; five truckloads of Chartres cognac delivered to U.S. 4th Infantry Division troops, each of whom also received two cigars; a special forces helicopter landing under fire on an embassy basketball court in Liberia, rotor blades chopping away the encroaching tree branches.

When civilians read or write military history, the genre often seems akin to an adventure story. Valor, vainglory, fear, audacity, good luck, bad luck—all are threads woven into a tapestry showing humans engaged in that most terribly human enterprise, war. But when military professionals read or write military history, it can also have the transcendent power of a morality tale, illuminating the profound consequences of good, bad, or indifferent leadership. The soldier-scholars who wrote these eleven chapters are never prescriptive; there is no blueprint pulled from the past that serves for the future. Collectively the authors have more than two centuries of military experience—as combat commanders, planners, thinkers, and teachers—and they know with the wisdom of veterans that yesterday never returns neatly as tomorrow. Yet they are not reluctant to draw lessons and to assert the latter-day pertinence of those lessons. Those seeking to do "the military thing automatically"—or to better understand what the "military thing" is—will find revelation in these pages.

Rick Atkinson

Preface

It is a curious fact of the military profession that its practitioners so rarely practice their craft. Many an able and successful soldier has served for decades and never heard a shot fired in anger. And while we may strive to bring realism to the training ground, the simple truth is that, despite our best efforts, battle and combat defy simulation to a remarkable degree. Battlefield noises, problems of terrain and weather, and the stress of decision making under complex conditions are things we can reproduce fairly simply. But replicating the enormous burden of leading in combat, where the price of failure can be almost incalculable, is beyond us. For centuries, commanders have therefore turned to military history as one way of overcoming the lack of battle experience. Just as the physician begins with the study of anatomy, the soldier must look to the history of battle if he is to approach, however indirectly, some understanding of the problems of battle command.

Or so one might think. Yet it is another curious fact of the military profession, at least as practiced in the United States, that a thorough grounding in military history is unusual. In a profession where business and management degrees are commonplace, the military historian is rare. This volume represents an attempt to encourage interest in military history as the wellspring of military professionalism. While only the uninitiated should think that past battles can tell commanders "what to do" in future ones, an intimate grasp of the history of battles and campaigns is clearly an invaluable tool for leaders thrust into the maelstrom of combat in the twenty-first century.

A fascinating dimension to *By Their Deeds Alone* is that its contributing authors are fighting men themselves. When H. R. McMaster writes about Kharkov, he knows something about the subject, because he personally demolished an Iraqi tank battalion at 73 Easting. John Tien and Dana Pittard fought on those same battlefields, as did Mike Fenzel—who appears in Dan Bolger's gripping account of the Liberia rescue mission as commander of the

Embassy Security Force in war-torn Monrovia. There are no dry academics here.

If there is one thread, one theme running through these stories, it is that *leadership*—not machines, not doctrine, not even logistics—is the supreme element in war. Successful commanders throughout history won because they imposed their will on their units, on the enemy, on the battle itself. To make good decisions under extreme stress—when one's own life, the lives of one's soldiers, and perhaps even the life of the nation itself are at stake—is perhaps the most difficult of human tasks. If future commanders—and the citizens who lead, support, or encourage them—take this message to heart, then this book will have served its purpose.

By Their Deeds Alone has been a labor of love chiefly because of its authors. Soldiers and scholars both, their quiet professionalism and love of country are both inspiring and reassuring. If, as I suspect, many of them become senior leaders in our armed forces, then the nation can look forward with the confident assurance that its army will be ready and its sons and daughters in uniform will be cared for well. For their friendship and comradeship I will always be grateful.

I am deeply indebted to all those who offered encouragement, helpful criticism, and constructive comments. Special thanks are due to: Rick Atkinson; Col. Mike Meese; Maj. Fred Hellwig; Col. (Ret.) Andy Berdy; Maj. Gen. Bill Caldwell; Col. (Ret.) Joe Collins; Maj. Gen. Rick Olson; Brig. Gen. (Ret.) Mitchell Zais; Col. (Ret.) Ladd Patillo; Brig. Gen. John Allen, USMC; and Capt. Harry Harris, USN. I particularly wish to thank Col. John Antal for his many years of wisdom, mentorship, and inspiration.

Finally, I absolve the authors of any errors of fact or interpretation that may have escaped my editorial eye. Any credit that may accrue from this book must go to them. I accept full responsibility for the rest.

Richard D. Hooker Jr.
Washington, D.C.

"I Order You to Die": Kemal at Gallipoli

How many armies have sworn to conquer or perish? How many have kept their oath?

—Ardant du Picq

On 25 April 1915, Allied forces began to land on the narrow beaches below Gaba Tepe on the Gallipoli peninsula, not far from the fabled Plains of Troy. From the high ground of Sari Bair above, a small band of Turkish infantry watched in terror, mesmerized at the sight of the British fleet disgorging its cargo. As the first Australian patrols approached, the peasant soldiers defending the heights began to stream to the rear. At that moment, a lean-faced, mustachioed Turkish colonel galloped up, his face a mask of utter disdain. "Where are you going?" he shouted. "Fix your bayonets and face the enemy!" The soldiers of the Turkish 19th Infantry Division obeyed instantly, for they knew their fiery commander well. Though unknown to the outside world, he would rise to greatness as the savior and father of the modern Turkish state. His name was Mustafa Kemal.

In the summer of 1915 the Allies—France, Britain, and Russia—faced stalemate and possible defeat on the continent of Europe at the hands of Germany and Austria. The nightmare of trench warfare had already settled over the battlefield in the west, while in the east the Russians had suffered catastrophes at Tannenberg and the Masurian Lakes. Seeking to break the stalemate, British First Lord of the Admiralty Winston Churchill suggested Gallipoli as a likely place to strike back with British sea power.

The Gallipoli peninsula, located on the northeastern corner of the Aegean Sea, controlled the approaches to the Dardanelles

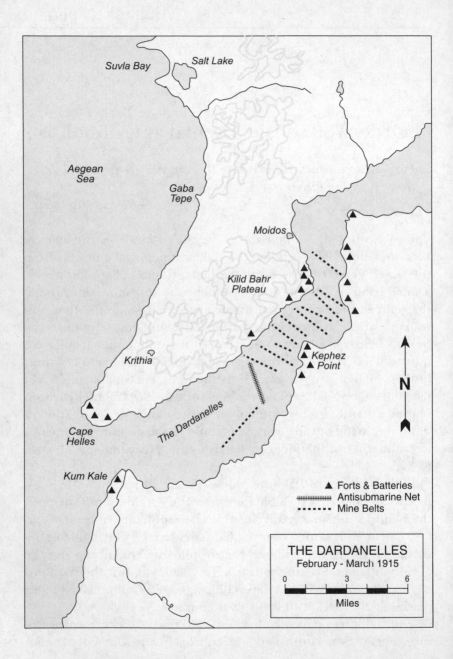

Suvla Bay

Salt Lake

Aegean
Sea

Gaba
Tepe

Moidos

Kilid Bahr
Plateau

Krithia

Kephez
Point

The Dardanelles

Cape
Helles

Kum Kale

N

▲ Forts & Batteries
⊞⊞⊞⊞ Antisubmarine Net
┅┅┅ Mine Belts

THE DARDANELLES
February - March 1915

0   3   6

Miles

Straits, Constantinople, and ultimately the Black Sea. For the Allies, control of the Dardanelles would open a sea-lane to key ports in Russia and, it was hoped, help encircle Germany. With Churchill its passionate advocate, the Gallipoli operation was given the grudging support of Lord Horatio Kitchener, the British war minister, who was always reluctant to draw forces away from the main theater of war. At first the British, with French support, attempted to force the Na on the Asiatic side with naval forces alone. When that failed with the loss of four warships, the Allies planned an amphibious assault to take the barren peninsula.

General Sir Ian Hamilton, a Kitchener protégé and veteran of the Boer War, commanded the Allied effort. Experienced, highly intellectual, and gentlemanly to a fault, the sixty-two-year-old Hamilton was known throughout the British army as a brilliant soldier and must have seemed an inspired choice. Hamilton's forces initially totaled some 80,000 troops and 118 guns, supported by powerful naval forces. The ground force consisted of two divisions of untested Australians and New Zealanders (30,000 men) under Lt. Gen. Sir William Birdwood, the regular army 29th Division (19,000 men) commanded by Lt. Gen. Sir Aylmer Hunter-Weston, the Royal Naval Division (11,000 men) led by Major General Paris, a French contingent of roughly division size commanded by General d'Amade, and service troops.[1]

Hamilton's opposite number was *Generalleutnant* Limon von Sanders, a distinguished German officer of strong leadership qualities and stable temperament. Sanders was a man of impressive authority with the trained habit of command. At Gallipoli he commanded the Ottoman Fifth Army, six divisions strong, drawn from all over the Ottoman Empire and stiffened by German staff officers and commanders. Two divisions protected the Asiatic shore, buttressed by German gunners under a German admiral. Another two guarded the Bulair lines to the north at the neck of the Gallipoli peninsula. One was stationed at Cape Helles, at the southern tip. The last was Kemal's division, posted in the center of the peninsula on the high ground running across its spine, ready to move wherever the Allies gained a foothold.[2] Watching von Sanders and his frighteningly efficient staff officers, members of the young Turkish officer corps, who had taken over the ailing government, were convinced that "it was not these generals who would lose."[3]

Mustafa Kemal was a study in contrasts. Brooding, driven, passionate, the young lieutenant colonel had just returned from Salonika. Trained at a formal military school in Turkey, his life's desire was to achieve military success and then use it as a springboard to political power. No dilettante, Kemal had served in the 1909 officer's mutiny and in campaigns in Albania, Tripolitania, and the Balkans—all of which enhanced his reputation in military circles.[4] A difficult subordinate who was proud, willful, and obstinate, Kemal possessed genuine military talent and was not afraid of responsibility. To his credit, von Sanders recognized these gifts and overlooked Kemal's abrasive personality.

Recalled from unimportant duties in the backwaters of the empire, Kemal had commanded in the area years before and was familiar with the unforgiving terrain and craggy cliffs that sliced into the Aegean. He wasted no time in readying his forces. The rumor spreading through Constantinople was that the Allies were going to attempt to breach the Dardanelles with a naval force. Pushing his men relentlessly, Kemal prepared them and himself for the ordeal that lay ahead.

General Ian Hamilton, though personally selected by Lord Kitchener to command the expedition, was essentially a staff officer, not a battlefield commander. Outstandingly brave as a younger officer in the late-nineteenth-century colonial wars, his greatest moment had come in the Boer War, where, as an acting lieutenant general, he had served as Kitchener's chief of staff. In a military career filled with achievement, Hamilton had never commanded a division or corps in a major campaign. Upon receiving his appointment to command the Mediterranean Expeditionary Force, Hamilton assembled a makeshift staff and left immediately for Gallipoli in HMS *Phaeton,* a Royal Navy cruiser capable of making thirty knots. In his briefcase he carried a travelogue and an out-of-date book on the Turkish army—all the intelligence that could be provided by the Imperial General Staff. He arrived in time to see the naval defeat of 18 March, when three obsolete battleships—

Ocean, Irresistible, and the French *Bouvet*—went to the bottom with more than seven hundred sailors after striking the Turkish minefields.[5]

The Allied forces assembling in the eastern Mediterranean faced daunting obstacles as they readied themselves for the amphibious assault on Gallipoli. No accurate maps or reliable information about the enemy were available. Moreover, with less than a month remaining before the scheduled 25 April landing, none would be forthcoming. None of the Allied troops had been trained in amphibious operations, which were in any case rudimentary since no doctrine or specialized equipment such as assault landing craft existed. The operation was makeshift in every sense of the word. Still, the Allied soldiers and sailors at Gallipoli belonged to professional armies and navies with great experience and strong traditions, and, at least in the beginning, Allied confidence was high.

The Turks Dig In

At the start of the campaign, Gallipoli was garrisoned by eleven forts with seventy-two guns between them, along with floating minefields and antisubmarine nets spread across the Narrows. The heavier guns were sited at Kum Kale and Sedd el Bahr at the mouth of the Straits. The Germans added eight 6-inch howitzer batteries that could change position rapidly and eight searchlights. Another hundred guns were deployed along the peninsula's eastern coast, although only ten were relatively modern and the Turks were short on ammunition.

With an Allied invasion clearly in the wind, von Sanders requested and received reinforcements. He departed Constantinople without his staff on 25 March. Arriving in the town of Gallipoli the next day, he immediately began to prepare to defend the peninsula. Recognizing that he could not defend everywhere, von Sanders predicted that Bulair, at the neck of the peninsula, and the beaches of Kum Kale on the Asiatic side would be the main Allied landing sites. This approach was sound and logical as those places provided the best opportunity to land large land forces and the best chance of moving inland successfully. Perhaps the Allies would have been better off pursuing this course of action.

Nevertheless, the outspoken Kemal disagreed, arguing that the brunt of the invasion would come at the center of the peninsula, at the base of the Sari Bair. He expected the Allies to land midway up the peninsula on the western side (avoiding the artillery massed in the Narrows), advance to clear the high ground, and rupture the Turkish defense without attacking it head-on. At the same time, he predicted the British would make a supporting attack from the southern tip of Gallipoli at Cape Helles and move northward to join the units making the main attack at the peninsula's center.

The Turks finished digging in by the third week in April. All that remained was to wait and watch.

"Now God Be Thanked"

Arriving without a plan, Hamilton and his chief of staff, Major General Braithwaite, extemporized. Hamilton intended to land his best division, the regular army 29th under General Hunter-Weston, on five small beaches at Cape Helles at the extreme southern tip of the peninsula. Ostensibly they were to seize the heights of the most prominent piece of high ground on the peninsula, Achi Baba, located six miles inland. General Birdwood's Australia–New Zealand Army Corps (ANZAC) was to conduct an amphibious assault nearly thirteen miles farther north between Gaba Tepe and the Sari Bair chain of hills. The ANZACs were then expected to clear the enemy in zone through the Sari Bair hills. Their objective was to reach Mal Tepe in the center of the peninsula.

The general idea was that the Turks engaging the 29th Division at Cape Helles would be cut off in their rear by the ANZAC forces. If they succeeded, the hills dominating the strait would then be in Allied hands and the way would be clear for naval forces to move safely through and head for Constantinople. The French force was asked to conduct a diversionary assault at Kum Kale on the Asiatic side of the Dardanelles. The Royal Naval Division was to conduct a similar assault to divert attention at Sedd el Bahr or S-beach, which lay at the base of the peninsula. Significantly, the plan called for the use of the French and Royal Naval Divisions in deception roles, limiting the forces that could be brought to bear for the main effort. If all went well, the Allies expected to control the lower half of the Gallipoli peninsula by the third day of operations.

Hamilton's commanders were hardly united in their enthusiasm for the plan. Hunter-Weston was so pessimistic that he thought the operation ought to be abandoned. Paris thought that it would be difficult enough to land even with the element of surprise, which, given the obvious signs of the Allied buildup, was highly unlikely. Birdwood thought it might be more favorable to go ashore at Bulair. D'Amade desired to go ashore on the Asiatic side, but he was unhappy at being relegated to a secondary role.

In the brief calm before the landings, the soldiers themselves felt the optimism common to all soldiers who have yet to experience combat. To a man they felt a sense of superiority over the Turks, who were thought to be dull, uninspired troops who would run at the sight of Europeans. None of the Allied units had fought on the western front, and the war was still young enough to fill green troops with thoughts of glory and conquest—and England. The spirit of the age was embodied by the young poet Rupert Brooke, whose ringing phrases had captured the imagination of a Britain not yet disillusioned by millions of deaths: "Now God be thanked who has matched us with his hour" might have been the motto of the young men assembled to fight and die at Gallipoli. Serving as a sublieutenant in the Royal Naval Division, Brooke died of fever on the isle of Skyros just before the landing, an ominous portent of what was to come.

The Landings

The landings on 25 April occurred in the early morning hours in no specific order. Each was to occur before the sun rose in order to mask the approach to the beach. On the Asiatic side, the French forces landed southwest of Kum Kale and made their way inland with little resistance. They secured their objective by nightfall. The

Allied force that approached Cape Helles was separated by nearly two miles. Hunter-Weston's 29th Division landed on three western beaches designated W, X, and Y Beaches. General Paris and his Royal Naval Division plodded forth in the black waters toward the southernmost point and landed on S and V Beaches. Well to the north, approaching the beach at the base of Gaba Tepe, was the intrepid but green ANZAC force. The legend of the "Diggers" began there.

The French success at Kum Kale was the only bright spot in an otherwise disastrous first day. In front of V Beach, the Royal Naval Division surged forward with its lead wave of five hundred men in towed boats. Behind them, two thousand more troops were embarked in the *River Clyde,* an obsolete collier towing more small boats on either side. The *River Clyde* was supposed to ground itself close to shore and then off-load its troops into lighters for the rest of the trip to the beach. A thirty-minute bombardment from HMS *Albion* would precede the assault. In the darkness and swirling tides, the *River Clyde* moved well ahead of the boats, and correcting the situation consumed the remainder of the night. It was broad, sunny daylight when the boats began their final approach to the beach. The silence that accompanied them was eerie and unnatural, and the British troops were uneasy as they neared the wire obstacles that marked the shore.

At that moment rifle and machine-gun fire ripped through the first troops to come ashore. The barrage then lifted and focused its fury onto those boats that had yet to unload. The beachhead was a mass of confusion. Casualties mounted alarmingly as the morning wore on. The boats continued doggedly toward shore amid the dead and dying. A British pilot flying three thousand feet overhead reported that the surf had been transformed into bloody red foam fifty meters out to sea. Unaware of the unfolding tragedy, one of the assistant division commanders and his staff approached a boat full of troopers that lay motionless a quarter of a mile from shore. As he pulled alongside he angrily asked the men what they were doing. It was only then that he realized they were all dead.

Only two short miles to the west was the 29th Division, which, like the French, had landed virtually unopposed. Once his forces were ashore, the division commander set the tone for the rest of the day by having his staff prepare the morning tea. There was no advance inland that morning; no reconnaissance patrols were sent forward. Hunter-Weston apparently believed that a successful landing was enough for one day.

At the center of the peninsula the ANZACs glided toward the shore in force. Naval gunfire roared over their heads and slammed into the hillsides as the boats approached the beaches. The first wave encountered only scattered resistance. The small Turkish security detachments along the ridgeline above had not expected to meet the main Allied thrust, and as the ANZACs streamed ashore they broke ranks in terror.

At this point, the terrain was more of an obstacle than the Turks. Landing on a narrow front, many troops were forced to pull themselves up the sheer faces of cliffs by grasping at tree roots and bushes. Boats filled with willing soldiers floated helplessly alongside the precipices of these rock formations. Some individuals and small groups made their way up the winding gullies, while others took to the high ground only to find themselves isolated. Eventually, most would abandon their positions to rejoin the main body of troops packed onto the beach. Inexplicably, no leader on shore showed the drive to move forward. Those patrols that did move inland found themselves gaining momentum as the enemy broke and ran at every encounter.

Mustafa Kemal, commanding the army's reserve division, galloped to a piece of high ground overlooking the ANZAC beaches. At a glance he recognized the danger. The attack was occurring exactly as he had envisioned, but he had no troops with which to stop the Allied invaders. Under orders from the army commander not to move without express permission, Kemal pondered his dilemma as a number of Turkish soldiers in full retreat approached. Kemal galloped into their path, stopped them, and faced them toward the enemy. At once the Australian patrol halted its advance.

"I Order You to Die"

Kemal realized that he must act quickly to prevent the Allied force from breaking out of the beachhead. He sent his orderly to bring the nearest battalion forward at once. As the battalion was being led into position, Kemal confronted its commander, who saluted and said, "Sir, what is it that you ask of us?" Kemal replied fiercely, "I do not order you to attack, I order you to die. In the time which passes until we die other troops and commanders can take our places." Fired with his zeal, the battalion went forward to delay the invaders.[6]

Kemal galloped furiously back to his division command post and ordered his battalions to deploy along the high ground of Sari Bair to block the Allied advance inland. Although a clear violation of his orders, this was perhaps the most critical decision of the entire campaign. Outnumbered three to one, the Turkish troops, led by Kemal's best regiment, the 57th Infantry, attacked fiercely and stopped the invaders cold.[7] By the end of the day, his division, although badly mauled, had begun to push the ANZACs back into their narrow enclave.

As darkness descended both sides looked fearfully toward the morrow. Kemal's 19th Division was badly shattered, and no reinforcements could be spared. But on the Allied side, Birdwood—despite his overwhelming superiority—considered his situation desperate. At the critical moment it was Kemal's determination and self-confidence that would win out, with incalculable consequences both for Turkey and the British Empire.

Meanwhile, the fighting sputtered along the rest of the front. For the next two days the Allies sheltered on the beach as Turkish forces flowed toward them, the outlines of the Allied plan now clearly apparent. Buoyed by success, the Turks and their German advisers became bolder, bringing up artillery, siting machine guns, and digging in as they arrived on the high ground. General Hamilton was awakened at 0200 on the twenty-seventh with an urgent message from General Birdwood. Hamilton, clad in pajamas aboard his flagship, read the report with mounting concern. Although the seventy thousand Allied soldiers ashore faced no more than twenty thousand Turks in and around the invasion beaches, Birdwood thought the situation was hopeless. He believed his corps was in great danger from Kemal's division, and he explained that his losses had been heavy. The dispatch concluded with a request to be evacuated by boat.

Hamilton was aghast. Not wanting to overrule his commanders, Hamilton sought the recommendations of Commodore Roger Keyes, who had staunchly advocated making another strong naval push through the Dardanelles after the 18 March debacle. Keyes told Hamilton they must stay and fight. Hamilton then sent Birdwood his reply:

> Your news is indeed serious. But there is nothing for it but to dig yourselves in and stick it out. It would take at least two days to re-embark you. . . . Meanwhile, the Australian submarine has got up through the Narrows and has torpedoed a gunboat at Chunuk. Hunter-Weston despite his heavy losses will be advancing tomorrow which should divert pressure from you. Make a personal appeal to your men and Godley's to make a supreme effort to hold their ground. . . . P.S. You have got through the difficult business, now you have only to dig, dig, dig, until you are safe.[8]

Thus was set the pattern for the Gallipoli campaign: "the action, the reaction, and the stalemate. The objective is set, the attempt is made, and it falls just short of success. . . . A wild unreality intervened between the wishes of the commanders and the conditions of the actual battle on the shore. The battle made its own rules, and it was useless for the generals to order the soldiers to make for this or that objective. . . . This was a simple exercise in killing, and in the end all orders were reduced to just one or two very simple propositions: either to attack or to hold on."[9]

Later events would show that the first landing had been the Allies' best chance to force the Turks off the peninsula and open the Straits. By the end of April the campaign had settled into a stalemate that would last for months. Incredibly, the combined naval and military might of two of the greatest powers in the world had been brought to bear against the scorned Turks, and the Turks had held. The nightmare, however, was just beginning.

For the next three months the armies watched each other warily, the Allies entrenched in their shallow beachheads, the Turks in command of the heights. Raiding parties raided, snipers sniped, and patrols incessantly patrolled. Several limited attacks were made on both sides with much hard fighting, but there were no more major offensives. As July wore on, Hamilton, acting on Birdwood's suggestion, decided to mount another major push to seize Sari Bair. To command the three fresh divisions sent to reinforce Hamilton, Kitchener sent out Lt. Gen. Sir Frederick William Stopford, an overage retired officer known principally as an administrator, but possessing the seniority required to issue orders to Hamilton's temperamental division commanders.

Renewed Hope

The operation was set for early August. It was to be a two-pronged effort, with British landings at Suvla Bay and the ANZACs attempting to break out from their beachhead below the Sari Bair ridge. The ANZAC assault was designated the main effort and Stopford's landing at Suvla Bay the supporting attack. Still unable to garrison the entire peninsula, the Turkish defense of Suvla Bay and along the Sari Bair ridge was sparse. The Turkish corps commander in Gallipoli's central corridor was Feizi Bey, an incompetent and wavering Turkish general who held his position more for political reasons than for military talent. The only troops readily at hand were eighteen hundred Turkish gendarmes led by a German major named Willmer.

Shortly after midnight on 6 August, twenty thousand fresh troops from the 10th and 11th Divisions began landing at Suvla Bay. The Turks were taken completely off guard and began to move back, offering little resistance. When the assault began at ANZAC Cove below Sari Bair, Major Willmer was ordered to send a battalion there, effectively depleting his already thin force of defenders. Electing not to defend on the beaches, Willmer allowed the ANZACs to move inland, hoping to counterattack.

Although several hours of darkness remained, the hills overlooking the Narrows were still some distance away. Two British divisions had made it ashore, but all was confused. Units were hopelessly mixed together. Now, when the situation called for prompt, decisive action, Stopford reversed his decision to come ashore with the landing force and remained on board ship.

A few miles away, General Birdwood and his ANZAC forces were fighting for their lives trying to break out at ANZAC Cove, making little progress toward the hills of Sari Bair. His force continued to press forward through the evening of 9 August. At this stage, any reasonable degree of communication between forces might have saved the operation. The best opportunity to break into the open was at Suvla Bay, but Stopford, unwilling to advance before landing all his artillery, procrastinated. Both forces inched forward, one facing staunch resistance and the other very little.

Kemal Takes Command

As the Allies muddled through the night, von Sanders took full advantage of the time he was given. After hearing of Feizi Bey's decision not to reinforce weakening positions, von Sanders promptly relieved him and promoted Kemal to corps command. This decisiveness contrasts markedly with Hamilton's detached theory of command and his relations with his own indecisive commanders. Kemal received the order to assume command of Bey's corps by one of von Sanders's German staff officers. Realizing that Kemal must command not only Bey's corps but also his own 19th Division, he remarked, "Isn't that too many troops to command?" Kemal retorted, "It's not enough" and rode off to direct his corps.[10]

After arriving on the Sari Bair ridge, Kemal moved from unit to unit, repositioning them and exhorting his commanders. He posted his forces on every piece of high ground in the area: Green Hill, Chocolate Hill, and Nibrunesi Point. Turkish casualties were light since only patrols had penetrated beyond the beach. His orders to subordinate commanders were unequivocal, often relating his intent to them in absolute terms: "Take that position if it costs every soldier's life, the freedom of Turkey depends upon you alone, do not let us down." His troops responded fiercely. In one incident above Suvla Bay, the commander of a battalion in the Norfolk Regiment led his command of sixteen officers and 230 other ranks onto the heights. None of them returned.[11]

At 0200 the following night Kemal was informed that Birdwood's ANZACs were threatening to take Tekke Tepe, the most critical piece of high ground in the central corridor and, next to Achi Baba in the south, the most commanding piece of terrain on the peninsula. Kemal knew that if the Allies succeeded in taking Tekke Tepe they would control the Narrows and the tide of the battle would irrevocably turn. Though drunk with exhaustion, having been awake for four days, Kemal rallied his troops and personally led two battalions across the uneven ground in a race to Tekke Tepe.

The ANZAC force made slow progress toward Tekke Tepe. Then, at 0330, they stopped to reorganize and prepare for what might be a struggle for that high ground. This delay proved fatal; as they approached the crest of Tekke Tepe at 0400 they were engaged by the Turkish force and driven from the steep slopes with heavy casualties. The race had been close, but Kemal's personal leadership in rallying his fatigued and thirsty troops led to the most decisive engagement of the campaign. His demands on himself were driven by the feeling that he alone stood between the Allies and Constantinople. Kemal was absolutely unwilling to allow an advance or breakthrough.

Once the ANZACs had been driven back, Kemal collapsed in exhaustion. After six months on the peninsula and three months of nearly constant fighting, he was evacuated to Constantinople even as the Allies began to lose faith in the conquest of the Dardanelles. As summer gave way to fall it became clear that the August battles had turned the tide. Many more lives would be lost to wounds, disease, and failed hopes, but for the Turks and their German allies the crisis had passed.

The aftermath of Gallipoli was stunning in its implications for British policy and for the entire war effort. Hamilton was relieved of his command and replaced by Lt. Gen. Sir Charles Monro. The Allies withdrew from the peninsula in December, making a masterful evacuation that presaged Dunkirk. On the morning of 19 December, the Turks awoke to find the trenches opposite them empty. In a final bitter paradox, the Allies achieved a harmony of effort in retreat they were never able to realize in the attack.

Recriminations followed, and the British government fell. Winston Churchill, the bold proponent of the expedition, went into the trenches in France as a reserve major. Allied losses, even by World War I standards, were staggering. Of the half-million Allied troops who fought at Gallipoli, 252,000 became casualties (Turkish losses were roughly the same). It marked the end of Hamilton's career.

Strategically, the outcome could not have been much worse. The Allied defeat released twenty Turkish divisions and cut off all contact with Russia and Romania. A million allied soldiers would ultimately fight in the Middle East and Salonika to subdue the Ottoman Empire, which did not fall until 1918. Except for the Australians and New Zealanders, the troops who fought at Gallipoli were never put to use in France; they remained in the Middle East for the remainder of the war.[12]

The Power of Personality

Eight decades later, the force of Mustafa Kemal's battlefield persona continues to dominate the Gallipoli campaign. Never comfortable as a follower, the very traits that made him a poor subordinate contributed to his greatness as a commander. Ruthless, driving, and aggressive, Kemal was also a profound student of his profession, a master of terrain, and was possessed of both extreme physical courage and moral force. To his great credit, von Sanders appreciated Kemal's gifts and valued them above the insubordination and constant friction which would trouble even the most gracious superior. Their mutually dependent relationship is worthy of study. Could such a leader survive and prosper in today's Western armies?

Any sketch of a commander in action risks devolving into a simple list of character traits, but there is food for thought in the tragedy that was Gallipoli. Almost to a man, the British commanders seemed so sunk in lethargy, so mired in stasis, that one almost wonders that they ever got ashore. Gentlemen all, they seemed to have no understanding of the value of time, or of the possibility that sudden, instant action might in the end save lives. These tendencies were so marked that the influence of the British system of promotion and command selection—so vital in any army that intends to wage war—must be faulted for choosing such men.

Kemal was the very antithesis of his counterpart, General Stopford. Young, fit, decisive, and imbued both with love of country and the desire to command, he rose to the moment and never wavered in his faith that the enemy could and would be overcome. Accounts of his leadership make almost no mention of a staff. His preference for personal reconnaissance and face-to-face orders became legendary. Time and again he would personally lead units into position, as much in command of a corps as a division. In a very real sense, Kemal succeeded in animating the Turkish forces with his own unshakable belief in victory. Above all, his instinct and penchant for bold action, tempered by careful study of the ground and the situation, mark him as one of the twentieth century's greatest commanders.

Notes

1. Eric Bush, *Gallipoli* (New York: St. Martin's, 1975), 69.

2. Eliot Cohen and John Gooch, *Military Misfortunes* (New York: Vintage Books, 1990), 137.

3. Alan Moorehead, *Gallipoli* (New York: Ballantine Books, 1956), 22.

4. A. L. MacFie, *Ataturk* (London: Longman Group, 1994), 40.

5. Moorehead, *Gallipoli*, 84.

6. Lord Kinross, "General Mustafa Kemal," in *The War Lords*, ed. Field Marshal Sir Michael Carver (Boston: Little, Brown, 1976), 97; Morehead, *Gallipoli*, 140.

7. In honor of its magnificent performance, the 57th Regiment's colors were later retired. No Turkish unit has ever been permitted to use its number since (George W. Gawrych, "The Rock of Gallipoli," in *Studies in Battle Command* [Fort Leavenworth, Kans.: U.S. Army Command and General Staff College, 1989], 89).

8. Moorehead, *Gallipoli*, 155.

9. Ibid., 164.

10. Ibid., 290.

11. Cohen and Gooch, *Military Misfortunes*, 153.

12. Morehead, *Gallipoli*, 361.

Epic at Narvik: The 3d Mountain Division in Norway

(Second Apparition): "Be bloody, bold and resolute; laugh to scorn the power of man!"

—William Shakespeare, *Macbeth*

On 9 April 1940, in a display of breathtaking audacity, the German armed forces launched the first truly joint operation in modern history—the invasion of Norway. Code-named *Weseruebung*, the invasion involved the simultaneous seizure of key points throughout Norway by Wehrmacht air, sea, and land units. The most remote objective, the port of Narvik, lay north of the Arctic Circle, more than 1,500 miles from Germany. Shrouded in mist and fog, snowbound Narvik was assigned to the German army's 3d Mountain Division for capture. In the coming weeks, the division's tough mountain soldiers would battle the elements and the odds to earn a victory that still stands as one of the outstanding tactical achievements of the war.[1]

Though remote and far from Germany, Narvik was considered crucial to the Reich. The principal city in northern Norway, it served as the terminus for the railroad that transported much of Germany's iron ore from Swedish mines to the east.[2] Loaded onto transports, the ore was moved southward by sea along the coastal leads to steel plants in Germany. To safeguard these vital raw materials, and to secure advance naval bases for German U-boats and surface raiders, German planners thought it essential to take Narvik before the Allies moved first.

The spring of 1940 found the 3d Mountain *(gebirgs)* Division resting and training outside Berlin after its successful role in the Polish campaign. German mountain divisions grew out of similar formations rooted in the old Royal Bavarian and Imperial Austrian armies and enjoyed a rich tradition as elite alpine formations. In the Great War, the German *Alpenkorps* earned widespread fame for its successes on the Italian front. A number of mountain soldiers, including a young officer named Erwin Rommel, won Imperial Germany's highest award (the *Pour le Merite*) there, and small mountain cadres were retained in the hundred-thousand-man postwar army dictated by the Versailles Treaty.

The 3d Mountain Division was formed in April 1938 out of the former 5th and 7th Divisions of the Austrian Republic and was part of XVIII Mountain Corps, along with its sister unit, the 2d Mountain Division. *Gebirgs* divisions were uniquely organized, with two infantry regiments instead of the standard three. Other units included a mountain artillery regiment of four battalions, an antitank battalion, a reconnaissance battalion, a pioneer battalion, and medical and signal troops. The 3d Division's principal units were the 138th and 139th Mountain Infantry Regiments *(gebirgsjäger)* and the 112th Mountain Artillery Regiment. Based in the Carinthian mountain provinces of Steiermark and Kaernten,[3] division soldiers, like all mountain troops, wore distinctive uniforms and were readily identifiable by the edelweiss badge worn on the cap. Although they expected to see service in the upcoming invasion of France, the hardy soldiers of the Mountain Corps were an obvious choice for a difficult cold-weather campaign. On 7 March 1940 Hitler formally assigned 3d Mountain Division to take part in the operation.[4]

To its great pride, the division was commanded by one of its own, *Generalmajor*[5] Eduard Dietl, an ethnic Austrian from Carinthia. Dietl served with distinction in the Great War as a young officer in Bavarian mountain units, earning the Iron Cross First Class and three awards of the Wound Badge. Unlike many of his Prussian general staff counterparts, Dietl enjoyed a reputation as a soldier's general. An outdoorsman, with a broad peasant dialect, Dietl proved to be a dynamic battlefield commander with an iron will. In the trial to come, his troops would need every ounce of his optimism and dogged determination to prevail.

The Plan

The German campaign plan for the invasion of Norway called for the simultaneous seizure of important population centers along the Norwegian coast, beginning with the capital, Oslo, in the south. To preserve the element of surprise, assault units were to move in fast warships at night. Discounting the chances of determined Norwegian resistance, German planners were more concerned about allied air and especially naval power in the early stages. Initially, isolated German detachments would establish lodgments throughout the country, supported from the air until reinforcements arrived overland by rail and road. If all went well, German possession of key ports would forestall Allied intervention with ground forces while the Luftwaffe held the Royal Navy at bay.

The senior German ground commander was *General der Infanterie*[6] Nikolaus von Falkenhorst, a veteran of the German intervention in Finland in 1918 and commanding general of XXI Corps. In an unusual move, the German armed forces high command (*Oberkommando des Wehrmacht* or OKW) bypassed the army high command (*Oberkommando des Heeres* or OKH) to task Falkenhorst directly with both planning and operational responsibilities. Although initially envisioned as the controlling headquarters for all forces operating in Norway, XXI Corps (later renamed XXI Group) controlled only ground formations, with air and naval units only "encouraged" to cooperate.[7] X Air Corps would control all Luftwaffe units. These command arrangements, complicated by the distance separating Dietl from his superiors, posed special problems for his detached force.

Of even greater concern were the slim forces given to Dietl to complete his mission. With just a handful of destroyers available to transport his force, only the 139th Mountain Regiment could be landed in addition to the division command post, small coastal artillery detachments to man captured guns, a single 75mm battery, and a small number of signal and support troops. (The division's other regiment, the 138th, would fight with 2d Mountain Division at Trondheim to the south.) It was hoped that a seaborne support echelon with supplies, artillery, and reinforcements would follow soon after the landing to strengthen these meager forces. Much faith was also placed in the Luftwaffe, which had played such a devastating role in Poland.

But it was the German navy that faced the longest odds. Most of the German surface fleet would be concentrated to cover the initial landings and the subsequent resupply convoys upon which so much depended. Warship Group 1, designated to transport and escort the division to Narvik, included the battleships *Scharnhorst* and *Gneisenau*, along with ten destroyers. Other groups would head for Trondheim, four hundred miles down the coast, and other key points on the Norwegian littoral. Facing them was the British fleet based at Scapa Flow on the northern coast of Scotland, at that time the most battle-worthy naval force in Europe. It was not at all clear that the Narvik assault force could land the troops safely; maintaining sea lines of communication was even more doubtful. Nevertheless that was not Dietl's concern. His task was to seize and hold Narvik.

The city lay inside the huge Vestfjord, a long, narrow inlet surrounded by cliffs on three sides which thrusts deeply into the Norwegian coastline before narrowing to become the Ofotfjord. Narvik itself is at the tip of a small peninsula formed by two smaller bodies of water, the Rombaksfjord to the north and the Beisfjord to the south. To the east, only twenty-five miles distant, is the Swedish border. The vital Kiruna rail line ran along the northern edge of the peninsula, flanked by bare mountains that run almost into the sea. A single improved road ran south along the coast. In early April, snow still lay three to four feet deep, with temperatures often ranging well below zero. Blizzards, biting wind, and deep drifts made climactic conditions some of the most challenging in the world.

Embarking shortly after midnight on 7 April, the 3d Mountain Division endured a difficult sea passage to its objective. Rough weather, attacks by British bombers, and reports of British warships scattered the convoy en route, but Dietl's force landed safely in Narvik harbor soon after daylight on the ninth. Quickly occupying the town, the *gebirgsjäger* disarmed a Norwegian battalion, in the process seizing large stocks of Norwegian weapons, ammunition, and other supplies intended for mobilizing units.[8] This windfall would loom large in the days to come, for despite the uneventful capture of the winter resort, the situation soon changed dramatically for the worse.

Things began to go wrong almost at once. Patrols quickly discovered that the coastal batteries thought to be guarding the sea approaches to Narvik did not exist—and without them in German hands, defending the harbor and town from the sea would be impossible. Disaster struck that same day with word that the vital freighters carrying fuel for the destroyers' return trip, as well as Dietl's equipment and supplies, had been intercepted and sunk or dispersed. The next morning, a British destroyer flotilla entered the fjord, evaded a screen of German U-boats, and engaged the German destroyers sheltering there. Attacking out of a swirling snowstorm, this force sunk or damaged five German destroyers.

Several days later, a stronger force led by the battleship *Warspite* and aircraft carrier *Furious* finished off the German destroyer force. In the course of the attack, British warships shelled German positions in the town heavily, causing a temporary panic that did not subside until it became apparent that there would be no immediate amphibious landing. Nevertheless, the loss of ten warships at Narvik was a crippling blow to the *Kriegsmarine*, depriving Dietl of all naval support. The situation now became critical. Cut off from the rest of XXI Group, lacking artillery and air defense, and hemmed in by British warships, the division deployed grimly against the Allied landings that were sure to follow.

Amid the crisis, Dietl displayed the initiative and grit so characteristic of German commanders. To replace his missing artillery, he recovered heavy guns and antiaircraft weapons from the damaged warships and mounted them overlooking the town, manned by naval crews. Radios, rations, and other supplies were also recovered from the stricken vessels. Organizing the grounded destroyer crews into naval battalions, he equipped them from Norwegian stores and employed them for static defense in the town. A second light mountain battery flown in soon after the landing improved morale, but lack of fire support remained a critical liability.

The 3d Mountain Division's tactical dispositions reveal the confidence Dietl had in his men and himself. Two of his three infantry battalions and one of his two batteries were deployed seventeen miles to the north on key terrain guarding the northern approaches to Narvik. The remaining battalion defended the town itself, while one company moved eastward to secure the railway to the Swedish border. To the southwest, small units established an outpost at Ankenes, to provide early warning of any advance from that direction. Widely dispersed, his units were well out of supporting distance, vulnerable to air and naval attack, and poorly protected against the elements. Dietl could only rely on training and discipline, air cover from X Air Corps, and early reinforcement to compensate for his lack of strength on the ground. He had taken Narvik, but could he hold it?

The Empire Strikes Back

Although British naval units failed to prevent the German landings, they responded quickly and decisively. Most of the German surface fleet was sunk or scattered, and control of Norwegian waters by the Royal Navy was quickly reestablished. Nonetheless, German units had occupied most of Norway's population centers, and the Luftwaffe posed a major threat to Allied naval action. It soon became apparent that Allied ground forces must go to Norway, not only to contest Nazi occupation but also to push back the air umbrella that threatened Britain's mastery of the North Sea.

Although there was some discussion of storming Narvik with a naval landing party following the destruction of the German destroyer force, this was dismissed early on as confusion descended on the British War Cabinet and military chiefs.[9] Plans existed to land forces in Norway—indeed, the British were on the verge of doing so when the Germans arrived—but the sudden appearance of strong Wehrmacht forces throughout Norway prevented their execution.

By midday on 11 April, a force had been assembled at Scapa Flow under Maj. Gen. P. J. Macksey, commander of the 49th Division.[10] Orders arrived that day directing Macksey to proceed to Norway, "eject the Germans" from Narvik, and secure the port and railway to the border. Macksey was told that four additional battalions would follow within thirty hours, and an additional two battalions would arrive within a week. The 24th Guards Brigade—consisting of the 1st Scots Guards, 1st Irish Guards, and 2d South Wales Borderers—sailed the next day, accompanied by the 146th Infantry Brigade in slower transports. British planners envisioned no opposed landing; rather, Macksey's force would disembark at Harstad, about thirty-five miles from Narvik, establish a base there, and advance overland supported by the fleet.[11]

En route, the 146th Brigade was diverted to Namsos to the south so that Macksey arrived off Harstad on the fifteenth with only the Guards Brigade. The hurried nature of the deployment had an immediate impact. Although antiaircraft troops accompanied the force, they had no guns with which to defend against German air attacks. Transport ships had not been loaded tactically, so quartermasters had no idea what supplies were stored where. Some battalions lacked mortar ammunition, and others had no motor transport. Artillery, landing craft, and reserve ammunition were completely lacking. Troops struggled ashore burdened with thirty-five pieces of winter gear, including fifteen-pound overcoats, and office furniture arrived before artillery shells.

Worst of all, the small fishing port of Harstad had almost no equipment for off-loading stores, so the transfer of supplies from ship to shore was agonizingly slow. Almost comically, all of the 146th Brigade's heavy equipment arrived even though the brigade itself had been diverted for other operations in central Norway, hundreds of kilometers away. Macksey thus found himself unable—and increasingly unwilling—to move quickly against Dietl's force in the face of such snarled logistics. Nor could he bring himself to agree with the naval commander, Admiral of the Fleet William H. D. Burke, the Earl of Cork and Orrery, that Narvik could be taken by a coup de main supported by heavy naval gunfire.

As an interim measure, several infantry battalions were moved forward to staging areas somewhat closer to Narvik while preparations were made to receive a follow-up force consisting of a mixed force of French *chasseurs alpins* and Polish troops. Liaison officers were sent out to make contact with several Norwegian battalions operating to the north of the city.

Meanwhile, the alpine soldiers improved their positions. The first sharp engagement occurred astride the Kiruna railroad on

13 April when a German company, sent out to reconnoiter toward
the border, struck a Norwegian battalion attempting to blow the
railroad bridge linking Narvik to the ore fields. In a three-day battle the *jäger* company decisively defeated the Norwegians, capturing
forty-five and driving another 150 across the border, where they
were interned.[12] The steady Allied buildup and incessant shelling of
the town caused worry in Berlin, but Dietl was ordered to hold
Narvik "to the last." In the same message he was informed of his promotion to *generalleutnant*, an honor accompanied by the Knight's
Cross—both clearly intended to bolster his pride for the ordeal
to come.

The Battle Joined

The first serious Allied attempt to shake Dietl's grip coincided with
the War Cabinet's decision on the twenty-first to place Lord Cork in
overall command of forces operating in the Narvik area. Three days
later a strong force led by HMS *Warspite* and including the cruisers
Effingham, Aurora, and *Enterprise* shelled Narvik for more than three
hours in the midst of a driving snowstorm. The Irish Guards, embarked in the warships, stood by to occupy the town in the event the
Germans surrendered, but despite heavy damage to buildings and
the waterfront there was no sign of collapse. Following this failure,
the Allies settled down to pursue a deliberate advance on Narvik
from both the north and south, using newly arrived French, Polish,
and Norwegian units as well as the British troops based at the entrance to the fjords.

On the same day, local Norwegian forces, reinforced from Norway's northernmost regions, attacked German outposts north of
Narvik at Lapphaug, a commanding elevation dominating the coast
road. Three battalions attacked frontally, while a fourth attempted
to maneuver behind the Germans to cut off their line of retreat. In
this area, the mountain infantry battalions manned a thin screen
consisting of machine-gun positions and observation posts.

Foot patrols covered the gaps between positions, but no continuous defensive frontage existed. Nor was there any tactical depth to
the defense. The shortage of troops and the great distances to be

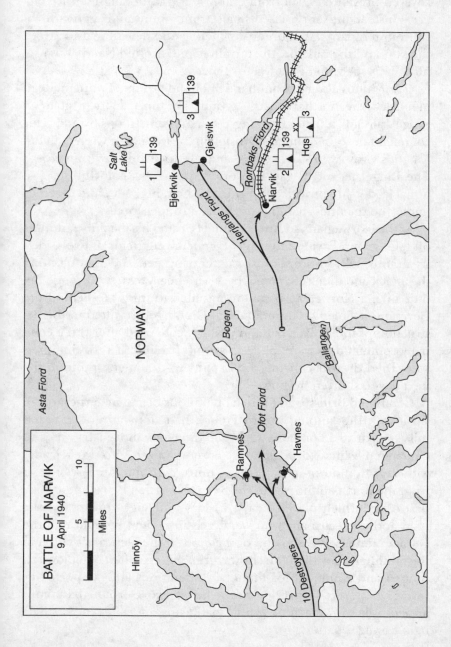

BATTLE OF NARVIK
9 April 1940

Miles
5   10

Hinnöy

Asta Fiord

NORWAY

Salt Lake

1 | 139
3 | 139

Bjerkvik

Gje svik

Herjangs Fiord

Rombaks Fiord

Narvik

2 | 139
Hqs | XX | 3

Bogen

Ballangen

Ofot Fiord

Ramnes

Havnes

10 Destroyers

covered prevented Dietl from employing traditional defensive tactics.[13] Instead, he emphasized small strong points and aggressive local counterattacks. A counterpuncher, Dietl knew that, aside from the port and the rail line, the terrain in and around Narvik was useful only as space to be traded for time.[14]

Oberst Julius Ringel, commander of the 139th Mountain Regiment, led the northern battle group. The mustachioed, goateed Ringel, already a legend among the mountain troops, would later command the 5th Mountain Division in the assault on Crete, win the Knight's Cross with Oak Leaves, and rise to *general der gebirgsjäger*.[15] The Ringel legend began in Norway, where his colorful, inspirational leadership provided the glue that held his command together under the relentless hammering of far stronger forces.

As the Norwegians advanced, Ringel posted his machine gunners on high ground, where they had commanding fields of fire. Aided by an unusually severe snowstorm, they succeeded in first blunting the attack and then throwing it back with heavy losses. Although the outflanking Norwegian battalion was able to infiltrate behind the Germans, a violent counterattack at Gratangen resulted in the destruction of the Nordic battalion, which collapsed after three company commanders were killed in action. Feeling the growing pressure, Dietl drew back from the Lapphaug-Gratangen position the next day to shorten his lines.

Combined British and French operations began in earnest on 28 April with the landing of two French battalions at Sjovegan, ten miles north of Lapphaug. One battalion was moved by water to Gratangen, while Norwegian forces, reorganized into two brigades with the addition of more arriving units, continued to press down from the north all the way to the Swedish border. Patrolling British destroyers, which placed heavy fire day and night on the coastal road and any Germans who wandered into view, complicated the German defense. By the end of the month, the tactical situation in the mountains north of the city was grim. Seven Allied battalions, all trained and equipped for mountain operations and supported by several batteries of artillery, now faced two German battalions armed only with machine guns, small arms, mortars, and a single light-howitzer battery.

Throughout this period the 3d Mountain Division endured terrible ordeals. The infantry battalions fighting to the north were fed a total of three hot meals from mid-April to late May.[16] Manning exposed positions around the clock, the alpine soldiers lived in the open air without special winter clothing, warming tents, cooking fires, or sleeping bags—all considered indispensable for cold-weather operations. As Allied strength grew, Norwegian units (now consolidated into the 6th Division, headquartered at Harstad) became bolder. Their persistent probes and attacks were gradually wearing down the German defenders.

Meanwhile, the Luftwaffe continued to attack British shipping and installations as flying conditions permitted, slowing the off-loading of supplies and movement of troops. Some indication of the ferocity of the air battle can be seen in the tally of downed aircraft: British fighters operating in the Narvik area claimed thirty-seven German aircraft shot down in less than a month, and antiaircraft fire accounted for twenty-three more over Harstad alone. In turn, German bombers attacked and sank the British antiaircraft cruiser *Curlew* and the Polish destroyer *Grom*, in addition to damaging HMS *Furious*.[17] Unfortunately for Dietl, the Luftwaffe's primary effort was directed against British shipping and shore installations. Although certainly necessary, these missions absorbed most of the limited air support, which had already been compromised by poor weather, British strength in the air, and the lack of nearby bases. The 3d Mountain Division could count on no coordinated close air support of the kind that had proved so decisive in Poland.

The failure of Allied land operations farther south prompted Hitler and XXI Group to send forces to help their embattled comrades to the north. In early May, the 2d Mountain Division and Dietl's own 138th Mountain Regiment were ordered to proceed north from Trondheim and relieve the defenders at Narvik. The task was not an easy one. Hundreds of kilometers of mountain terrain lay between the rescuers and the besieged, traversed by a single road defended by substantial Allied and Norwegian forces. The mountain soldiers set out at once, making steady progress through areas judged "impassable" by Allied intelligence officers. Still, the Allied buildup continued in the north. With central and southern

Norway now lost, Narvik assumed even greater importance as a political objective for the Allies. The Germans must be beaten somewhere, and if not at Narvik—at the farthest extremity of Germany's strategic reach, where Britain's air and sea power were strongest—then where?

On 6 May two battalions of French Foreign Legionnaires arrived from North Africa. These hard-bitten soldiers approached arctic campaigning phlegmatically; one legionnaire commented picturesquely: "At home we are used to crossing the desert on camels, and you give us boats and ask us to cross the water. But perhaps it will be all right. Yes, I think so." Fifteen destroyers, supported by the cruiser *Aurora,* the battleship *Resolution* (replacing *Warspite),* and the aircraft carrier *Ark Royal* (replacing the damaged *Furious)* enabled the British to blanket the coastline with fire for miles inland. With a total of twenty-four artillery pieces in the Narvik area, these reinforcements, plus a Polish brigade of *chasseurs de montagne* (though battle-hardened in the invasion of Poland, few had ever seen a mountain), gave the Allies an overwhelming preponderance of strength on the ground, aided appreciably by the spring thaw now well under way. As trafficability improved, they moved out to tighten the noose.

On 10 May, Operation *Gelb,* the German invasion of France and the Low Countries, began with a roar. With it went General Dietl's last hopes for substantial reinforcements. The invasion of France immediately consumed the attention of Hitler and the General Staff, which argued that all resources should be directed to the main theater of operations. Still, some reinforcements were dropped into Narvik by parachute, including one *falschirmjäger* (paratroop) battalion and two mountain companies, hastily trained in parachute operations, together with small numbers of artillerymen and specialists, all totaling no more than eleven hundred men. Throughout the month of May, with victory in France by no means certain, Narvik's defenders watched as the balance tipped sharply against them.

As Allied strength rapidly increased, the Norwegians fought even more vigorously, scoring an important success on 13 May by seizing the Kuberg Massif above Narvik, bringing them to within seven miles of the coastline and almost within sight of the city. Attacking uphill, the Norwegians succeeded in displacing an entire German battalion from the three-thousand-foot elevation. A few miles to the west, the Legionnaires landed on the coast and seized Bjerkvik, ten miles north of Narvik, and a German supply depot in Elvegaard nearby.[18]

Marching hard to the east, these forces joined hands with the *chasseurs alpins* moving down from Gratangen. Now hemmed in from the north and west, Ringel drew his northern battle group back to a final line of defense short of the town itself. For the final stand he selected a difficult position in the hills northeast of the city, facing in two directions to ward off the Norwegians and parry the French. Just behind him lay the divisional supply base at Bjornfjell. Under the watchful eyes of troops on the Kuberg and pounded by Allied naval guns, the exhausted mountain men scraped at the stony soil, seeking cover from the elements and the fire raining down on them from the sea. Sensing a crisis, General Dietl grimly notified Falkenhorst and XXI Group that he would hold on to Narvik as long as possible, then fall back along the railroad toward Sweden.

As the Allies tightened their hold on Narvik, the ineffectual Macksey was replaced by Lt. Gen. (later Field Marshal) Claude Auchinleck, who was given direct control of land and air forces in northern Norway under Lord Cork. Noting with satisfaction the strong performance by the French mountain units, Auchinleck deployed his British army units southward to assist in delaying the German relief columns trudging remorselessly toward Narvik.

However, the self-assured Auchinleck brought no instructions from Whitehall urging unity of effort with the Norwegian army. Throughout the campaign in northern Norway, the Allied policy of divided command prevented close cooperation between the Norwegians and their British counterparts.[19] Both the local Norwegian division commander, Maj. Gen. Curt Fleischer, and the Norwegian commander in chief, Maj. Gen. Carl Otto Ruge, proved able soldiers with an intimate grasp of climate and terrain. For their part, the British administered their operational areas largely without reference to Norwegian authorities, while withholding many of their plans and intentions from Ruge. The newly promoted *Generalleutnant* Dietl could take some comfort in the continuing poor liaison between the uneasy Allies.

As the German army continued to pour across the Meuse, pressure mounted on British commanders to reach a decision at Narvik. The final assault was set for 27 May. The plan called for a two-pronged advance, with the Poles attacking Ankenes from the southwest before pushing on to the head of the Beisfjord. Two Foreign Legion battalions (assisted by a Norwegian battalion) were ordered to cross the Rombaksfjord at night in assault craft to seize the Taraldsvikfjell, the high ground northeast of Narvik, before driving into the town to finish the job. British naval units would fire directly into the town from the fjords, suppressing machine-gun positions and disrupting any German counterattacks, while the Norwegians would thrust southward to cut the railroad—the only line of retreat.

The assault began at midnight with a crushing naval bombardment. By 0400, two battalions were safely ashore and moving up the Taraldsvikfjell, although German Stukas delayed the third battalion and scattered the British destroyers. Opposite Narvik, the Poles made good progress, advancing with two battalions abreast to seize the Ankenes outpost. With less than a thousand troops in and around Narvik itself, many of them sailors untrained in land warfare, Dietl now faced not only the loss of the town and its port but the possible destruction of his force altogether.

Despite heavy damage to the town, the outnumbered German garrison had survived the bombardment in reasonably good shape, and throughout the morning the defenders launched violent counterattacks against both threats, throwing the opposing infantry back. After regrouping, the Allies pressed on, supported by British warships and heavy artillery. By noon it was clear that Narvik must fall, and the *gebirgsjäger* began to disengage and draw off to the east along the rail line, leaving between three hundred and four hundred casualties and prisoners behind. To the east, the Norwegians and *chasseurs alpins* forced Ringel back toward the railroad in a fighting withdrawal.

At the end of May, the 3d Mountain Division lay exhausted in a shallow perimeter along the railway in the hills east of Narvik. The newly arrived 1st Battalion, 1st Parachute Regiment, which had sustained severe losses since jumping into the Narvik pocket earlier that week, defended the rail line itself. The 139th Mountain Regiment was a shadow of its former self, its 3d Battalion destroyed altogether and the others barely company strength. The remnants of the 1st Battalion held the northern part of the perimeter, with the survivors of the 2d Battalion and a small naval group in the south. Bereft of supplies and with fewer than a thousand men fit for combat, the division faced a total of six elite French battalions, four Polish battalions, and two Norwegian brigades.

In one of the greatest feats of marching endurance of all time, the 2d Mountain Division continued to advance, fighting all the way. With time running out, the division formed special Narvik companies manned with its toughest troops. Jettisoning all heavy weapons and equipment, these men pressed on night and day. But it soon was clear that the division would not arrive in time to save the day.[20] Conscious that they had performed a memorable feat of arms, the German troopers at Narvik were nonetheless well aware of their situation. Soon the Allies would attack again. There could be only one outcome.

The Miracle of Narvik

Despite their weakness, the Germans continued to patrol their front actively in the first week of June. They knew that a strong attack by the entire Allied force could quickly crush their small pocket and destroy the division or drive it in fragments over the border. Yet no attack came.

What Dietl and Ringel did not know was that the collapse of the front in France had doomed Allied operations in Norway. Even before the 27 May assault on Narvik, the British government had directed that all forces be withdrawn as soon as a face-saving victory had been won. In early June, while Norwegian forces made small attacks to distract the Germans, the Allies assembled and sailed away, carrying King Haakon VII and the Crown Prince and leaving Norway to its fate. On 8 June the last Allied soldier, ironically a Frenchman, departed from the quay of the devastated port. On that day, the railhead, airfields, and dock facilities all having been destroyed, the gallant General Ruge met with astonished German commanders to discuss terms for a cease-fire. The Norwegian government subsequently surrendered and the Norwegian army, which had fought so stubbornly, was disarmed. The Battle of Narvik was over.

In the aftermath, honors rained down on the gaunt survivors. Dietl became the first German soldier to be awarded the Knight's Cross with Oak Leaves. He went on to command first a mountain corps and then, as a *generaloberst* (colonel general), a mountain army fighting the Russians in Finland, only to die in an air crash in 1944. Ringel was promoted to command of the 5th Mountain Division, soon to endure a Calvary of its own on Crete—the "graveyard of the German paratroops." In an unprecedented act for the tradition-conscious Wehrmacht, a special sleeve device was awarded to every participant in the battle. For the rest of the war, to be a "Narvik soldier" was a mark of distinction.

How to account for the 3d Mountain Division's triumph against the odds? Surely its status as an elite infantry formation had something to do with its performance in battle. Fully manned with well-conditioned soldiers inured to the cold, the division could draw on long traditions of success to foster esprit and sustain morale. Well trained and recently blooded in Poland, it was as combat ready as any unit in the German army.

A certain sense of desperation, coupled with a strong sense of combat superiority, undoubtedly spurred the *gebirgsjäger* on. Isolated in the far north, with nothing but their own efforts to sustain them, they fought with unusual determination and resolve. Their opponents were no raw militia. The French units were among the very best in the French army, and the Norwegians were fit, well acquainted with local topography, and fighting for the best of causes—their national survival. Still, the mountain soldiers maintained a striking level of resistance, not easily explained when comparing forces and weapons.

The German preference for maneuver in the offense and defense also served them well in the Narvik battle. Rejecting a passive defense, German commanders deployed well away from the town to ensure the maneuver room they would later use to such effect. Local Allied successes always met with violent counterattacks delivered to the flanks and rear. This aggressive spirit and preference for fluid tactics kept the Allies off balance and fostered a fear and respect the mountain troopers did not hesitate to exploit.

That leadership played a dominant role is an inescapable conclusion. The two senior commanders present on the German side, Dietl and Ringel, were both profoundly experienced leaders with extensive combat experience in the Great War and many years of service with mountain units. Both were decisive men with infectious optimism. Both would display the same qualities of leadership that loomed so large in the Narvik campaign on many other battlefields. Their ability to inspire their troops and their aggressive leadership under duress were undoubtedly the single most important factors in prolonging what seemed to be almost hopeless resistance. Their example of self-confidence and imperturbability spread throughout the division, welding it together against the thunderbolts that threatened to tear it apart at any moment.

Was Narvik a German victory? Strictly speaking, the 3d Mountain Division failed in its mission to defend its assigned objective. But in war there are many kinds of victory. To remain in control of the vital railway, to deny the Allies the political triumph they so desperately needed, even to keep up the fight and continue to resist—all these were victories in their own right. For their part, the Allies made no boasts about their performance. German mountain soldiers reoccupied Narvik within days of retreating from it and presided at the Norwegian surrender.

But it was their survival as a fighting organization that constituted the biggest victory of all. For weeks, the 3d Mountain Division faced not only defeat but also total destruction. The collapse of a single key unit or position might have spelled ruin, yet the division retained not only its cohesion but also its ability to maneuver and counterattack against superior forces. Even at the end, when all seemed lost, the chain of command continued to function. Key weapons remained manned. Tactical integrity was maintained. Though the youngest *soldat* knew the seriousness of the situation, the remnants of the division stood firm, ready to fight to the end. And because they did, a famous victory was won. That it was won in the service of perhaps the worst cause in history cannot detract from the defenders' achievements as soldiers, for at Narvik they fought not to advance National Socialism, but for the most timeless cause of all: They fought to see the dawn.

Notes

1. For an account of the German invasion of Norway from the campaign perspective, see the author's "Operation Weseruebung: Maneuver Warfare and the Operational Art," *Joint Force Quarterly* 1, no. 1 (summer, 1993).

2. In 1939, 9 million of the 11 million tons of iron ore used in Germany came from Swedish mines. Francis Kersaudy, *Norway 1940* (New York: St. Martin's, 1991), 15.

3. James Lucas, *Hitler's Mountain Troops* (London: Arms and Armour, 1992), 15–17.

4. Earl F. Ziemke, *The German Northern Theater of Operations, 1940–1944* (Washington: Center for Military History, 1959), 19.

5. Roughly equivalent to a U.S. brigadier general. However, a German *generalmajor* typically commanded a division, since one-star assistant division commanders did not exist in the German army.

6. General of infantry, the equivalent of a U.S. lieutenant general.

7. Opposition from the air force (*Oberkommando der Luftwaffe* or OKL) and naval (*Oberkommando der Kriegsmarine* or OKM) high commands ensured that each would retain control over their units in Norway. Consequently, OKW exercised operational control over all services fighting in Norway from Berlin—a precedent that was to have doleful consequences for German arms throughout the war (Ziemke, *German Northern Theater*, 18).

8. Included in captured stocks were eight thousand rifles and 315 machine guns, weapons that would later play a major role in the obstinate defense offered by the lightly equipped mountain soldiers. See Christopher Buckley, *Norway: The Commando's Dieppe* (London: HMSO, 1952), 125.

9. T. K. Derry, *The Campaign in Norway* (London: HMSO, 1952), 51. This is the official British history of the campaign.

10. Macksey had previously served as commander of a brigade in Palestine, an interesting résumé to bring to command of cold-weather operations in Norway.

11. Ibid., 145–46.

12. Lucas, *Hitler's Mountain Troops*, 31.

13. Derry, *Campaign in Norway*, 156–57.

14. James Lucas, *Alpine Elite* (New York: Jane's, 1980), 34.

15. *Oberst* is the equivalent of a U.S. colonel; *general der gebirgsjäger* (general of mountain troops) is the equivalent of a U.S. lieutenant general.

16. Lucas, *Alpine Elite*, 34.

17. J. L. Moulton, *The Norwegian Campaign of 1940* (London: Eyre and Spottiswoode, 1966), 233.

18. Derry, *Campaign in Norway*, 197–99.

19. "General Fleischer was furious at the British, with whom he had had no liaison for three weeks" (Kersaudy, *Norway 1940*, 198).

20. Lucas, *Alpine Elite*, 35.

The Ghost Division: The 7th Panzer Division in France

Forget the flanks. Run the panzers!
            —*Generaloberst* Heinz Guderian

In May and June 1940, the German army electrified the world with its lightning conquest of France. Although outnumbered in men, tanks, and artillery, the Wehrmacht smashed the French army and its British allies in a mere six weeks. In the most crucial phase of the invasion, the crossing of the Meuse River, the German 7th Panzer Division set the pace for the rest of the German army, led by its inspiring commander, a junior general named Erwin Rommel. Throughout the campaign it traveled farther and faster than any other division, earning it the title *Gespensterdivision* (Ghost Division).[1] The operations of the 7th Panzer Division from 10–19 May 1940 provide an outstanding case study of the armored division in attack and pursuit—lessons that are as interesting and valid today as they were almost sixty years ago when Erwin Rommel burst upon the stage of military history.

Birth of a Legend

In the winter of 1939–40, the 2d Light Division, actually a motorized division, was redesignated 7th Panzer in the reorganization that followed the Polish campaign. The division fought with distinction in Poland under the strong and aggressive leadership of *Generalmajor*

Georg Stumme. Rated as one of the army's best panzer division commanders, General Stumme was very popular with his soldiers.[2]

On 6 February 1940, three months before the invasion of France, newly promoted *Generalmajor* Erwin Rommel assumed command of the division. Rommel, a distinguished infantryman and World War I recipient of the *Pour le Merite* (the German equivalent of the Medal of Honor), had never commanded tanks before. Following in the footsteps of an accomplished panzer commander, Rommel was viewed with some skepticism by the division, which had been groomed by a master tank commander. Many questioned whether an infantryman could successfully command tanks.[3] Rommel, however, would soon dispel any doubts about his ability to lead a panzer division.

More a listener than an assertive talker, Rommel established an easy rapport with his men, despite his demand that they achieve higher standards. Within three weeks of assuming command, he relieved a battalion commander and noted with some satisfaction that the dismissal would send shock waves throughout the division.[4] Rommel believed in commanding from the front because opportunities present themselves fleetingly on the battlefield and are manifest only to those at the critical point. In battle he would show a rare gift of *coup d'oeil*, an expressive term for the ability to quickly size up a situation and make an accurate decision in the midst of chaos.

The leadership of subordinate commanders, staff officers, and combat soldiers within the 7th Panzer Division complemented and often emulated Rommel's aggressive style. *Oberst* Karl Rothenburg, commander of the 25th Panzer Regiment, the division's lone panzer regiment, and another recipient of the *Pour le Merite*, was one of the best tank officers in the German army.[5] *Oberstleutnant* Frolich, commander of the 78th Artillery Regiment, and *Oberst* Friedrich Furst, commander of the infantry brigade (*Schützen* Brigade 7), were also very competent. The two infantry regimental commanders, *Oberst* von Unger (6th Rifle Regiment) and especially *Oberst* von Bismarck (7th Rifle Regiment), consistently displayed competence and aggressiveness under fire. *Major* Muller, the commander of the six-hundred-man signal battalion, used aggressive and innovative techniques to keep communications systems up during the campaign.[6]

The division and subordinate-unit staffs were small compared to a modern U.S. Army armor division. It had no chief of staff or assistant division commanders, and the subordinate units lacked executive officers. Clearly less bulky and less bureaucratic than modern equivalents in the U.S. Army, the streamlined 7th Panzer Division staff had a direct relationship with the division commander.[7] This allowed both division staff officers and subordinate commanders to clearly understand the division commander's intent. The division operations officer (Ia) ran the internal affairs as well as the operations of the division. The 7th Panzer's Ia, Maj. Otto Heidenkamper, was young but extremely competent, a General Staff officer and graduate of the demanding *Kriegsakademie* who would rise to the rank of *generalleutnant* by the end of the war. *Major* Ziegler, the division intelligence officer (Ic), would later accompany Rommel to the Africa Corps, where he also served with distinction.

The 7th Panzer Division's subordinate-unit commanders had a common approach to warfighting that allowed them to maintain momentum through maneuver. This common approach gave them great speed, flexibility, and a tremendous talent for communicating with clarity in few words—sometimes in no words at all. A review of typical division message traffic between the division commander, division staff, and subordinate units shows an amazingly brief, concise construct.[8] By understanding the commander's overall intent and by using "thrust lines," leaders within the division lessened the need for lengthy message traffic.

The thrust line was an innovative and offensive-oriented technique employed by the 7th Panzer Division staff and leaders. The division commander or the division Ia designated the thrust line for given periods of time and directed the maneuver of subordinate units along it. Rommel or Heidenkamper designated the thrust line in terms of clearly identifiable beginning and ending points on a map. Thrust lines would most often begin with zero and were always tick-marked at one-kilometer intervals over their entire length. Units within the division would communicate in terms of locations along thrust lines. For example, "twelve left, one km" meant twelve kilometers along the line and one kilometer left. Thrust lines helped all leaders within the division focus on the mission and reduced the need for lengthy verbal and written message traffic.[9]

The tactic of always attempting to fire first to seize the initiative during tactical engagements was also evidence of a common approach to warfighting used throughout the division. This controversial technique called for shooting at possible as well as actual enemy locations. Division units often fired indiscriminately at suspected enemy positions in wooded or urban areas while continuing to move. Rommel wrote, "The action of opening fire immediately into the area which the enemy is believed to be holding, instead of waiting until several of one's own tanks have been hit, usually decides the issue."[10] This technique often caught French and Belgian units by surprise and helped 7th Panzer Division units maintain momentum by taking and holding the initiative in tactical engagements.

Gaining and maintaining momentum in combat through aggressive maneuver was a key to the division's success in the French campaign, born from aggressive leadership at all levels as well as a shared doctrine that demanded decisive action and stressed rapid mobile operations. But other factors also applied.

Organization, Equipment, and Training

The idea behind the panzer division, as conceived by Heinz Guderian in the 1930s, was to create a powerful mobile formation centered on tanks. This formation included mobile infantry, artillery, antitank, and antiaircraft units.[11] The 7th Panzer Division had only one panzer regiment with three tank battalions instead of the standard two panzer regiments with two tank battalions in each regiment. In addition to the panzer regiment, the division had two rifle regiments, an artillery regiment, a reconnaissance battalion, a motorcycle battalion, an engineer battalion, an antitank battalion, and an attached antiaircraft battalion.[12]

When operations began on 10 May 1940, the division had 218 tanks instead of the 276 to 324 tanks found in six of the ten panzer divisions used in the French campaign. Nearly half of the tanks in the 7th Panzer Division were Czech-built PzKpfw 38(t)s.[13] In tank versus tank combat, most of the division's tanks could not penetrate the armor of French Char B1 or British Matilda tanks, but what German tank crews lacked in equipment they more than made up for with experience, superior training, and overall tactical expertise.

The Allies were numerically superior to the Germans in the total number of artillery pieces available. However, the French did not have any self-propelled guns, only horse-drawn artillery. In the area of antitank (AT) weapons, the Germans were initially inferior to the French. The French fielded 47mm AT guns, whereas the German 37mm AT guns were no match for the heavier French and British tanks. Once the Germans began using the excellent 88mm antiaircraft gun in a ground-support role, the antitank advantage shifted to the Germans. The Luftwaffe's "flying artillery"—Stuka dive-bombers operating in direct support of ground units—also helped to compensate for the German deficiency in artillery. Because the British withheld many aircraft to defend the British Isles, the Germans were superior in total number of aircraft, their only numerical edge.[14]

In March and April 1940, Rommel put the division through an intensive final training period in the Rhoen Mountains. Divisional units went through an exhausting program of live gunnery and small arms firing. The division practiced movement and traffic-control drills, coordination of all arms in various tactical field exercises, and trained in communications between commanders and staffs at all levels. Rommel organized field-training exercises in all types of weather, day and night, emphasizing communicating on the radio quickly and efficiently.[15]

The division commander visited every tactical unit almost daily, emphasized teamwork, and insisted that the same units work together in order to establish habitual relationships. By the end of April 1940, the subordinate commanders in the 7th Panzer Division had created a motivated and trained team in a very short but intense training period.[16] At the beginning of May, the division moved to its final staging area in the Eiffel Mountains in western Germany to prepare for the invasion of France.

Case Yellow

The German plan for the assault in the west, known as *Fall Gelb* (Case Yellow), had undergone several revisions since its initial publication in 1939. The final plan, often called the Manstein Plan, had three distinct but related phases. An airborne assault and subsequent overrunning of the Netherlands, in order to protect the northern flank of the German armies advancing into Belgium, Luxembourg, and France, would begin the invasion. Next, air and ground attacks by *Generaloberst* Fedor von Bock's Army Group B, in the north, aimed to draw the Allied armies forward into Belgium and away from the planned German main attack in the south. Finally, the main attack through the Ardennes Forest and Luxembourg, led by powerful armored forces under Gen. Gerd von Rundstedt's Army Group A, had the mission of seizing bridgeheads across the Meuse River in the Sedan area.

Generalleutnant Erwin von Kleist's panzer group, a part of *Generaloberst* Siegmund List's Twelfth Army, was Army Group A's main effort. Panzer Group Kleist had *Generalleutnant* Guderian's XIX Panzer Corps of three panzer divisions and *Generalleutnant* Georg Reinhardt's XLI Panzer Corps of two panzer divisions.[17] The 7th Panzer Division, along with *Generalmajor* von Hartlieb's 5th Panzer Division, made up the XV Panzer Corps, commanded by *Generalleutnant* Hermann Hoth. The aggressive and experienced Hoth had also commanded XV Panzer Corps during the 1939 Polish campaign. XV Panzer Corps was a subordinate unit in *General der Artillerie* Günther von Kluge's Fourth Army (fourteen divisions in total). The Fourth Army was the most northerly army within Rundstedt's Army Group A.

7th Panzer Division's mission, as a part of XV Panzer Corps, was to attack through the northern part of the Ardennes and cross the Meuse River between Givet and Namur in order to guard the right (northern) flank of Panzer Group Kleist, the Army Group's main effort. Following the crossing of the Meuse, the general intent for XV Panzer Corps was to continue to attack to the west to protect the right flank of Panzer Group Kleist.

At 0530 on 10 May, the 7th Panzer Division crossed the German-

Belgian border heading for Dinant on the Meuse River 120 kilometers away. Led by its reinforced reconnaissance battalion on motorcycles, the division moved through the Ardennes Forest along a single axis. Reinforcing the 7th Motorcycle Battalion was a motorized rifle company, engineer platoon, antitank platoon, artillery battery, and an antiaircraft battery. The initial going was very slow. Moving an armored division through the densely wooded Ardennes, with its twisting narrow roads, defiles, steep embankments, and many natural and man-made obstacles, proved a daunting challenge.

The efforts of unit traffic control personnel and the Luftwaffe made the challenge of moving through the potentially vulnerable Ardennes much easier. Staff officers in the XV Panzer Corps did a remarkable job of developing and marking inevitable route changes brought on by numerous man-made obstacles. An armored division strung out and stuck on winding trails is a tempting target for aerial attack. The Luftwaffe maintained local air superiority throughout the two-day movement through the Ardennes. The Allied air forces made no serious large-scale attempt to disrupt the huge German advance through the difficult terrain.[18]

A light Belgian screening force, the *Chasseurs Ardennais,* opposed the 7th Panzer Division. The Belgians barricaded and blew deep craters in most roads and forest trails. Luckily for the Germans, the Belgians left the majority of the roadblocks undefended. The 7th Panzer Division bypassed some of the obstacles by going around them and by moving on side roads. If units were unable to bypass, then the engineers quickly cleared the obstruction. When the Belgians did fight, they fought bravely. This kept the division from reaching its objective, the Ourthe River, on the first day—an unacceptable development to the leaders of the 7th Panzer Division. Quickly learning lessons from the first day of movement, the division's leaders concentrated and reorganized units on the evening of 10 May.[19]

At dawn on the eleventh, the division advanced along two axes instead of one. The reinforced 7th Motorcycle Battalion led the advance on the northern axis, while the reinforced 37th Armored Reconnaissance Battalion led the advance in the south. By the end of the morning, leading elements of the division had smashed

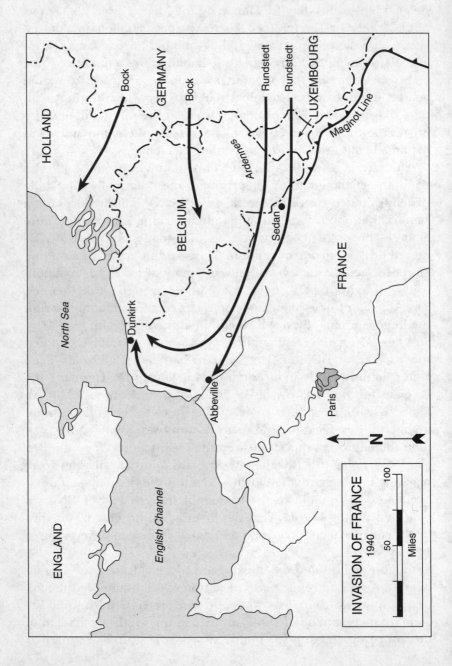

INVASION OF FRANCE
1940

Miles
0   50   100

through Belgian resistance to reach the Ourthe River, the previous night's objective and the only major obstacle on the way to the Meuse. Along the Ourthe, the French 4th Light Cavalry Division (DLC) waited to pick up the fight from the Belgians.[20]

Seventh Panzer Division units crossed the Ourthe River in two places: the 7th Motorcycle Battalion south of Hotton and the 37th Reconnaissance Battalion north of La Roche. At this point the division began to pick up speed. The 7th Motorcycle Battalion fought a small engagement northeast of the road junction at Marche against mechanized elements of the 4th DLC.[21] Advancing south of the motorcycle battalion, the 37th took the town of Marche itself. By the evening of the eleventh, the division had units west of Marche, only thirty-five kilometers from the Meuse.

Both friend and foe noted the 7th Panzer Division's success. Strong French forces set up a blocking position near the town of Leignon to prevent Rommel from reaching the river. On the evening of 11 May, Rommel decided to commit his main body in order to clear a path to Dinant. At XV Panzer Corps, *Generalleutnant* Hoth noted that the 7th Panzer Division was moving much faster and making more progress than its neighbor, the 5th Panzer Division.[22]

Jumping the Meuse

The 25th Panzer and 7th Rifle Regiments attacked at 0700 the next morning and broke through the French defenses three hours later. The 25th Panzer captured the towns of Ciney and Leignon, just sixteen kilometers from Dinant. As the division continued its push toward the Meuse, a large gap developed between it and the 5th Panzer Division. Rather than hold up Rommel's progress, *Generalleutnant* Hoth decided to reinforce his success and temporarily transferred the 5th Panzer Division's advance element, *Oberst* Werner's 31st Panzer Regiment, to Rommel. This gave the 7th Panzer Division an additional 150 tanks, but also widened the division's frontage and area of responsibility.

The 7th Panzer Division now aggressively raced to the Meuse River with hopes of capturing a bridge intact. The 7th Motorcycle

Battalion and 31st Panzer Regiment reached the Meuse Valley by the afternoon of the twelfth. At 1620, the bridge at Dinant blew up just as tanks from 25th Panzer Regiment arrived. In the north, scouts in armored cars from Werner's 31st Panzer Regiment found a bridge intact at Yvoir at 1630 and attempted to cross it. With a huge explosion, the French blew the bridge, destroying two of Werner's armored cars in the process.[23] The French had managed to destroy the last of the bridges across the river. Leading elements of the 7th Panzer Division now swarmed around the east bank of the Meuse between Dinant and Yvoir looking for additional crossing points.

Just south of Yvoir, in the vicinity of the village of Houx, soldiers from the 7th Motorcycle Battalion found a small stone dam connected to a narrow island in midstream. A lock gate connected the other side of the island to the river's west bank. *Oberst* Furst, the infantry brigade commander, ordered the motorcycle battalion to cross the river on foot that night. Initial patrols went over the dam without provoking a French reaction. Eventually, two companies of the 7th Motorcycle Battalion crossed the Meuse and dug in on the west bank. Thus, shortly after midnight on the twelfth, the 7th Panzer Division held a tenuous bridgehead on the west side of the Meuse.

Gaining an early foothold on the west bank of the Meuse proved to be a remarkable feat. Army Group A's main effort, Panzer Group Kleist with five panzer divisions and the support of an entire army group, did not reach the Meuse until that evening. Panzer Group Kleist, which included *Generalleutnant* Heinz Guderian's XIX Corps and the support of virtually every available Luftwaffe ground-attack aircraft in the theater, planned to begin crossing the Meuse at 1600 on the thirteenth.[24] The German high command, focusing on Panzer Group Kleist in the south, was unaware of the 7th Panzer Division's rapid advance. Allotted only a secondary flank security role to the main effort, the division already had established a foothold on the far side of the river and was developing a major offensive of its own. Rommel, with very little air support allocated to his division, ordered the attack to begin at dawn—twelve hours before the main attack in the south.

The division pushed elements across the river at first light and achieved two secure bridgeheads after several hours of intense fighting. The 7th Motorcycle Battalion and the 6th Rifle Regiment secured the northern bridgehead near Houx. The 7th Rifle Regiment, with assistance from the 25th Panzer Regiment, secured a southern bridgehead near Dinant. These successes owed much to the leadership and energy of the division commander. Rommel's command presence and aggressive style came to the forefront during the critical crossing of the Meuse, a day that would spell disaster for the French army and for France itself.

At 0400 on the thirteenth, after checking the readiness of the artillery support, Rommel drove to Dinant with his adjutant, Captain Schrapler. Rommel received a quick report from his engineer battalion commander, *Major* Brinkau, and *Oberst* Furst, the infantry brigade commander. The situation looked bleak. French direct and indirect fire thwarted attempts by the 7th Rifle Regiment to get across the river in rubber boats. Dinant and most of the Meuse Valley were being pounded by French artillery. Antitank fire from the west bank had knocked out a number of German tanks approaching the river. Furthermore, the early morning mist, which had provided invaluable concealment to the motorcycle battalion in the north at Houx, was dissipating. To make matters worse, several times during the meeting, French shellfire landed near Rommel himself. Rommel, *Oberst* Furst, and *Major* Brinkau took cover on the ground as the meeting progressed.[25]

The need for smoke to conceal the division's southern river crossing was obvious. No smoke unit was available, however, so Rommel ordered that several houses along the Meuse be burned to provide a makeshift smoke screen. As soon as smoke began to cover the area, the crossing began anew. Rommel then moved to the northern crossing site near Houx.

In the north, most of the 7th Motorcycle Battalion had reached the west bank of the Meuse. However, French resistance there stiffened. Direct and indirect fire prevented the movement of German antitank guns to the west bank. Deadly enemy fire also wounded a company commander and killed the battalion adjutant and another lieutenant. The 7th Motorcycle Battalion's commander, *Major*

Steinkeller, took charge of two companies himself and attacked and seized the hamlet of La Grange on the high ground just above the crossing area. There were still numerous pockets of enemy resistance between *Major* Steinkeller's position and the crossing area, however. Heavy French gunfire prevented further river-crossing operations, effectively severing the 7th Motorcycle Battalion from the east bank.[26]

The situation in the north did not please Rommel when he arrived. He felt that *Major* Steinkeller should have first expanded the west bank zone laterally and cleared the zone thoroughly to protect the crossing area from direct fire before attacking inland.[27] Rommel ordered the 6th Rifle Regiment to clear the west bank of all French units that could place direct fire on the crossing site. Rommel also feared that the lightly armed 7th Motorcycle Battalion, without antitank guns, was vulnerable to a French armored counterattack.

Rommel left the northern crossing site and returned to the southern crossing site just north of Dinant at about 0800. While en route, his command group came under fire from French forces on the west bank of the river. A shell burst wounded *Hauptmann* Schrapler.[28] When Rommel arrived, *Oberst* von Bismarck reported that his 7th Rifle Regiment had managed to get only one company across the river because of the heavy French direct and indirect fire.

The division commander soon realized that his only hope of getting more men and equipment across was to neutralize the French strong points on the west bank with powerful artillery and tank support. Returning to his command post (CP) around 1000 hours, he met with the corps commander, Hoth, and the Fourth Army commander, *General* der Artillerie Kluge. Both had followed his progress with interest. Rommel quickly briefed his higher commanders and then discussed the situation with his Ia, *Major* Heidkämper. After coordinating for additional firepower, Rommel returned to Dinant to get the southern crossing moving. En route, a Luftwaffe aircraft accidentally bombed his vehicle. Luckily for Rommel there were no injuries.[29]

Additional German tanks and artillery arrived at the southern crossing site around noon. Rommel personally directed the tanks to slowly move up and down the east bank with turrets traversed at ninety degrees, firing across the river at French positions about one hundred to two hundred meters downrange.[30] Under cover of the tanks' gunfire, the crossing slowly got under way again. The division commander was everywhere—with the engineers, leaping on tanks to give them targets to shoot, pushing additional firepower assets forward, and whipping up the morale of badly shaken riflemen. At one point, Rommel took temporary command of the 2d Battalion, 7th Rifle Regiment, from *Major* Bachman and crossed the river in a rubber boat.[31]

Rommel reached the west bank of the Meuse just in time to be on the receiving end of a French armored counterattack against the two German rifle companies. All of the German tank and antitank support remained on the other side of the river. Rommel told the company commanders to have their men fire small arms at the tanks to make the French tanks button up. The ruse worked and the tanks withdrew.[32]

Late in the afternoon, Rommel recrossed to the east bank, mounted a tank from the 25th Panzer Regiment, and drove to the northern crossing site near Houx to find the crossing in full swing. At least twenty antitank guns had forded the river, the infantry brigade headquarters and the 7th Motorcycle Battalion were safely on the west bank, elements of the 6th Rifle Regiment were moving across, and the engineers had begun building a bridge. Rommel was pleased with the progress in the north until he noticed that the engineers were building an eight-ton bridge that could not support tanks. He immediately ordered them to cease work and start building a sixteen-ton bridge so tanks could get across as quickly as possible. French direct and indirect fire continued to disrupt efforts to build the sixteen-ton bridge. Several pontoons were hit and a number of engineers, including the engineer battalion commander, *Major* Brinkau, were killed.[33]

While Rommel was on the east bank of the northern crossing site, the French launched a counterattack on the west bank against the bridgehead established by the 7th Motorcycle Battalion. The battalion succeeded in halting the counterattack, but the unit sustained numerous casualties, including its commander, *Major* Steinkeller. Rommel immediately crossed the Meuse and went to the infantry brigade headquarters to personally survey the situation.

Determining the need for immediate tank support, he ordered a panzer company, to be followed later by the entire panzer regiment, to cross the river by ferry on the evening of 13 May. Ferrying tanks across the river was a slow process, and by first light only fifteen tanks had made it to the far shore.[34]

After four full days of moving and fighting the division was show-ing clear signs of exhaustion. The 7th Panzer Division had moved far ahead of the divisions on each of its flanks. The 5th Panzer Division to the north was several kilometers behind, and the 32d In-fantry Division to the south was just approaching the Meuse. Con-ventional wisdom might have called for the division to wait for its neighbors.

The corps commander, Hoth, had other ideas.[35] Ordered to con-tinue the attack through the night, Rommel instructed *Oberst* von Bismarck's 7th Rifle Regiment at the southern crossing site to ad-vance against the village of Onhaye, five kilometers west of the Meuse. The division commander reinforced the regiment with ele-ments of the 42d Antitank Battalion and a tank platoon from the 25th Panzer Regiment.[36]

During the early morning hours of 14 May, while still under cover of darkness, Rommel received a message that the 7th Rifle Regi-ment was in trouble. He immediately ordered *Oberst* Rothenburg and all available tanks from 25th Panzer Regiment to move to On-haye to assist. Rommel, riding in a tank, moved behind Rothen-burg's tank. En route, Rommel learned that the 7th Rifle Regiment did not need help after all.[37] However, as the tanks of the 25th Panzer Regiment approached Onhaye, they came under attack by heavy and accurate French direct and indirect fire. Rommel's tank was hit twice, and shell fragments struck him in the cheek. Rommel, blood pouring down his face, abandoned the tank, taking the crew with him to seek cover in the woods. They barely escaped being cap-tured by French troops.[38]

This temporary setback lasted for only a couple of hours. By mid-morning the 7th Rifle Regiment, aided by the tanks that Rommel had brought forward and close air support by Stuka dive-bombers, had repelled several French counterattacks. During that eventful morning, Hoth decided to place all 5th Panzer Division units west of the Meuse under Rommel's control. Hoth's action showed considerable faith in the progress and audacity of Rommel and the 7th Panzer Division. By midnight, the division had moved about twelve kilometers west of the Meuse and, after nearly five continuous days of combat, Rommel and his men were given a much-needed break until the next morning.

The 7th Panzer Division's crossing of the Meuse River was the first of three successful German crossings on 14 May. However, it was the first German division to really exploit the Meuse crossing. Far to the south, all three panzer divisions from Guderian's XIX Panzer Corps crossed the Meuse near Sedan. Reinhardt's XLI Panzer Corps, also a part of Panzer Group Kleist, held on to a narrow bridgehead across the Meuse. The Meuse crossing so unbalanced the French defenses that they never properly regrouped. Trying to contain three German crossings was too much for the French Ninth Army Commander, General Corap, who decided to fall back from the river line to the next main defense line farther to the west, along the rail line east of Philippeville, fifteen miles west of the Meuse.[39] This decision in all likelihood lost the campaign and the war for the French army.

Breakthrough and Exploitation

On the morning of 15 May, the 7th Panzer Division, acting on orders from XV Panzer Corps, attacked in the direction of Avesnes, seventy kilometers to the west. The division's intermediate objective was the town of Philippeville, which was about twenty-two kilometers away. Rommel met with his operations officer, *Major* Heidkämper, and the division artillery commander, *Oberstleutnant* Frohlich. The three agreed to draw the division thrust line from the church at Rosee to the church at Froidchapelle. Commanders at all levels marked the thrust line and the indirect fire targets on their maps.[40]

The division led with the 25th Panzer Regiment followed by elements of the division artillery, the 37th Reconnaissance Battalion, and the 7th Rifle Regiment. Rommel initially rode on *Oberst* Rothenburg's command tank. Receiving his highest allocation of air support since the beginning of the campaign, Rommel called for Stuka dive-bombers to attack just ahead of the regiment's lead tanks.[41]

Soon after beginning the advance on the morning of 15 May, the 66th Tank Battalion, the lead battalion in the 25th Panzer Regiment, fought a brief engagement against French armor at Flavion. Though outgunned by the heavier French tanks, the German tank commanders surprised and outfought the French. After mauling the enemy, the 25th Panzer Regiment continued to advance toward Philippeville with gun tubes traversed over the sides, firing at possible enemy targets in woods and farmhouses, and at villages. The combination of tanks firing on the move at all actual or suspected enemy positions and the terrifying Stuka dive-bombing completely unnerved, shocked, and paralyzed many French units. Enemy soldiers began to surrender in droves.

The 25th Panzer Regiment reached Philippeville by midday. The tankers were now in the French Ninth Army's rear area, causing havoc. Having outstripped its neighboring units on both flanks by at least ten to fifteen kilometers, the 7th Panzer Division was in a potentially dangerous situation. It would have to rely on speed and momentum for its flank security. Fortunately, the French were unprepared for the division's rapid tempo and continuous movement.

The division continued to advance. About four kilometers west of Philippeville, the 25th Panzer Regiment ran into stiff French resistance. It was at this point that Rommel realized that the rest of the division was lagging at least ten kilometers behind the tanks. A huge gap existed between the 37th Recon Battalion and the 25th Panzer Regiment. Rommel left *Oberst* Rothenburg's tank and drove east with a reinforced tank company as escort to bring the rest of the division forward.[42]

The division commander soon discovered that the French had taken advantage of the large gap between his units to counterattack the trailing 37th Recon Battalion and 7th Rifle Regiment. The Germans recovered quickly and destroyed numerous French tanks and equipment. Rommel was still not satisfied with the slow movement of *Oberst* Furst and the infantry brigade, which had caused the gap in the first place.[43] By late evening, the gap between the 25th Panzer

Regiment and the rest of the division had been closed and the division halted in the vicinity of Cerfontaine. It was now nearly forty kilometers west of the Meuse and at least fifteen to twenty kilometers ahead of the nearest friendly units.

At 0400 on the sixteenth, the reconnaissance battalion occupied Froidchapelle in preparation for an attack later in the day through the northwestern extension of the French Maginot Line. Thinking that the Maginot Line fortifications would be difficult, Rommel planned initially to lead with his tanks. Upon reaching the French fortifications, the two infantry regiments and supporting engineers would then pass through and, covered by tank and artillery fire, conduct a deliberate breach of the fortifications.

Following a visit by Kluge, Rommel moved out once again on *Oberst* Rothenburg's command tank. With the reconnaissance battalion in the lead, the 7th Motorcycle Battalion, 58th Engineer Battalion, 25th Panzer Regiment, and the infantry brigade followed. The division occupied the town of Sivry without incident, the combat engineers along with the motorcycle battalion clearing obstacles. The tanks bypassed the town of Clairfayts and continued to advance. At this point, everything was going as planned.

When the engineers finished breaching obstacles west of Clairfayts at about 2200, Rommel sensed a golden opportunity. Reacting intuitively, he decided to forgo the planned deliberate breach of the Maginot Line by the engineers and infantry. Instead, he ordered the 25th Panzer Regiment to advance at maximum speed, followed closely by the 37th Recon Battalion and the 7th Motorcycle Battalion. The division artillery had the mission of screening their flanks with indirect fire and covering the roads and villages in front of the advanced detachment. Unfortunately, the infantry regiments once more lagged behind. The division's advance now became a "mad nocturnal pursuit."[44]

At about 2300 on 16 May, near the village of Sar-Poterie, the advance detachment came under French direct and indirect fire. The tankers fired all their weapons with gun tubes to the side and continued to move. The French defensive zone began to collapse as surprised French soldiers watched German tanks attack what was once a safe and secure rear area. By midnight, the 25th Panzer Regiment was in Avesnes. Thousands of French soldiers surrendered to the division in the early morning hours of the seventeenth.[45]

Rommel and the leading elements of the 25th Panzer Regiment next moved west of Avesnes, only to encounter a French tank battalion that had slipped between the lead battalion and the trailing 2d Tank Battalion. *Oberst* Rothenburg lost contact and tried to regain radio contact with the trail battalion. General Rommel, on board the same tank, attempted to raise both the division CP and the XV Panzer Corps. One can only imagine the frustration and difficulty of a division commander and a regimental commander feverishly attempting to establish communications from the same tank.

Meanwhile, a fierce firefight took place in Avesnes between the French tank battalion and the 2d Tank Battalion, which was commanded by *Oberstleutnant* Ilgen. The battle ended just before 0400 on the seventeenth with the destruction of the French tank battalion. At first light, the 7th Panzer Division found itself strung out over a forty-five-kilometer stretch between Avesnes and Philippeville. General Rommel had no contact with his division headquarters, his infantry brigade, or with the corps headquarters. His advance detachment was so far forward that there were no friendly units on his flanks. Following the firefight in Avesnes, it was time to rest and consolidate the night's gains, reestablish contact with subordinate units and XV Panzer Corps, and make plans for the next movement. Rommel, however, had other plans.

With plenty of good reasons to stop and regroup, Rommel sensed what Clausewitz meant when he wrote, "No victory will be effective without pursuit; and no matter how brief the exploitation of victory, it must always go further than an immediate follow-up."[46] At least a division's worth of French soldiers and equipment had surrendered to the 7th Panzer Division in the last eighteen hours. The smell and look of French defeat were everywhere. Rommel felt that if he stopped attacking, he would end up allowing the French to recover from their initial shock at finding German tanks in their rear areas. Most importantly, Rommel wanted permission to seize a bridge on the Sambre River, the next major obstacle. Out of contact with corps headquarters, Rommel decided to act without orders. He advanced with what he had on hand: two tank battalions and the motorcycle battalion. His objective was to seize a bridge over the Sambre, eighteen kilometers to the west, at the town of Landrecies. Convinced that the rest of the division was behind him and would eventually catch up, Rommel moved out with the advance detachment.[47]

Unknown to Rommel, around midnight that same night, *Oberst* Furst moved the infantry brigade headquarters and 6th Rifle Regiment to rest positions near Sivry, twenty kilometers to the east of Avesnes. Furst also gave permission to the 7th Rifle Regiment to move to rest positions even farther to the east.[48] This meant that, except for the motorcycle battalion, there would be no infantry support that evening. At this point, Rommel himself truly did not know the location of the rest of the division and he could not control it because he was out of radio range. To make matters worse, the 25th Panzer Regiment's tanks were running low on fuel and ammunition, primarily due to the divisional tactic of liberally firing on the move against actual and suspected enemy positions.

Despite his supply and communications problems, Rommel and the advance detachment attacked toward Landrecies through the morning of 17 May. Numerous shocked French units began to surrender to Rommel and his fast-moving mobile force. The advance detachment soon reached the town and seized the bridge over the Sambre River intact. Still believing that the rest of the division was close behind, Rommel ordered the 25th Panzer Regiment to continue to attack west toward the town of Le Cateau. The advancing units halted just east of there, approximately fourteen kilometers west of the Sambre River. When Rommel looked back to the east and saw no follow-on units from the rest of the division, he finally stopped.[49] He ordered the 25th Panzer Regiment to move into defensive positions near Le Cateau and had the 7th Motorcycle Battalion secure the bridge. He then turned his attention to concentrating the division. Rommel left the advance detachment at midmorning and, with a tank escort, drove the twenty-eight kilometers back to Avesnes, arriving there at about 1500.

On French and German situation maps the 7th Panzer Division's position looked like a long, thin, forty-kilometer dagger stabbing west into the French defensive zone. The 7th Panzer Division's leaders now concentrated on consolidating and clearing the extended division zone. Firefights between 7th Panzer Division and French units within the zone continued during this consolidation period. The Germans captured thousands of French soldiers and scores of tanks, armored cars, artillery, and other equipment throughout the day.

That evening, General Hoth ordered Rommel to seize the bridge over the Sambre at Berlaimont, thirteen kilometers northwest of Avesnes, and hold the bridge open for the 5th Panzer Division, which was at least a day behind. Showing remarkable flexibility, the 7th Panzer Division operations staff dispatched the 1st Battalion, 6th Rifle Regiment, reinforced with an artillery battalion, to seize the bridge at Berlaimont. The battalion completed its mission without incident late in the evening on 17 May.

With the situation well in hand, General Rommel finally decided to get some rest. The respite did not last long, however. At a little after midnight, XV Panzer Corps ordered the 7th Panzer Division to continue the attack the next morning through Le Cateau toward Cambrai. Unfortunately, the 6th Rifle Regiment encountered a large French armored force around the Pommereuille Wood area, between Landrecies and Le Cateau, a dangerous development since resupplying the 25th Panzer Regiment in Le Cateau was imperative before mounting an attack toward Cambrai. The division succeeded in defeating the French force near Pommereuille Wood by midday.

The division finally launched its attack toward Cambrai at about 1700 on 18 May, moving along two axes centered on French National Route 39. The 25th Panzer Regiment, 7th Motorcycle Battalion, and 1st Battalion, 6th Rifle Regiment, reinforced with artillery and antiaircraft units, attacked north of Route 39 to seize the communications center of Cambrai. The 7th Rifle Regiment attacked along the southern axis, south and southeast of Cambrai. The attacks made good progress. By 2100, the 25th Panzer Regiment had fixed the French in Cambrai while 1st Rifle Battalion and 7th Motorcycle Battalion skirted the city to the north and seized bridges over the L'Escaut Canal. The 7th Rifle Regiment seized the area south and southeast of Cambrai. By 2300, Cambrai was firmly under the division's control. Rommel now had his units assume a defensive posture in order to fight off strong French counterattacks throughout the division's zone. The French counterattacked around Le Cateau and also against Landrecies, along the Sambre River. Pushing fuel and ammunition forward in this environment was a challenge. By midnight on the eighteenth, the 7th Panzer Division's left flank neighbor, the 12th Infantry Division, was still fifty-two kilometers to the east. The 5th Panzer Division, on the right flank, was twenty-nine kilometers behind.

During the morning and afternoon of 19 May, the 7th Panzer Division consolidated, rested, and reorganized. Over the next two days, the division attacked toward Arras and met a British counterattack in that vicinity. It blunted the British attack on the twenty-first, but not before the British counterattack caused alarm among the senior leaders of the German army.[50] Driving toward the sea, Rommel continued to attack from 22–28 May, helping to force the British evacuation at Dunkirk. Following a short rest period, the 7th Panzer Division next participated in the attack across the Somme River on 5 June and the rapid movement from the Seine River to Cherbourg. With the capture of Cherbourg on 19 June 1940, the campaign in France ended for the newly christened "Ghost Division."

The Campaign in Review

The 7th Panzer Division's success during the campaign in France significantly affected the overall success of the German army. Crossing the Meuse River on 13 May, the division wrested the tactical initiative from the French Ninth Army. However, the Meuse crossing, by itself, did not cause the French defeat. The division's ability to create and maintain momentum caused the collapse and defeat of French forces within the division's zone of attack. It maintained this momentum by continuing to attack faster than the French could physically and mentally prepare to defend. The psychological effect on the opposing French commanders was profound. Maneuvering deep into the French rear areas caused shock, confusion, and eventually paralysis throughout the French Ninth Army, generating effects out of all proportion to the division's actual blows.

The aggressive leadership and will of *Generalmajor* Erwin Rommel strongly animated the division during the first ten days of the French campaign. Leading from the front and not from a rear command post, Rommel made timely decisions and was able to sense and rapidly take advantage of fleeting windows of tactical and sometimes operational opportunities. An austere, professional division staff much leaner than its modern U.S. Army counterpart was able to quickly process orders and execute the intent of the division commander. The aggressive style and leadership of leaders throughout the 7th Panzer Division fed its extraordinary momentum during operations. The first example of this occurred during the operations leading up to the Meuse crossing and the subsequent expansion of the bridgehead. Another example occurred during the night attack on the evening of 17 May that culminated in the seizure of a bridge over the Sambre.

A common approach to warfighting displayed by leaders at every level throughout the division revealed itself again and again as the 7th Panzer Division continuously wrested the initiative from its opponents. Firing on the move, both day and night, at confirmed as well as unconfirmed enemy positions kept the French off balance. Simple, functional command techniques such as the use of thrust lines also helped to maintain momentum by encouraging a sense of offensive purpose, brevity on the radio, and rapid orientation in quickly changing situations.

Today, particularly after the 1991 Persian Gulf War, the idea of a lightning campaign based on mechanized ground forces and air support is not revolutionary. In 1940, however, few knew what to expect from mechanized ground forces during a fast-moving campaign. The 7th Panzer Division in 1940 fought and defeated larger and better-equipped opponents because it had forward-leaning leaders at all levels who pushed to gain and maintain momentum through aggressive maneuver. Boldness, the use of surprise, a readiness to accept risks, and an intuitive sense of the importance of momentum on the battlefield distinguished Rommel's exercise of command in this, the German army's greatest hour.

In the twenty-first century, American commanders similarly find themselves in charge of highly digitized, lethal, but increasingly smaller combat formations. Though much has changed, much remains the same in the clash of wills that still defines modern warfare. In searching for answers to the challenges of fighting outnumbered, they will find much to learn from the Ghost Division and its indomitable commander.

Notes

1. David Fraser, *Knight's Cross: A Life of Field Marshal Erwin Rommel* (New York: HarperCollins, 1993), 191–92; Correlli Barnett, ed., *Hitler's Generals* (New York: George Weidenfeld and Nicolson, 1989), 298. The title of "Ghost Division" was certainly earned by the 7th Panzer Division's overwhelming success, swiftness, and unexpected appearance on the battlefield time after time. It is unclear, however, if the title came from French commentators or German propaganda. It is known that German propagandists used the nickname Ghost Division to help make Erwin Rommel a national hero in Germany in 1940.

2. George Forty, *The Armies of Rommel* (London: Arms and Armour, 1997), 38. General Stumme was to meet Rommel again in North Africa.

3. Hans von Luck, *Panzer Commander* (New York: Dell, 1989), 35. Von Luck was initially a company commander in the 37th Armored Reconnaissance Battalion at the beginning of the campaign. He later became the battalion commander when his commander, Major Erdmann, was killed on 28 May 1940.

4. Fraser, *Knight's Cross,* 161; Forty, *Armies of Rommel,* 38.

5. Forty, *Armies of Rommel,* 39. *Oberst* is the German equivalent of colonel in the U.S. Army.

6. Ibid., 43. *Oberstleutnant* is the German equivalent of lieutenant colonel in the U.S. Army.

7. R. H. S. Stolfi, *A Bias for Action: The German 7th Panzer Division in France and Russia, 1940–1941,* Perspectives on Warfighting, no. 1 (Quantico, Va.: Marine Corps University, 1991), 14–15.

8. Stolfi, *Bias for Action,* 13–16. According to Stolfi: "The messages show a remarkably stark but also streamlined style. They also show that the officers writing them shared a common, no-nonsense operational language." The following is an example of a typical message exchange between 7th Panzer Division headquarters and a subordinate unit. Division headquarters to the 7th Rifle Regiment on 13 May at 0550: "How are you doing?" The reply at 0640: "7th Rifle Regiment crossed the Maas River at 0600."

9. Ibid., 12. Fraser, *Knight's Cross,* 173.

10. Basil H. Liddell Hart, ed., *The Rommel Papers* (New York: Da Capo, 1988), 7. Units from the 7th Panzer Division would drive through woods, towns, and villages with guns blazing. This technique often caught French defenders by surprise, but it was controversial because of its potential for causing unnecessary French civilian casualties.

11. Heinz Guderian, *Panzer Leader* (New York: Ballantine Books, 1957), 11–20.

12. Alistair Horne, *To Lose a Battle: France 1940* (Boston: Little, Brown, 1969), 249. Liddell Hart, ed., *Rommel Papers*, 4.

13. Horne, *To Lose a Battle*, 262; Liddell Hart, ed., *Rommel Papers*, 4; Forty, *Armies of Rommel*, 39. Most sources claim that the 7th Panzer Division began the campaign with 218 tanks. George Forty claims it had 225. A possible reason for this discrepancy may be found in Forty's categorization of seven or eight specially built command tanks as line tanks.

14. Horne, *To Lose a Battle*, 176. The French and British deployed approximately 450 bombers and dive-bombers in France compared to approximately 1,740 bombers and dive-bombers employed by the Germans.

15. Luck, *Panzer Commander*, 35.

16. Ibid., 35–37.

17. Erich von Manstein, *Lost Victories*, ed., Anthony E. Powell (Novato, Calif.: Presidio Press, 1982), 107–111, 123; Forty, *Armies of Rommel*, 53.

18. Horne, *To Lose a Battle*, 205–06; Fraser, *Knight's Cross*, 164, 165.

19. Horne, *To Lose a Battle*, 223.

20. Ibid., 223; Forty, *Armies of Rommel*, 55.

21. Liddell Hart, ed., *Rommel Papers*, 7.

22. Stolfi, *Bias for Action*, 6.

23. Horne, *To Lose a Battle*, 249–50.

24. Guderian, *Panzer Leader*, 78–79; Stolfi, *Bias for Action*, 7.

25. Liddell Hart, ed., *Rommel Papers*, 8.

26. Horne, *To Lose a Battle*, 265.

27. Liddell Hart, ed., *Rommel Papers*, 9.

28. *Hauptmann* is the equivalent of captain in the U.S. Army.

29. Ibid., 9; Fraser, *Knight's Cross*, 168.

30. Horne, *To Lose a Battle,* 266.

31. Liddell Hart, ed., *Rommel Papers,* 10. Forty, *Armies of Rommel,* 56. A division commander taking personal charge of an infantry battalion in modern combat is certainly rare. Rommel felt that the troops in the 2d Battalion, 7th Rifle Regiment, were badly shaken and needed strong leadership.

32. Fraser, *Knight's Cross,* 169; Liddell Hart, ed., *Rommel Papers,* 10.

33. Horne, *To Lose a Battle,* 268; Forty, *Armies of Rommel,* 43. The 7th Panzer Division had a high number of officer casualties during the campaign. This was probably due to the officer corps's emulation of Rommel's "lead from the front" style. Leaders within the division were up front and visible. They also made inviting targets. Rommel was shot at several times during the French campaign and luckily was wounded only once. Unfortunately, many of his subordinate leaders were not as lucky.

34. Liddell Hart, ed., *Rommel Papers,* 11.

35. Stolfi, *Bias for Action,* 9. This was a gutsy call by General Hoth. The soldiers of the 7th Panzer Division had been on the move since 10 May and had been fighting continuously since the twelfth. Units within the division must have been close to physical and mental exhaustion by the evening of the thirteenth. Knowing this, Hoth still ordered a night attack. Rommel probably would have ordered the same attack also, but Hoth beat him to the punch. Both Rommel and Hoth clearly understood the need to maintain momentum through aggressive and ruthless maneuver, even if it meant pushing subordinate units to the breaking point.

36. Stolfi, *Bias for Action,* 9.

37. Ibid., 10; Liddell Hart, ed., *Rommel Papers,* 12. The original radio message received by the 7th Panzer Division headquarters from the 7th Rifle Regiment was that the unit was surrounded *(eingeschlossen).* However, the actual message sent by the 7th Rifle Regiment was that the unit had been struck or hit by a French counterattack *(eingetroffen).*

38. Horne, *To Lose a Battle,* 310.

39. Liddell Hart, ed., *Rommel Papers,* 14.

40. Fraser, *Knight's Cross,* 173; Forty, *Armies of Rommel,* 58.

41. Horne, *To Lose a Battle,* 339; Fraser, *Knight's Cross,* 174.

42. Liddell Hart, ed., *Rommel Papers*, 15.

43. Ibid., 16–17.

44. Horne, *To Lose a Battle*, 403.

45. Stolfi, *Bias for Action*, 20–21.

46. Carl von Clausewitz, *On War*, ed. and trans. Michael Howard (Princeton, N.J.: Princeton University Press, 1976), 263. Clausewitz's insight on following up a victory with a ruthless pursuit in Chapter 12 of Book 4 is compelling. Clausewitz writes that few commanders are able to think beyond the present moment at the end of a battle to conduct an aggressive pursuit. Clausewitz also states that successful pursuits occur primarily due to the commander's ambition, energy, and quite possibly his callousness.

47. Liddell Hart, ed., *Rommel Papers*, 22.

48. Stolfi, *Bias for Action*, 21, 23.

49. Fraser, *Knight's Cross*, 177.

50. Ibid., 187. The initial shock of the British armor counterattack at Arras affected the nerves of the Fourth Army commander (Kluge) and the Army Group A commander (Rundstedt). Hitler in turn sensed their anxiety.

"A Most Daring Enterprise": The Conquest of Fortress Singapore

> Our Army and Navy . . . have harried and hunted a strong enemy and broken through his defenses at every point, capturing Singapore with the speed of the gods.[1]
>
> —Emperor Hirohito

The Japanese campaign to conquer Malaya and seize the British naval base at Singapore was a pivotal event in the struggle for Japanese hegemony during World War II. In seventy days of brilliant fighting, from 8 December 1941 to 15 February 1942, the three divisions of the Japanese Twenty-fifth Army, advancing through "impenetrable jungle,"[2] captured the Fortress of Singapore—"the Gibraltar of the East"—and dealt the United Kingdom the greatest defeat in its long, proud history.

The opponents in the battle for Malaya possessed sharply contrasting styles of warfare. In spite of the growing threat of war in the Far East and two years of conflict in Europe, the British, Australian, and Indian troops in Malaya were ill prepared for combat. Lieutenant General Sir Arthur Percival, commander of Commonwealth troops in Malaya, repeated many of the same mistakes that marked the British defeat in France in 1940 at the hands of the German blitzkrieg. Naked British courage, the traditional last resort of the British army, could not stem the Japanese tide without a bodyguard of competent planning, intelligence, technology, and generalship.

The Japanese, on the other hand, displayed an "inextinguishable daring and explosive energy" and maintained a tempo of attack that preempted an effective British defense of Malaya.[3] The plan to conquer Malaya was one of the "more complicated operations carried out by the Japanese in the entire war" and one of the most decisive campaigns of World War II.[4] The Japanese Twenty-fifth Army, commanded by Gen. Tomoyuki Yamashita, demonstrated in Malaya what the Japanese army could do when led by a master of the operational art.

The Japanese conquest of Malaya ranks as one of the greatest military campaigns in history, yet it is rarely studied by Westerners. A well-known rule of military science states that an attacker should have a three-to-one advantage over the defender to ensure success. If the defender occupies prepared positions in rugged, restricted terrain, the required ratio can rise dramatically in favor of the defender. How did the Japanese beat a force twice its size in the restricted jungle terrain of Malaya? What lessons can be gleaned from the Japanese victory?

Brilliant campaigns ending with lopsided victories are unusual in war. Malaya, in particular, defies the ledger-logic of force comparisons and demonstrates the intangibles of war, what one Japanese writer called the "spiritual power" of the Japanese.[5] The study of short, decisive campaigns therefore becomes an important primer for anyone interested in war as an act of policy.

Japan stood at a crossroads in 1941. Germany had already conquered France, pushed England off the continent, and invaded Russia. Russia was reeling from the Wehrmacht's assault and tottered on the verge of capitulation. In Japan, the final impetus for war came when Japanese economists reported that the U.S. oil embargo would exhaust Japanese fuel reserves within eighteen to twenty-four months. That looming threat, added to a bellicose war party that had swept into power, pointed Japan irreversibly on the road to global war.

A Divided Strategy

Within the Japanese military, two camps contended for strategic primacy. One wished to strike north into Russia to seize territory before the Germans succeeded in knocking the Soviets out of the war. The other wanted to strike south to secure the rich resources of

Southeast Asia. A critical player in these debates was Lt. Col. Masanobu Tsuji, a socially prominent officer and brilliant planner whose thinking heavily influenced the decisions of the Imperial General Staff. A participant in the bitter fighting at Khalkhin Gol in 1939, Tsuji wanted no part of another disastrous Russian campaign.

Based on this strategic assessment, and their current intelligence assessments, the Japanese Imperial General Staff decided to strike south to seize all of Southeast Asia and create an island defensive zone of "unsinkable carriers" to secure the Empire. In a series of rapid campaigns, the Japanese General Staff planned to attack Pearl Harbor, the Philippines, and Malaya before consolidating to defend against the inevitable Anglo-American counterattack. "The concept of achieving decisive victory by one surprise blow lay deep in the Japanese character."

The Malayan campaign was planned and directed by Tsuji, a brilliant zealot called the "God of Operations."[6] In the months leading up to the campaign, Tsuji, "an idol of the most radical young officers,"[7] forcefully touted Singapore as "the key to Southeast Asia. Its seizure will emancipate the oppressed peoples of Asia and will also exert a powerful influence to bring about settlement in China."[8] Seldom has a lowly lieutenant colonel played such a critical role in the fortunes of war. With ties to the Japanese Imperial Court, a brilliant mind, and a large following, Tsuji "played a remarkably significant part in accelerating Japan's progress toward war."[9] General Hideki Tojo selected Tsuji to command a ten-man staff cell, called the *Doro Narwa* Unit, to plan the conquest of Malaya and Singapore. In addition to campaign planning, the group also developed tactics, techniques, procedures, and equipment for combat in the jungles and islands of Southeast Asia. Tsuji's pamphlet *Read This Alone—And the War Can Be Won,* published and issued to each soldier in the Imperial Army in 1941, became an influential document that was studied as a primer on combat operations in Southeast Asia's rugged terrain. In addition, the pamphlet offered a moral and political justification for war: "If we remain patient any longer, Japan's aircraft, warships and road transport may be forced to a standstill . . . the final reckoning of our holy crusade will come on the battlefields ahead."[10]

Tsuji's plan for the Malaya campaign was brilliant and bold. In the first phase, Japanese forces would "land in southern Thailand, brave the intense heat and the long distance of eleven hundred kilometers, and advance through dense jungle,"[11] to seize critical airfields and capture Kuala Lumpur. In the next, decisive phase of the campaign, the Twenty-fifth Army would attack to capture Singapore from the north, where defenses were the weakest. Japanese planners were well aware that the combined might of the Americans, British, and Dutch could work against Japan. Surprise and speed thus lay at the heart of the operational plan.[12] The goal was to stun the enemy with one swift blow and force his early capitulation.

A simple look at a 1941 terrain map of Malaya reveals clearly how difficult the campaign would be. The region's few roads roughly followed the eastern and western coastlines. A ridge of mountains running north to south divided Malaya down the center. The mountains stopped at Johore. The eastern side of the country was dense jungle. A single-track railway from Gemas to Kota Bharu to Thailand was the main route of transport. The only main road of importance ran from Kuantan across the central range to Raub. The eastern coast had sandy beaches dotted with mangrove, offering plenty of landing sites to an invader.

The western coastal strip, on the other hand, had an improved road net that ran from Johore Bahru to the Thai border. The western half of the country was heavily farmed and contained most of the rice-growing areas, rubber plantations, and tin mines. However, with less jungle and better roads, it offered fewer beaches suitable for amphibious landings. In addition, Penang Island, placed like a natural fortress on the west flank of the Malayan isthmus, could pose a serious obstacle to an attacker.

Tsuji pored over the intelligence reports, looking for a weakness in the British defenses. The Japanese had taken a keen interest in the construction of "Fortress Singapore" since the early 1930s. For years a dedicated network of Japanese spies had reported on British preparations in remarkable detail. From these reports, Tsuji discovered that Singapore's defenses were strong facing the sea in the south and east, but almost nonexistent to the north, along the Johore Strait. In spite of several official British studies that warned of the danger of an attack from the north, "the British took only half-hearted measures to fortify the northern approach."[13] The British believed that an assault from the north through the dense jungle would take months if not years. Tsuji, who was aware of the British plans, quickly determined that Singapore—a diamond-shaped island of immense strategic military, economic, and political importance—could be taken from the rear or landward side in spite of the difficulties the terrain would impose. He also decided that the main attack would strike down the western side of the Malay Peninsula.

From the beginning, Tsuji realized that success hinged on close coordination between Japanese naval, air, and land forces. Lacking the ships to land all his forces simultaneously, Tsuji realized that surprise and timing would have to make up for this deficiency. The plan called for the invasion fleet to depart Samah on Formosa and conduct seven separate night amphibious landings in Thailand (at Prachuap, Chumphon, Bandon, Nakhon, Singora, Thephau, and Patani) and one on Malaya's eastern coast at Khota Bharu. By landing in Thailand, Tsuji hoped to preempt a prepared British defense of northern Malaya. Once ashore, the advance forces would attack rapidly to seize their first vital objectives: the British airfields located close to the east coast.

Tsuji was convinced that airpower would play a decisive role in the campaign—if the British airfields in Malaya could be seized quickly and put to use by Japanese air units. After the airfields were secured, the invaders would simultaneously drive west, then south, bypassing enemy resistance. Eventually, the main attack by the Twenty-fifth Army would strike down the western coast, seize Johore, and conduct the assault on Singapore Island. Surprise, speed, and unrelenting pressure were required to win within the one hundred days allowed by the Imperial General Staff to complete the campaign.

The key points of the plan for the assault on Singapore Island itself were "to crush the enemy to the north of the Johore Strait; to block them in the sector east of the Dyke road (the

Causeway); to assault from the Causeway to the west; to advance first of all to the strategic line on the heights of Bukit Timah; and after that to occupy the whole island."[14]

General Yamashita, known to his men as the "Lion of Manchuria" for his exploits in China, was selected to command the Twenty-fifth Army on 5 November 1941.[15] Yamashita was renowned throughout the Japanese army as a determined and brilliant commander. Tsuji, having worked on the Malaya campaign plan since September 1941, presented the plan to Yamashita. The forces approved for this campaign consisted of three divisions and one tank brigade with air and naval support.

Yamashita quickly concurred with Tsuji's plan. Yamashita was so confident of victory that he decided that the three divisions allocated for the attack would be more than ample to defeat the British—in spite of the fact that the British outnumbered the Japanese two to one. Although a fourth division was allocated as a reserve for the attack, Yamashita believed that he would not need it. The "Lion of Manchuria" understood the difficulty of supplying units in restricted jungle terrain. He believed that three divisions, moving swiftly, could accomplish the mission and would be all that his stretched logistics could support.

The British at Bay

Winston Churchill, the imperturbable prime minister of Great Britain, saw Malaya, and especially Singapore, as an impregnable bastion of British strength in the Pacific. He believed that the British defenses in Malaya were solid and that Fortress Singapore could not be seized from the sea in a quick coup de main. If the Japanese were foolish enough to attack from the north, down the narrow roads along either coast, there would be plenty of time to stop them as they struggled through the difficult jungle terrain. The Royal Air Force (RAF) would either stop the Japanese on the beaches or smash them as their infantry trudged south. Churchill was also confident that the U.S. Pacific Fleet, anchored at Pearl Harbor, Hawaii, would race to Britain's aid.

On paper Churchill's view seemed logical, especially from far-off London. The British had a large, well-equipped force to defend Malaya and Singapore. British forces in Malaya consisted of almost 90,000 men: 20,000 British, 15,000 Australian, and 37,000 Indian troops. Supporting arms included an impressive array of 754 artillery pieces and 158 aircraft. Singapore itself was a formidable defensive work, consisting of reinforced concrete bunkers, ammunition storage areas, and fighting positions. The island of Singapore was naturally easy to defend. If properly employed, the civilian and military labor force available to the British there could shape the island's defenses into an impregnable fortress that would be difficult for any attacker to overcome.

Facing the sea, batteries of fifteen-inch guns dominated the eastern mouth of Johore Strait and protected the vast military barracks at Changi. The naval fortifications and gun emplacements were constructed of steel and concrete, with some of the world's most powerful coastal artillery. The military airfields on the island "were good bases for a large air force . . . the fortress took nearly ten years to build, cost over ten million pounds sterling, and was completed in February 1938."[16] To reinforce the garrison, the battleship *Prince of Wales* and the battle cruiser *Repulse* arrived in November 1941 to deter Japanese naval activity.

The true state of British defenses was, however, altogether different from outward appearances. British, Australian, and Indian units were woefully unprepared for combat. Training levels in almost all the British units were poor. Many of the men in the Australian units that arrived in 1941 were green recruits with only rudimentary military training. The state of the Indian troops was particularly bad, as would be seen in the fighting to come. Most alarming was the lack of new aircraft in sufficient numbers to patrol, defend, and intercept Japanese aviation. All of the British aircraft in Singapore were obsolete by 1941 standards, since the newest aircraft were needed to defend the skies over Great Britain.

To add to this sad state of affairs, the leadership of the British forces was second rate. Most of the best British and Australian commanders were in North Africa, fighting the Germans. The commander of all British forces in Malaya, Lieutenant General Percival, was not the dynamic, staunch leader needed to command Britain's vital strategic base in the Pacific. Essentially a polished staff officer, not a fighting commander in the mold of Maj. Gen. William Slim or Lt. Gen. Richard O'Connor, Percival lacked decisiveness and was consumed with doubt. Lacking confidence in his troops and worried about the lack of equipment (particularly airpower), Percival argued in vain with local government authorities for civilian labor support and generally failed to prepare for what many saw as the impending typhoon of war.[17] His commanders, particularly Maj. Gen. Henry G. Bennett of Australia, did not trust his leadership. Passive, rigid, obstinate, procrastinating, and dogmatic, Percival would prove no match for Yamashita.

Percival, however, was not blind to the possibility of a Japanese attack from the north. The British plan, code-named Matador, accounted for this possibility. In the event of a Japanese attack into Thailand, the British forces planned to rush north into Thailand and defend along the narrow and defensible Isthmus of Kra. At the same time, the RAF, operating from airfields in northern Malaya, would strike the aggressor before his forces could land on Malaya's shores. "Although the Japanese were firmly established in southern Indochina and had airfields from which the whole of Malaya and Singapore Island was within range of their bomber aircraft, it was obvious that, to support an advance down the western side of Malaya, they would in the first instance require airfields in southern Siam and northern Malaya."[18] British forces thus planned to primarily protect airfields rather than defeat the attacker in a battle of maneuver. In Malaya, the RAF was Britain's "silver bullet."

Tsuji's plan called for a swift battle of maneuver. Yamashita's Twenty-fifth Army consisted of the 5th and 18th Infantry Divisions and the Imperial Guard Division, a total of approximately sixty thousand men. His troops were confident, well trained, superbly disciplined veterans of the fighting in China. In addition, Yamashita had the 3d Tank Brigade with eighty light and medium tanks and forty armored cars, about four hundred artillery pieces of all types, and, most importantly, 617 modern airplanes. Many of these aircraft were excellent Zero-sen fighters. Japanese naval forces, however, were limited to one cruiser, ten destroyers, and five sub-marines. Tsuji rationalized the numerical disadvantage in ground forces by counting Japanese quality over British quantity.[19] Confi-dent of victory, he accepted risk in the area of naval forces and be-lieved that a surprise landing would provide security for the inva-sion forces. He also believed that the air force would gain air superiority everywhere over the battle area and could negate British sea power. Most importantly, Tsuji expected to benefit from the use of unorthodox tactics. The Japanese Twenty-fifth Army would fight as a combined-arms force, using infantry, tanks, engineers, and ar-tillery in close cooperation with air and naval forces.

Tsuji expected the Japanese forces to use the indirect approach, infiltrating and enveloping enemy defenses and exploiting battle-field opportunities as they occurred. He believed that the pace of the attack must be resolute and continuous. "If a man can pass, so can a motor vehicle. If a road is too narrow, cut a way through . . . force your way ahead, even if you have to carry the thing on your shoulders."[20] He understood that Japanese tactics would frame the operational victory as long as "the Japanese did not adhere to the established rules."[21]

The Battle for Malaya

The battle for control of the Malay Peninsula can be divided into three stages: the Japanese landing and the battle of Jitra; the Japa-nese crossing of the Perak River and the rush to Gemas from Kuala Lumpur; and the battle for Singapore Island. Thorough planning, tactical concentration, combined arms, and a singleness of purpose were written into each phase of the Japanese campaign. Tsuji's plan profited not only from the "unexpected choice of such a difficult route but by the opportunities for unexpected infiltration which the thick vegetation often provided."[22]

On 4 December the invasion fleet carrying the Twenty-fifth Army left Formosa. Tsuji's plan left nothing to chance. The convoys moved in bad weather and passed beyond the range of reconnais-sance aircraft, sailing with strong air escort by day to conduct landing operations under cover of darkness in the early hours of 8 December. The landings coincided roughly with the attacks on American forces at Pearl Harbor and in the Philippines.

Rough seas and bad weather greeted the Japanese invasion fleet as it prepared to land, causing great concern. Landing operations became so hazardous that troop barges and boats were scattered all along the eastern coast. Nevertheless, the landing continued. Japanese infantry climbed down cargo nets into small boats and struggled to shore. Luckily for the Japanese, surprise was complete and only the landing at Khota Bharu was opposed. Thailand, a neutral country, agreed to a cease-fire the first day and signed an alliance with the Japanese a few days later. Unwilling to upset Thailand's neutrality, the British decided not to move into Thailand prior to hostilities.

The only Japanese landing in Malaya occurred at Khota Bharu and was initially met by fierce British resistance. After a desperate fight and heavy casualties, the Japanese gained a foothold on the southern edge of the beach and turned the British defense. The invaders quickly moved inland as the British forces disengaged. Tanks and motor vehicles were unloaded, placed on steel barge boats, and rushed ashore. True to their plan, the Japanese seized the airfield at Khota Bharu intact, before its supplies of ammunition, bombs, and fuel could be destroyed. The seizure of this airfield and several others achieved the first major objective of the campaign. With the aid of these airfields, and excellent flying by determined pilots, the Japanese gained complete air superiority in four days. The capture of the airfields with their large stocks of fuel and ammunition was a serious blow to the Allies.[23]

Knocked off balance by the surprise Japanese attack, the British abandoned Matador, which called for mobile forces to move forward to stop the Japanese landings. Canceling orders to move troops to the north, Percival instructed his forces to defend the Malaya-Thai border at Jitra. He believed that it would take weeks for the Japanese to fight through the rugged, restricted jungle terrain. He was wrong. Within two days of the initial landings, Yamashita had established his forces in Malaya and was pushing inland. The Japanese advanced aggressively, shifting their forces from the east coast to the west while the British tried to decide what to do.

On 10 December the Japanese shocked the world with a tremendous victory at sea. Japanese planes searching for the British fleet caught the *Prince of Wales, Repulse,* and several destroyers steaming in the South China Sea. The British had sailed under heavy fog without air support, hoping to catch the Japanese invasion fleet unaware. As the fog suddenly cleared, Japanese torpedo planes attacked and sank the *Prince of Wales* and *Repulse.* "The effect of losing the ships was shattering . . . for the forces on the mainland the effect on morale was immediate and deadly."[24] The British went into shock and Singapore suddenly became a port without a navy. Coupled with the stunning Japanese victory at Pearl Harbor, the rapid destruction of the two most powerful ships in the British Far East Fleet and the quick seizure of the airfields in Malaya gave the Japanese a tremendous psychological and operational advantage.

Yamashita's main forces immediately pushed west across the neck of the Malay Peninsula north of Singora and began their attack down the west coast. By landing on the east coast, which contained the most difficult terrain, and then shifting forces to the west coast before driving south, Yamashita hoodwinked Percival into believing that the main Japanese attack would come in the east. In spite of multiple reports to the contrary, Percival continued to believe that the main Japanese attack would come along the east coast. Accordingly, he deployed a large portion of his force in the east to meet this threat.

Advancing remorselessly, the Japanese marched seventy-five miles from Patani to a position forty miles north of the Malaya border known as "the Ledge." On 9 December the Japanese advance guard—a motorized column from the 5th Division consisting of two battalions, a light artillery battery, a tank company, and some engineers, led by tanks—moved down the main road with their headlights blazing. They met a Punjabi battalion near the Ledge, losing their two lead tanks to antitank fire. The Punjabis, who had been ordered to delay and not defend, immediately withdrew to new positions six miles south of the Thai frontier.

By the eleventh, Yamashita's advance guard had penetrated ten miles behind British lines and smashed two battalions of the 11th Indian Division. The 11th Division withdrew to Jitra, but the position was not prepared—before the Japanese invasion, Percival had considered digging positions bad for morale. At Jitra the Japanese advance guard, again led by armor, once more met and smashed the Punjabis. The defense by the 11th Division was "so singularly inept that whatever cohesion it had was dissipated even before the battle was joined."[25] Panicking, the British blew up the bridge at Jitra too soon and abandoned most of their antitank guns and transport to the Japanese. "The overall result was a disaster that was nothing short of shameful and a disgrace to British arms."[26]

Maintaining the pressure, the Japanese conducted a night attack and penetrated the British lines in the pitch dark and pouring rain. The defense along the Jitra line failed to stem the Japanese advance. "A mere two battalions of Japanese infantry, supported by a company of tanks, defeated the 11th Indian Division and drove it from its initial position within 36 hours."[27] The British commander ordered a retreat, and the rout was on.

Suddenly the British were consumed in "chaos and confusion unrelieved by the vestiges of competent generalship."[28] What could the British have done to stop Yamashita's advance? The obvious solution was to deny the enemy use of the north-south rail and road nets,[29] but the rapid and aggressive Japanese advance preempted this option, revealing the sluggishness and lack of resolution that underlay Percival's defense. The Japanese land forces moved forward rapidly, "so perfectly choreographed and so unbelievably economical"[30] that they forced the stunned British into an endless retreat down the Malay Peninsula. Official British reports chronicled the retreat with savage accuracy: "There was considerable confusion . . . the Japanese advanced more quickly than expected . . . the Japanese tanks came as a great surprise . . . the troops were very tired . . . the jungle gave the men a blind feeling."[31]

The speedy, highly skilled attacks by Japanese forces spread confusion and panic in the British ranks. Penang Island was evacuated without a fight and the British troops fell back from one poorly prepared defensive line to the next. Wherever the British, Indian, or

Australian regiments stood and fought, the Japanese found a way through the jungle, enveloped the defenses, and compelled the British to begin what one contemporary observer called the "Great Run" south to Singapore.[32] The British were rudely awakened to the fact that they were "outmatched by better soldiers."[33] Again, Tsuji writes: "On the average our troops had fought two battles, repaired four or five bridges, and advanced twenty kilometers every day. Our small boats, without armaments, had maneuvered and carried out landings up to six hundred and fifty kilometers behind the enemy's lines on the western coast, and even surpassed the achievements of the troops on land."[34]

Japanese command of the air and sea, the adept use of tanks, and their tactics of outflanking the British defenses forced the defenders to fall back toward Johore to avoid encirclement and capture. To defend Johore, the key to the defense of Singapore Island, the British withdrew forces that were positioned north of Kuala Lumpur to the south. On 11 January 1942 Kuala Lumpur fell.

During the difficult advance the Japanese used every conceivable means to maintain the mobility of their forces and their freedom of maneuver. In preparation for the offensive, each Japanese division was provided with bicycles. The tactical technique was one of envelopment and constant movement to the south.

> Motor vehicles and bicycles were substituted for horses. Each regiment of infantry was allotted roughly fifty trucks for the transport of heavy machine-guns, battalion guns, regimental guns, heavy ordnance, quick-firing guns and the like, as well as ammunition. All officers and men who did not ride with the trucks were provided with bicycles . . . almost without exception, bridges were demolished in front of our advancing troops . . . it would have taken over a year to break through eleven hundred kilometers. With the infantry on bicycles, however, there was no traffic congestion or delay. Wherever bridges were destroyed the infantry continued their advance, wading across the rivers carrying their bicycles on their shoulders, or crossing on log bridges held up on the shoulders of engineers standing in the stream. It

was thus possible to maintain a hot pursuit of the enemy along the asphalt roads without giving them any time to rest or reorganize.[35]

Japanese commanders typically attacked directly along the roads. Upon contact, the Japanese moved into the jungle to infiltrate, out-flank, and encircle the British, appearing behind the defenders to block the roads. British infantry, tied to their trucks for mobility, were cut off by the faster-moving Japanese troops equipped with bi-cycles. At the same time, Japanese bombers and fighters attacked British columns along the narrow roads. Daily bombing attacks on the city of Singapore, its airfields, and military depots added to the psychological calamity and created a strong sense of impending doom. As the Great Run neared Singapore Island, the situation worsened for the British: "Errors by commanders; insufficient or in-adequately trained troops . . . nerves frayed, morale and discipline and efficiency constantly diminishing."[36] As one observer of the British debacle put it:

No wonder that the Japanese never slowed down, no won-der that time after time British, Australian or Indian troops were annihilated by skillful Japanese enveloping tactics. On the British side wrong decisions were made. Communications broke down. Orders went astray. Whole pockets of troops were cut off. The first Japanese tanks appeared and "came as a great surprise" to the British who had not one single tank in Malaya. In a jungle country where the British had insisted that tanks could never operate, the Japanese tanks moved easily between the spacious rows of rubber trees.[37]

Disorganized, demoralized, and exhausted, the British survivors of the battle for Malaya fled to Singapore Island on 31 January 1942, hoping that the wide Johore Strait would stop the Japanese ad-vance. In a flurry of explosions, the British destroyed the vital cause-way that crossed the strait. The British gained fresh courage and of-ficers told their troops to prepare for a twelve-month siege. The British still believed they could use their firepower—a two-to-one advantage in the number of artillery pieces—to destroy the Japanese as they crossed the strait. The strait was a deep, fast-flowing channel "fifteen hundred meters wide at high tide."[38] Thanks to this wide natural antitank ditch, the British felt they had gained time to mount a defense that would result in heavy casualties and defeat for the Japanese.

Unknown to the Japanese, the British force on Singapore Island had swelled to 138,000 combat troops as reinforcements were rushed to the island. Unfortunately, many of these troops were of dubious fighting quality, unarmed, and untrained. To add to Percival's problems, the landward defenses facing north were completely unprepared. Hasty positions were quickly dug and wire obstacles were erected, but time was running short.

By the end of the first week of February 1942, the entire northern bank of the Johore Strait was in Japanese hands and they were ready to attack Singapore Island. Yamashita, however, was worried. Japanese reconnaissance confirmed that the British defenders had registered their artillery at critical crossing points along the strait and positioned dozens of searchlights to counter a night crossing. He knew he faced a stern challenge in the conquest of Singapore, no matter how weak the northern defenses were reported to be. His forces, living mostly off of captured British supplies, had been fighting continuously since early December. His supply lines were extended to the point of breaking. A landing of emergency ammunition supplies at Endau at the end of January helped, but did not solve, his supply problems. The shortage of food, fuel, ammunition, and especially artillery shells threatened to postpone the offensive. In early February the Japanese supply of rifle ammunition was less than a hundred rounds per rifleman.

Yamashita now had about seventy thousand combat soldiers for the attack on Singapore, and he erroneously believed that the British force was only about thirty thousand strong. In spite of his ammunition problems, he continued to press the attack. With characteristic efficiency, Yamashita and Tsuji prepared the battlefield through expert reconnaissance and security operations. Next, Yamashita ordered his forces to clear the battle area of all civilians, thus denying the British an important source of intelligence information,

especially since the British had no air force left with which to conduct reconnaissance.[39] To support the crossing, the Japanese
scrounged a wide assortment of landing craft, civilian boats, and
rafts to support the assault crossing.

In spite of the strain of combat and limited supplies, Japanese
morale was high. Yamashita's veteran soldiers smelled blood. "Singapore, the British stronghold which for over a hundred years had
dominated Asia, now lay before our eyes pawing the ground in its
last moments."[40] They were eager to attack and were fired with the
will to win by their recent victories over the Indians, British, and
Australians. As Tsuji relates: "The Singapore we had once seen in a
dream we now saw under our eyes from the heights . . . Each of us
received, in the lid of a canteen, a little of the Imperial gift of *Kiku-
masumune* [special wine] and we drank a toast: it is a good place to
die. Certainly we will conquer."[41]

Into the Breach

The Japanese assault on Singapore Island began on 7 February. The
attack was led by Lieutenant General Nishimura's Imperial Guards
Division, which conducted a night amphibious assault to seize Pulau Ubin. Nishimura's attack achieved complete surprise and the island fell without difficulty. A few hours later, Yamashita's artillery
moved to Pulau Ubin to support the main attack. By 2245 the Japanese guns were shelling the British defenders at Changi fortress and
blasting positions all along the northern section of the island.

The attack on Pulau Ubin was a feint designed to draw attention
away from the main attack, which came across the Johore Strait at
the causeway on the night of the seventh. Fifteen thousand veterans
from Lt. Gen. Takuro Matsui's 5th Infantry Division and Lt. Gen.
Renya Matagouchi's 18th Infantry Division floated across the strait
on rafts, boats, and barges supported by fierce Japanese artillery
fires. The landing forces were opposed by the Australian 22d
Brigade, which repulsed the first two assaults with heavy Japanese
casualties. Though spirited, the Australian defense was disjointed,
lacking artillery or searchlight support due to haphazard British
communications. Yamashita pressed the attack and the Japanese

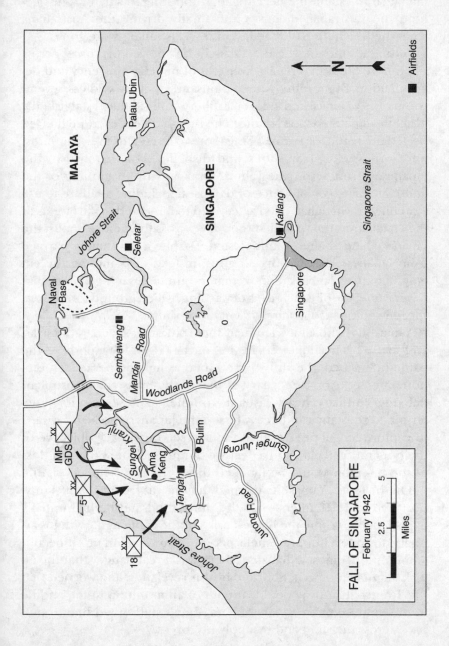

MALAYA

Palau Ubin

Johore Strait

SINGAPORE

Naval
Base

Seletar

Sembawang

Mandai Road

Woodlands Road

Kallang

Singapore

Singapore Strait

IMP
GDS

5

18

Sungei Kranji

Ama
Keng

Bulim

Tengah

Sungei Jurong

Jurong Road

Johore Strait

N

Airfields

FALL OF SINGAPORE
February 1942

Miles

2.5   5

managed to establish a beachhead, infiltrating in small groups behind the Australian defenses and finally driving the Australians from the beach. By 0100 the last of the Australians were gone.

All night long the "Lion of Manchuria" moved his forces across the Johore Strait in a remarkable feat of military efficiency and determination. By morning, fifteen thousand Japanese soldiers, several companies of tanks, and a dozen artillery batteries had established a beachhead on Singapore Island. The British defenders, who had expected the battle for Fortress Singapore to last ten or twelve months, were overwhelmed by shock and disbelief. For the British, the Japanese thrust across the Johore Strait was the beginning of the end: "Thanks to the absence of defenses, including a failure to use searchlights which had been assembled to blind and make targets of the attackers as they paddled their way across the Johore Straits, the Japanese landed almost unmolested. Despite a devastating barrage from Japanese artillery, British guns, instead of pounding the enemy's point of embarkation, remained mute, awaiting orders that never came. Despite the weeks of warning, Allied ground forces were speedily outflanked, encircled, cut off or routed."[42]

Yamashita, who always led near the front, moved across the strait and set up his headquarters in view of the city of Singapore. As the battle intensified, the British grew increasingly desperate. The Johore line broke on 9 February, although the British and Australian defenders inflicted heavy casualties on the Japanese. In spite of determined resistance and heavy losses, the Japanese pressed forward to capture Singapore's critical water reservoir—a key objective of their operational plan and a decisive point. Tsuji knew that the "loss of the reservoir would be fatal" to the British, and he was right.[43]

On the tenth, Yamashita learned that he was facing about eighty-five thousand defenders—not the thirty thousand he had initially expected. Now came the biggest crisis of the campaign. With his artillery down to a hundred shells per gun and rifle and machine-gun ammunition almost exhausted, there was a real danger that the attack might sputter out. Shocked by this revelation and worried that the Twenty-fifth Army would run out of ammunition in the middle of the fight, some members of Yamashita's staff urged him to pull back across the strait and resupply his forces.[44]

Yamashita disregarded their words of caution and charged ahead. He based his decision not on stubbornness, but on an intuitive appreciation of his counterpart. Gambling that the British and their vacillating commander would soon crack, Yamashita moved on 11 February to seize Bukit Timah, the most strategic point on Singapore Island, although nearly all his ammunition had been fired off during the assault crossing. Too much of a samurai to retreat, he now faced the real possibility that continued British stubbornness could turn the tide of battle against him. His staff told him that the British had only a few days of water left, but still retained plenty of ammunition. The question was: Would Yamashita's ammunition run out before the British ran out of water?

As he stared failure in the face, a forward unit reported that a British delegation had arrived under a flag of truce to discuss surrender terms. Bluffed by Yamashita's threat of impending attack, General Percival surrendered Singapore on 15 February, seven days after pulling his forces inside the fortress defenses. The campaign ended with the loss of 138,708 British troops—130,000 as prisoners. British equipment lost to the Japanese included fifty-four fortress guns, three hundred field guns, two hundred mortars, two hundred armored cars, ten thousand automobiles, a thousand trucks, and vast stores of food, fuel, and ammunition. In eight weeks of fighting, the Japanese advanced at an average of twenty kilometers a day, fought ninety-five engagements, destroyed five British brigades, and repaired 250 bridges—all at a cost of 9,656 Japanese killed and 6,150 wounded.

Unquestionably, the fall of Singapore was a crushing blow to the Allies in the Pacific. "Even more than the retreat of the Americans from the Philippines, the fall of Malaya and Singapore was a psychological defeat for the Allies of great importance."[45] Fortress Singapore would remain in Japanese hands until after the signing of Japan's surrender. In the words of British prime minister Winston Churchill, the debacle in Malaya was the "worst disaster and largest capitulation in British history."[46]

The Changing Face of War

What relevance does a study of the Japanese campaign in Malaya have today? Although technology has affected the way that wars are fought, it has not altered the nature of war. War may change, but the principles remain much the same. These principles become the rules that guide commanders in planning campaigns. "The rules are not rigid prescriptions, like algebraic formulas, but concepts, which must be applied artfully as circumstances call for."[47]

If the Japanese had conducted a direct naval and amphibious attack against Fortress Singapore, attacking the main strength of its defenses, it seems likely that the British would have won a defensive victory. Lieutenant Colonel Tsuji recognized this possibility and developed a plan to bypass the British preparations. He was aware of Japan's overall strategic weaknesses vis-à-vis the United States and Great Britain.[48] Tsuji therefore sought an unconventional solution that offered the greatest chance of producing a rapid tactical and operational victory. An important lesson of the Malaya campaign is that the balance of power can be overturned by a smart, thinking enemy who does not play by the established "rules."

For their part, the British completely underestimated their enemy. Overconfidence and racial pride interfered with British judgment before the war began. This arrogance was quickly replaced by despair and panic after the loss of *Repulse* and *Prince of Wales* and the failure of the Jitra line. The long list of British errors in Malaya is difficult to fathom, until the absolute contempt that many British officers and soldiers felt for the Japanese is factored in. "There can be no extenuating circumstances to explain away the fact that three Japanese divisions, only one of which ever deployed its full infantry component, handed out a hiding to a force more than twice its size."[49]

By any standard of measure, the Japanese campaign in Malaya is "one of the most brilliant feats of arms in the war, perhaps in modern military history."[50] If the British proved inept, the Japanese proved to be brilliant, especially considering the arduous conditions and daunting odds they faced, and their performance paved the way for their eventual success in the first days of the campaign.

Japanese training, skill in the employment of combined arms and joint operations, and ability to achieve air superiority quickly proved to be a decisive, campaign-winning combination. Yamashita and Tsuji forced the British onto the horns of a dilemma by conducting continuous, rapid, converging, combined-arms attacks that forced the weary defenders back from one defensive line to another. By the time the British fell back into their citadel on Singapore Island, they were so psychologically shaken that they could hardly mount an effective defense.

In future wars the United States may oppose enemies who will not match our conventional military capability. Because of their weakness, potential enemies may seek to employ unorthodox means to set the conditions of battle. These opponents will face the same dilemma that Lieutenant Colonel Tsuji faced in 1941: how to use a weaker force and avoid the enemy's strength to gain a decisive victory in minimum time. If this is true, a study of the Japanese campaign to conquer Malaya and Singapore has immediate relevance to the professional soldier and military historian today.

The Malaya campaign is an example of operational dislocation and paralysis through dominant maneuver, not overwhelming firepower. Japanese success depended on speed and excellent information about the enemy—concepts which relate directly to the key operational concepts of dominant maneuver and information dominance that inform our warfighting doctrine today. The speed with which the Japanese broke through and enveloped the British defenses, their willingness to take risks to continue the tempo of the attack, and their exploitation of gaps in the British lines by every means available became the soul of the Japanese campaign. These tactics gained tremendous temporal and psychological advantages for the Japanese and set the conditions for the operational campaign. The pace of Japanese operations was so fast, when compared with the British, that the British were unable to think ahead of each cascading crisis. The daring, rapid maneuver of Japanese land forces became the handmaiden of victory and earned Yamashita the title of the "Tiger of Malaya." As Lieutenant Colonel Tsuji stated: "The Malaya campaign seemed undoubtedly the most daring military enterprise in Japanese history."[51]

Notes

1. Yoshihara Yanosuke, ed., *Dai Shori no Kiroku* [Records of the Great Victories]—*Dai Toa Senso Dai-ichi-nen* [The First Year of the Greater East Asia War] (Tokyo: Bunshodo Shoten, 1943), 151.

2. James Leasor, *Singapore, The Battle That Changed the World* (New York: Modern Literary Publications, 1968), 22.

3. Russell Braddon, *Japan Against the World, 1941–2042: The 100-Year War for Supremacy* (New York: Stein and Day, 1985), 21.

4. H. P. Willmott, *Empires in the Balance: Japanese and Allied Pacific Strategies to April 1942* (Annapolis, Md.: Naval Institute Press, 1982), 161.

5. Shiga Naoya, *Soshun* [Early Spring] (Tokyo: Oyama Shotten, 1942), 144. Shiga was one of the best-known novelists in Japan. In 1942 he wrote about the early British and American defeats of the war: "They are saying in America that they were defeated because they underestimated Japan's capability. But what does the American view of Japan's capability mean? America has made a demonstration to the whole world of her gigantic war budget, her reliance on her own economic power. But the fact that no one has raised the issue of how poor a country can be in spiritual power—this the Japanese feel to be very odd."

6. In 1934 Masanobu Tsuji graduated with distinction from the Japanese staff college and was appointed to tutor Prince Mikasa, Emperor Hirohito's younger brother. He became a favorite of the Imperial Court and secured a level of influence well beyond his military rank. He was credited for planning the invasions of Malaya and the Philippines with a mere eleven divisions—using unorthodox tactics to make up for his lack of numbers. He survived the war, hid from war crimes tribunals, surfaced again to write a book on the conquest of Malaya, became a member of the Japanese Diet, and then vanished again in Southeast Asia in the 1960s.

7. John Toland, *The Rising Sun: The Decline and Fall of the Japanese Empire* (New York: Bantam Books, 1970), 172.

8. Colonel Masanobu Tsuji, *Japan's Greatest Victory; Britain's Worst Defeat* (New York: Sarpedon, 1993), 17.

9. Tsuji, *Japan's Greatest Victory,* iv. This reference is from the publisher's note.

10. Ibid., 348. Tsuji articulated the operational concept as follows: "Our candid ideas at the time were that the Americans, being merchants, would not continue for long with an unprofitable war, whereas we ourselves if we fought only the Anglo-Saxon nations could carry on a protracted war; that after we had achieved some great victories in the south the Republic of China would be willing to conclude an unconditional peace treaty based on the principles of an East Asia Co-Prosperity League; that Russia would break away from her western allies; and that after conclusion of peace with China it would be possible for us to move a million troops from that country to Manchuria, which would be sufficient to deter Russia from any further adventure in that direction or to deal with any attack which might develop there."

11. Ibid., 218.

12. Toland, *Rising Sun,* 172.

13. In fact, Singapore had *no* landward defenses. The plans to defend Singapore involved the forward deployment of forces further north, supported by armor and air cover. This plan, Operation Matador, was not resourced (it had no armor and little air support—the priority for these resources demanded that they be sent to Europe) and was preempted by the surprise Japanese attack. In any event, Lieutenant General Percival was unable to effect changes in Singapore's defenses in time to stem the Japanese attack.

14. Tsuji, *Japan's Greatest Victory,* 223.

15. The Japanese army did not refer to groupings of divisions as *corps,* but instead used the term *army.*

16. Tsuji, *Japan's Greatest Victory,* 218.

17. Ibid., 186–87. "According to the statements of officer prisoners, Lieutenant General Percival was strongly of the opinion that it was necessary to strengthen the rear defenses of the fortress, but against the opposition of the Governor-General he could not carry out the necessary construction and consolidation. The reason that had been given for this decision was that fortifying the rear 'would make the civilian population of Malaya uneasy.'"

18. Maj. Gen. S. Woodburn Kirby, CB, CMG, CIE, OBE, MC, *Singapore: The Chain of Disaster* (New York: Macmillan, 1971), 107.

19. Kirby, *Singapore*, 114.

20. Tsuji, *Japan's Greatest Victory*, 215.

21. Ibid., 260.

22. Ibid., 222.

23. B. H. Liddell Hart, *History of the Second World War* (New York: G. P. Putnam's Sons, 1970), 202.

24. Norman F. Dixon, *On the Psychology of Military Incompetence* (New York: Basic Books, 1976), 141.

25. Willmott, *Empires in the Balance*, 169.

26. Ibid., 171.

27. Ibid., 170.

28. Kenneth Attiwill, *Fortress: The Story of the Siege and Fall of Singapore* (Garden City, N.Y.: Doubleday, 1960), 46.

29. Dixon, *Psychology of Military Incompetence*, 143.

30. Kirby, *Singapore*, 114.

31. Braddon, *Japan Against the World*, 25.

32. Attiwill, *Fortress*, 49–50.

33. Gen. Sir Henry Pownall, the British commander in chief, Far East, during the battle for Malaya, from *The Listener*, 2 January 1986, 2.

34. Tsuji, *Japan's Greatest Victory*, 213.

35. Ibid., 183–84.

36. Attiwill, *Fortress*, 50.

37. Noel Barber, *Sinister Twilight, The Fall of Singapore* (Glasgow: William Collins and Son, 1968), 60–61.

38. Tsuji, *Japan's Greatest Victory*, 213.

39. The British lost fourteen aircraft trying to oppose the Japanese landing at Endau. After this disastrous setback, the Royal Air Force withdrew all surviving British aircraft to the Netherlands East Indies, abandoning the aerial defense of Singapore on 30 January 1942.

40. Tsuji, *Japan's Greatest Victory*, 213.

41. Ibid., 221–22.

42. Dixon, *Psychology of Military Incompetence*, 143.

43. Tsuji, *Japan's Greatest Victory*, 221. "The reservoirs on Singa-

pore Island were storage reservoirs only, being fed by pipeline from Jahore across the Causeway. When subsequently the Causeway was demolished and the reservoirs and distributing pipes were damaged by shellfire, there was not enough water to supply the island's population of one million people for more than a few days."

44. Toland, *Rising Sun,* 269.

45. S. L. Mayer, ed., *The Japanese War Machine* (Secaucus, N.J.: Chartwell Books, 1976), 150.

46. Louis Allen, *Singapore 1941–1942.* 2nd rev. ed. (London: Frank Cass Publishers, 1993), 186. General Percival continuously underestimated the Japanese ability to execute a successful operational plan. In many ways it seems that the British were doomed to failure—a theme that is conveyed repeatedly in Allen's book. It was almost impossible for the British to think "outside of the box" [in today's parlance] about their enemy.

47. Bevin Alexander, *How Great Generals Win* (New York: Avon, 1993), 28.

48. As Adm. Isoroku Yamamoto, commander in chief of the Imperial Japanese Navy from 1939 to 1942, remarked: "I can raise havoc against the Americans for one or two years. After that the issue is in doubt" (Toland, *Rising Sun,* 102). The Japanese failure in World War II thus was not impossible to predict. Japan's defeat was more the result of "fatal delusions of invincibility and an incorrigible aversion to any departure from an agreed plan" (Braddon, *Japan Against the World,* 49). A critical lesson of the Malaya campaign, therefore, is that even the most brilliant operational victories seldom rescue a flawed strategy.

49. Willmott, *Empires in the Balance,* 334.

50. Ibid., 334. It is hard to believe that a great power at war since 1940 could make so many mistakes and perform so ineptly.

51. Ibid., 172.

H. R. McMaster

"Flashing Sword of Vengeance": The Kharkov Counteroffensive

> A sudden and powerful transition to the offensive—the flash-
> ing sword of vengeance—is the greatest moment for the de-
> fense.[1]
>
> —Carl von Clausewitz

The 1943 German counteroffensive between the Dnepr and
Donets Rivers in the Donbas region of the Ukraine was one of the
most stunning reversals in military history. In mid-February 1943,
two Soviet fronts had penetrated the German defenses along the
Donets River, advanced 150 miles in thirty days, and threatened
the very survival of German Army Group South. Less than four
weeks later, three Soviet armies and part of a fourth, as well as
an entire armored group, had been destroyed as fighting organizations and German forces had regained all of the territory lost
during the Soviet offensive. German success stemmed in large
measure from Soviet blunders and weaknesses. While the Soviets
presented the Germans with opportunities, German commanders
and units were capable of discerning those opportunities and possessed the courage and skill to exploit them.

The Red Army Ascendant

On 17 February 1943, Adolf Hitler traveled to the eastern front to
consult with the commander of Army Group South, *Feldmarschall*
Erich von Manstein.[2] During his flight over the sparsely vegetated
rolling hills and frozen marshes of the Ukraine, the Nazi dictator

might have reflected on the disasters of past months. The human and military cost of operations on the eastern front had reached staggering proportions. Stalingrad had fallen just two weeks earlier, and the once-powerful Sixth Army was gone. In and around Stalingrad alone, the Soviets swept five armies (the Sixth and four German allied) off the battleground. Thirty thousand wounded had been evacuated from the besieged city. More than 150,000 German and Romanian troops were either killed in action or died of hunger or exposure. The Red Army took 91,000 prisoners (only 5,000 of whom would survive the war).[3]

The blow to Hitler's prestige was perhaps as damaging to Germany's fortunes, for it encouraged increasingly irrational behavior in the *führer*. Prestige was important to Hitler mainly because he was calling on his people and his allies to make great sacrifices in a murderous campaign in Russia and the Ukraine. Although the disaster at Stalingrad resulted mainly from Hitler's inflexibility and failure to confront the strategic and operational realities of the eastern front, the dictator could not afford to admit any degree of responsibility lest the illusion of his infallibility evaporate completely. Instead, Hitler blamed his allies and his own generals.[4]

After the fall of Stalingrad, Hitler faced an even more dangerous crisis. Soviet headquarters, *Stavka*, believing that the imminent surrender of the German Sixth Army had created "favorable conditions" for a general offensive, ordered "the encirclement and destruction in detail of the Donbas, Caucasus, and Black Sea enemy groups."[5] At the end of January, four Soviet armies had attacked across a six-hundred-mile front between the Donets and Dnepr Rivers. Initially, Soviet formations outnumbered the defending German units by a ratio of eight to one.[6] The Voronezh Front, under Gen. Col. Filip Ivanovich Golikov, attacked to secure Kharkov and Kursk while Gen. Nikolai Fedorovich Vatutin's Southwest Front executed its orders to "cut off all enemy groups located in the Donbas and Rostov regions, encircle and destroy them and prevent their withdrawal to the west and evacuation of their equipment." The combined offensive quickly surrounded two German corps and recaptured the major cities and transportation hubs of Kursk, Kharkov, and Rostov. Vatutin's Southwest Front bypassed stiff German resistance at Slavyansk and accelerated its attack west and south to Dnepropetrovsk and Zaporozhye to cut off what the Soviets believed would soon be a German retreat across the Dnepr River. Manstein's First Panzer Army, Group Hollidt, and Fourth Panzer Army had been forced to withdraw to the angle of the Donets and Mius Rivers and Soviet forces were pouring around them to the north.[7] As Hitler arrived at Manstein's headquarters in Zaporozhye, the Soviet First Guards and Sixth Armies were continuing to advance between the right flank of Army Group Kempf in the vicinity of Krasnograd and the left flank of the First Panzer Army.[8]

Manstein, however, seemed more concerned about Hitler's interference than advancing Soviet armor. Having sealed the fate of the German Sixth Army with his orders to retain Stalingrad at all cost, the dictator now insisted that Manstein adopt a static defense that would leave the initiative with the advancing Soviet armies. Manstein recalled years later that Hitler had "turned his back on reality." Hitler began to "overestimate his own will-power," which rendered him unable to gain an accurate appreciation for the situation. While retaining an inflated belief in the strength of his own will, Hitler recoiled from risks in military decisions. Hitler's "aversion to accepting any risk in mobile operations when its success could not be guaranteed in advance, and his dislike of giving up anything voluntarily— such were the factors which influenced Hitler's military leadership more and more as time went on."[9] Manstein was determined to stand up to Hitler and demand the latitude needed to conduct operations consistent with his appreciation of the situation.

Hitler's and Manstein's personalities were incompatible. Hitler wanted yes-men, and Manstein did not hesitate to argue against what he regarded as unwise decisions or unsound tactics.[10] In contrast to Hitler, who favored holding ground, Manstein believed that the strength of the German army lay in its ability to conduct mobile operations aimed at achieving surprise and seizing the initiative with rapid, concentrated attacks from unexpected angles. Manstein also believed that the main object in war must be the destruction of the enemy army, whereas Hitler was anxious to retain prestigious cities and areas of economic benefit to the Reich.[11]

The loss of Kharkov on 15 February further infuriated Hitler, who had ordered *Generaloberst* Paul Hausser, the SS Panzer Corps commander, to hold the city "to the last man." Hitler did not seem to recognize that it was only Hausser's disobedience of those orders, and his SS Panzer Corps's fighting withdrawal from Kharkov, that saved it from a fate similar to the Sixth Army's at Stalingrad.[12] Hitler expected absolute obedience and intended to exert tight control over his forces. Manstein believed that subordinates must be granted the greatest possible freedom of action.[13] The men seemed on a collision course. When Hitler arrived in Zaporozhye, he had all but made up his mind to relieve Manstein.[14]

On 17 February, Manstein briefed Hitler on the situation. Group Hollidt continued to defend against three Soviet armies along the naturally strong position of the Mius River line. The gap between the First Panzer Army in the area of Stalino and Army Detachment Lanz in the area of Pavlograd had widened to 110 miles. A Soviet armored group under Gen. Col. Markian M. Popov was attacking toward Slavyansk and threatened to envelop Group Hollidt's defenses from the north. General Lieutenant F. M. Kharitonov's Soviet Sixth Army was driving to the Dnepr and had orders to cross the river just north of Manstein's headquarters. The Soviets were accelerating the offensive based on the mistaken conclusion that the SS Panzer Corps's withdrawal from Kharkov presaged a general withdrawal of German forces across the Dnepr.[15]

Manstein outlined his plan to seize the initiative from and defeat the Soviets. He intended to launch concentrated attacks against the exposed flanks of the Soviet Sixth Army and Popov's armored group. Infantry units were to fix the enemy main attack and hold shoulders to the north and south of the Soviet penetration. Mobile armored formations were to attack to sever Soviet lines of communication, destroy enemy forces, and reestablish a defensive line along the Donets River. Emphasis would be on speed and attacks in depth to fragment the Soviet armies and paralyze their command and control. Manstein would create the mobile reserves he needed by pulling out all the panzer divisions from the Mius River line. Group Hollidt, minus those divisions, would continue to defend there.[16]

Hitler objected, concerned about the possible collapse of the Mius River defense. Greatly distressed, Hitler threatened over a two-day period to water down Manstein's plan by committing German forces piecemeal into static defensive positions. Hitler also continued to press Manstein for an immediate attack to retake Kharkov.[17]

Manstein, however, saw possibilities where Hitler saw only difficulties. Clearly the Soviet objective was ambitious, the Soviet weakness apparent in the overextension of the attack. The farther the Soviets advanced to the west and southwest, the more effective would be the counterattack. He observed that Stalin was "going for the big prize and he is not afraid of risks. We've got to lure him into taking extreme risks. That's our only chance!" The German commander acknowledged the weakness of the Mius River line, but told Hitler, "We've got to face that danger." Manstein argued that committing the SS Panzer Corps to a direct attack on Kharkov would squander a valuable asset needed to strike the counterblow against enemy weakness.[18]

Finally, Soviet action on 19 February forced the issue and the sheer desperation of the situation redounded to Manstein's benefit. The Soviet XXV Tank Corps thrust from Pavlograd and cut the only direct rail line to Group Hollidt. When enemy tanks closed to within forty miles of Manstein's headquarters, Hitler's entourage urged the dictator to flee. As Hitler's airplane took off from Zaporozhye, the lead Soviet unit had closed to within six miles of the airfield. Now free to act, Manstein immediately issued orders for the counterattack.[19]

An Iron Fist

The first blow of the counteroffensive fell against Popov's armored group. The 7th Panzer Division, which had disengaged from Slavyansk under the cover of fog, attacked the IV Guards Tank Corps. Simultaneously, SS Motorized Division "Viking" attacked the 12th Guards Tank Brigade in the western portion of Slavyansk. Heavy German air attacks hit the Soviet forces in depth. Those strikes marked a change in momentum, but the Soviets remained unaware of what was happening. The Soviet high command had not appreciated either the German potential for a massive counterattack or the weakening of their own forces. Indeed, an air of

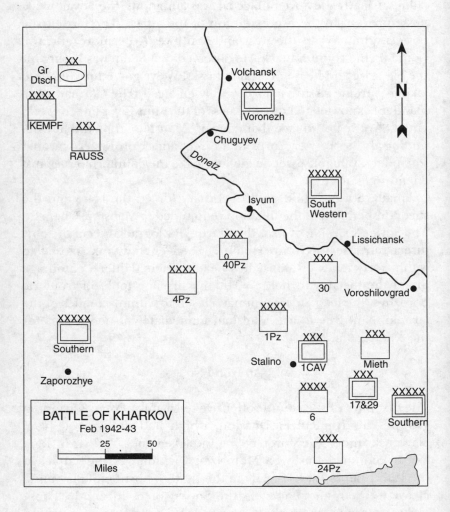

Gr
Dtsch XX
        ⬭

XXXX
KEMPF

        XXX
        RAUSS

Volchansk •

XXXXX
Voronezh

Chuguyev •

Donetz

        XXXXX
        South
        Western

Isyum •

        XXX
        0
        40Pz

        XXXXX   Lissichansk •
        30

        XXX   Voroshilovgrad •
        30

XXXX
4Pz

XXXXX
Southern

Zaporozhye •

        XXXX
        1Pz

        XXX   XXX
        1CAV   Mieth

Stalino •

        XXXX   XXX   XXXXX
        6   17&29   Southern

BATTLE OF KHARKOV
Feb 1942-43

25   50

Miles

        XXX
        24Pz

optimism persisted at both Stavka and the Southwest Front head-quarters.

The intelligence failure was not due to a lack of information. On 19 and 20 February, Soviet air reconnaissance observed large German tank concentrations near Krasnograd, noted the forward movement of equipment from Dnepropetrovsk, and detected the regrouping of tank forces from the east toward Krasnoarmeisk. The chief of staff of the Southwestern Front, Gen. Lt. S. P. Ivanov, assessed the movements as a withdrawal from the Donbas to Zaporozhye. Based on that assessment, Vatutin ordered the Sixth Army to continue its attack and demanded that the front mobile groups "fulfill their assigned mission at any cost." The Voronezh Front adopted a similar attitude. Well after the German counteroffensive was under way, *Stavka* reported that it had "exact data that the enemy . . . is withdrawing in dense columns from the Donbas."[20]

Complicating their failure to discern changes in the enemy situation, the Soviets had not recognized the weakening of their own forces. By 17 February, Popov's armored group with its four corps was down to thirteen thousand men and fifty-three of its original 137 tanks. Half of the entire strength of Vatutin's Southwest Front was out of action and the front reserve could muster only 267 tanks. Golikov's Voronezh Front had suffered comparable losses. The two tank brigades in the Third Tank Army, for example, had only six operational tanks between them.[21]

As the weakened Soviet formations blundered forward, the Germans attacked at high speed into their flanks and rear. Manstein ordered the First and Fourth Panzer Armies to attack with the object of destroying Tank Group Popov south of a line from Pavlograd–Lozovaya–Barvenkovo. In his order to the Fourth Panzer Army, *Generaloberst* Hermann Hoth emphasized that the main objective was the destruction of six tank corps and one guards rifle brigade to open maneuver space for a continuation of the attack to the north. Emphasis was on speed to fragment Soviet combat formations and render them ineffective. The orders of *Generaloberst* Gotthard Heinrici, commander of the XL Panzer Corps, are representative. He told his division: "Don't waste time fighting against villages and towns. Keep moving!"[22] By 20 February, the German XXX Corps had encircled Tank Group Popov northwest of Stalino while the XL Panzer Corps attacked into the flank with three divisions abreast.

Simultaneously, the SS *Das Reich* Division attacked toward Novo-moskovsk and turned east toward Pavlograd, trapping a large Soviet force south of the Samara River and eliminating the threat to the Dnepr crossings.[23] The Soviet command's failure to recognize the German counteroffensive sealed the fate of their forces east of the Donets. As the panzer corps attacked, German bombers struck Soviet reserves and logistical formations in great depth and pro-vided close support for divisions that had outrun their artillery. On 23 February, Tank Group Popov's headquarters reported its com-munications cut and that panic in the ranks was being suppressed "by the harshest measures."[24]

However, both Vatutin and Golikov continued to assume that they were conducting a pursuit to the Dnepr. When Popov re-quested permission to withdraw twenty miles to the north, Vatutin denied the request as being "counter to the assignments given to the group and to the situation as it stands, when the enemy is doing everything he can to speed the withdrawal of his forces from the Donbas to the Dnepr."[25] The XXV Tank Corps received similar in-structions and continued its attack to the west. Its lead division ran out of fuel as the XLVII Panzer Corps encircled the main force. The Soviet corps abandoned its vehicles and its soldiers joined a grow-ing mob trying to escape to the north and east.[26]

On 28 February, German tanks broke through to the Donets. *Stavka* finally responded. The Third Tank Army was detached from Golikov's right wing and placed under the control of Vatutin to counterattack against the German armor formations in the Sixth Army's rear. However, German bombers devastated the Third Tank Army as it marshaled for the attack. By 2 March, the Third Tank Army was surrounded and had only fifty tanks remaining. Vatutin's First Guards and Sixth Armies were in full retreat. Although the frozen river allowed Soviet soldiers to escape to the eastern bank of the Donets, both formations were severely beaten and four of their tank corps practically destroyed.[27]

Manstein shifted the counteroffensive to the north against Go-likov's southern flank and toward Kharkov. The German forces raced both the retreating Soviets and the thaw that threatened to immobilize both armies. The Fourth Panzer Army and the SS Panzer Corps attacked north on 7 March, covering twenty miles in two days and separating the Sixty-ninth Tank Army from the Fortieth Army and the remnants of the Third Tank Army. On 10 March, the SS Panzer Corps encircled Kharkov and cut the Third Tank Army's escape routes to the Donets.[28] Against orders, *Generaloberst* Hausser launched a costly, ill-conceived attack on Kharkov, but recaptured the city on the fourteenth after three days of brutal urban fighting.[29] After Kharkov fell, Soviet resistance west of the Donets collapsed completely. German forces seemed poised to break through into the rear of the Central Front and encircle Soviet forces west of Kursk. *Stavka* diverted the Sixty-second and Sixty-fourth Armies from Stalingrad to hold the line north of Kharkov.[30]

Manstein declared the operation completed on 17 March, and the spring thaw soon brought mobile operations to a halt. The front stabilized and the Soviets continued to reinforce what would become the southern flank of the Kursk salient. The Germans had regained the Donets-Mius line and removed the immediate threat to Army Group South.

Keys to Victory

Generalmajor Friedrich W. von Mellenthin observed that "it may be questioned whether any achievement of generalship in World War II" could approach Manstein's performance in command during the first months of 1943.[31] Manstein certainly deserves credit for developing a plan that seized the initiative from the enemy through surprise and aggressive maneuver. He fended off Hitler's calls for a more conservative approach that would have committed German forces against the Soviets' strength. Manstein knew that attacks against the enemy's flanks and rear could turn the mass of the Soviet armies against them. He created depth by allowing Tank Group Popov and the Soviet Sixth Army to move forward while German forces held the shoulders of that penetration. He set conditions for simultaneous attacks that struck the enemy from unexpected angles and fell against weak, elongated flanks. German air forces extended the counteroffensive in even greater depth and disrupted Soviet operational reserves.[32]

Manstein was sensitive to the human dimension of war and developed a plan that gained a psychological advantage through surprise and a temporal advantage by rapid, simultaneous attacks to which enemy commanders could not respond effectively. Hitler had equated movement with risk. Manstein, however, understood that the riskiest course of action was to cede the initiative to the enemy by remaining in static defensive positions and permitting the enemy to concentrate overwhelming strength against him.

Manstein orchestrated the offensive at the operational level, but did not attempt to centralize control over his formations. He assigned appropriate tasks to the appropriate formations. Refusing to immobilize his armor, Manstein used his infantry to protect the flanks of his armored attacks and to fix the enemy's main attack. Artillery fires were concentrated in areas only thinly held by ground troops, to assist in fixing enemy formations and to deceive the enemy as to the size of his maneuver forces in the area.[33] He integrated the Fourth Air Force into his plans and was able to retain the initiative by striking Soviet reserves simultaneously with the initiation of the ground offensive. His orders established objectives and determined the timing of the counterattack, but did not restrict subordinate commanders.[34]

For his part, Manstein credited the victory to the German troops and their commanders who, "convinced of their superiority as soldiers, stood their ground in the most desperate situations." Soldier and unit confidence, Manstein observed, "did much to compensate for the enemy's numerical preponderance."[35] That confidence came from superior German training and leadership. One German officer who fought with Army Group South observed that German advantages over the enemy stemmed from "standards of training." He recalled that "the training of tank crews never ceased, even in combat." What the U.S. Army now calls after-action reviews were held after every engagement and "successes and failures were discussed, just as after peacetime exercises."[36]

The German qualitative advantage at the small-unit level appears even more dramatic when placed in the context of Soviet weaknesses at that level. In contrast to the German ability to respond immediately to orders and take initiative based on the situation, Soviet units at the beginning of 1943 were a composite of understrength veteran units and new, inexperienced formations.[37] As a result, Soviet companies and battalions were prone to panic and disintegration when faced with unexpected circumstances. Manstein recognized his advantage over the enemy at the small-unit level and took action to capitalize on it.[38]

However, the blame for Soviet failure must lie principally with the high command. Flushed with the success of Stalingrad, the attack was conceived as the pursuit of already defeated enemy formations.[39] Military philosopher Carl von Clausewitz observed that "in war, the subjugation of the enemy is the end and the destruction of his forces the means." He observed further that "the attacker is not interested simply in reaching its objective: he must get there as victor."[40] Soviet front commanders confused the occupation of ground with progress toward defeating the enemy. Rather than basing their plans on seizing key terrain that might facilitate the destruction of enemy forces, Soviet units simply attacked along the line of least resistance without connecting their advance clearly to the purpose of the operations.[41] What the Soviets had construed as an indication of impending victory—the gaining of ground—was actually setting conditions for defeat.

Clausewitz observed that an attacker can either "perish by the sword or by his own exertions." Both factors conspired against the attacking Soviet formations in the Donbas. The rapid Soviet advance created vulnerabilities in their own forces. Soviet strength eroded due to the skillful German defense and the weakening effects of time and distance on a force operating at the end of extended supply lines. Clausewitz described the "culminating point" of an attack as the point beyond which the "scale turns" and the attacker is vulnerable to a counterblow. Manstein recognized that vulnerability.[42]

The Soviet advance diminished an already limited ability to sustain combat forces logistically. Lead elements of the Third Tank Army ran out of fuel and were destroyed in place. Most elements at the front were perilously low on ammunition and many went days without food. Inoperable tanks were evacuated to large centralized repair facilities and most never made it back to their units. Although *Stavka,* the Southwest Front, and the Voronezh Front had conceived of the operation as pursuit, they did not embed robust logistical formations forward into the attacking units. Supply bases remained 250 to 300 kilometers to the rear.[43] German signal intelligence made Manstein aware of the perilous logistical condition of the Soviet forces, which was a vital element of his decision to strike a counterblow.[44]

Soviet logistical estimates depended on many assumptions, such as the level of enemy resistance and rates of advance by their own forces, which proved to be wildly inaccurate. When those assumptions did not hold true, logistical assets remote from the front and under centralized control proved useless. Indeed, efforts to achieve efficiency in logistics are often founded on the unrealistic expectation that logistical requirements can be predicted with certainty and precision. In 1943, due to limited assets, the Soviet army had to rely on centralization to ensure efficient use of scarce resources. Not until late 1943 and early 1944, when Soviet industry began to recover and the Soviet army began to reap the full benefits of the lend-lease program, were the Soviets able to decentralize logistical support and organize effectively to sustain a strategic offensive against Germany. As the U.S. Army contemplates reorganizing its logistical infrastructure, the Russian experience at Kharkov may prove instructive. Despite claims to the contrary, today's information technology cannot forecast changes in tempo that typify armored combat because those changes depend primarily on factors that defy prediction. Because of imponderables, such as how strongly the enemy will resist or where and when opportunities will arise, logistical support must be located well forward and be capable of surging immediately to meet unforeseen requirements. Unlike the United Parcel Service or Wal-Mart, redundancy in military logistics is a virtue, and centralization in the name of efficiency is a recipe for disaster.

Complicating the logistical breakdown was a lack of depth in Soviet formations. The advancing Soviet armies concentrated virtually all of their combat power at the front. Without combat formations arrayed in depth, they were unable to sustain the speed and power of the offensive and were unable to respond effectively to attacks against their flanks.

The question remains as to why the Soviets continued to advance at high speed despite their weakened state and vulnerability to counterattack. The Soviets had very good information on their own weakness and the enemy's strength. In retrospect, the information available seemed to lead inexorably to the conclusion that disaster loomed for forces advancing on the Dnepr unless those forces paused and assumed a defensive posture. The minds of Soviet commanders, however, were set inflexibly on one course of action. Their behavior seems to fit Clausewitz's general observation that an "attacker, reinforced by the psychological forces peculiar to attack, will in spite of his exhaustion find it less difficult to go on than to stop—like a horse pulling a load uphill."[45]

The Soviet command's inability to discern changes in the situation demonstrates that information does not equate to intelligence. The Soviet intelligence breakdown was due primarily to faulty assumptions about the enemy's *intentions*. Historian David Glantz observed that Soviet commanders "permitted optimism and overconfidence to cloud judgment" in the "clearest case of self-deception on the Eastern Front."[46] *Stavka*'s intelligence chief, Gen. Maj. Sergei M. Shtemenko, observed in retrospect that the entire plan for the offensive "had arisen on the basis of misinterpretation of the enemy's actions" and assumptions that "only appeared to correspond to the actual situation."[47] Because the Soviets had assumed only one enemy course of action—withdrawal—Manstein was able to achieve surprise and seize the initiative. Surprise inflicted a psychological defeat on the Soviets disproportionate to their physical losses.

The Soviet experience in February and March 1943 provides a strong caution for those who believe that advances in information and surveillance technology will lead to certainty in war. Curiously, reports from long-range surveillance platforms provided information that confirmed the high command's faulty assumptions. General Ivanov, chief of staff of the Southwestern Front, reported on 21 February, three days after the German counteroffensive against Tank Group Popov and the Sixth Army had begun, that "movements of enemy forces discovered by aerial reconnaissance sections . . . confirm our view that the enemy is continuing his withdrawal toward Zaporozhye." Reports from units actually engaged with the enemy challenged those assumptions, but were ignored. After Tank Group Popov reported the enemy counteroffensive, for example, it received the following instructions from the Front Military Council: "Fully restore the situation. Do not, in any case, permit an enemy withdrawal." It was not until five days after the German offensive began that *Stavka* revised its estimate of the enemy's intentions and not until nine days later that it realized the scope of the Soviet disaster.[48]

Manstein sought to create the appearance of weakness along Soviet lines of operation, and Soviet aerial reconnaissance proved vulnerable to deception.[49] If long-range surveillance platforms displace ground-based manned reconnaissance, future commanders may find themselves unable to discriminate between deception and accurate intelligence. Commanders must divert their eyes periodically from sensor downlinks and tune their ears to reports from soldiers and units engaged in actions against the enemy. Reconnaissance units may have to fight for the information that matters most, such as the nature of enemy intentions and the competence of the enemy. After March 1943, the Soviets recognized their deficiency in ground reconnaissance and formed specially trained reconnaissance companies and battalions to collapse German security zones, determine strength and weakness along the enemy's main defensive belt, and pull Soviet combat formations into battle under advantageous conditions.[50]

Bitter Fruits

The Kharkov counteroffensive was Germany's last great operational success on the eastern front in World War II. Like the German I Corps in Prussia in 1914, Manstein's Army Group South was unable to convert its victory into a larger success that could set conditions for a strategic decision. The German victory in February and March 1943, coupled with Hitler's reluctance to surrender ground, set the stage for the battle of Kursk. Disregarding Manstein's advice, Hitler delayed Operation Citadel, the German attack on the Kursk salient, for 111 days after the Kharkov counteroffensive ended in order to field newer German tanks. The Soviets used that time to create one of the strongest defensive sectors in the world. Indeed, none of the features that were present as Manstein initiated his brilliant counterstroke in February would be present at Kursk in July. In a tragic denouement to the brilliant victory at Kharkov, Kursk would become the "Death Ride of the Panzers," a disastrous battle of attrition that destroyed the Wehrmacht's ability to contend with the Red Army in the East. For the rest of the war, the German army would move in only one direction: to the west.

By late 1943, the Soviets had developed an offensive capability that permitted them to launch a bitter and bloody offensive all the way to Berlin. They built strong reconnaissance formations, pushed combined-arms capabilities to lower levels, integrated deception and supporting attacks into all offensives to immobilize enemy reserves, attacked in echelon to protect against culmination and preserve flexibility, and integrated muscular logistical units into combat formations to sustain offensives without pause. Under the strain of continuous fighting on the eastern front and with the Allied invasion on the western front, the German qualitative edge on the battlefield narrowed, and then disappeared completely. Germany tried but failed to compensate for diminished unit effectiveness with wonder weapons and increased firepower.[51] Meanwhile, the resolve of the Soviet people and the increasing flow of lend-lease equipment ensured that the quantitative gap between the Germans and the Soviets grew progressively larger.

Despite the temporary nature of the German victory in February and March 1943, the engagements in and around Kharkov demonstrate that winning in battle depends less on numerical superiority and firepower than it does on qualitative advantages and initiative gained through surprise and speed. Clausewitz advises practitioners of the military art to study history with an eye toward "tracing effects back to their causes."[52] Soviet weaknesses and failures as well as German strengths and successes contributed to the outcome. The Soviet command's failures included an ambiguous concept of the operation, faulty assumptions about enemy intentions, inflexibility, and an overreliance on long-range surveillance. Soviet weaknesses in combat and logistical organizations exacerbated the failures of commanders and staffs. Manstein's Army Group South was able to take advantage of Soviet weakness through the German command's willingness to accept risk and ability to discern and act on opportunities. At Kharkov, a sharp sword wielded by an expert practitioner defied all odds to win perhaps the most striking operational victory of the war in the East.

Notes

1. Carl von Clausewitz, *On War,* ed. and trans. Michael Howard and Peter Paret (Princeton, N.J.: Princeton University Press, 1976), 370.

2. On 13 February 1943, Army Group Don (Manstein) and Army Group B (*Generaloberst* Maximilian M. von Weichs) were combined into Army Group South under Manstein's control.

3. Soviet casualties in and around Stalingrad reached nearly one-half million. See David M. Glantz and Jonathan M. House, *When Titans Clashed: How the Red Army Stopped Hitler* (Lawrence, Kansas: University Press of Kansas, 1995), 141–42.

4. On this point, see Gerhard Weinberg, *A World at Arms: A Global History of World War II* (New York: Cambridge University Press, 1994), 669.

5. David Glantz, "From the Don to the Dnepr: A Study of Soviet Offensive Operations, Dec. 1942–Aug. 1943" (unpublished paper, School of Advanced Military Studies, U.S. Army Command and General Staff College, Fort Leavenworth, Kans.), 104.

6. Paul Carell, *Scorched Earth. The Russian-German War, 1943–1945,* trans. Ewald Osers (Atglen, Pa.: Schiffer Military History, 1994), 175. Estimates on the actual ratio vary due to reinforcements and attrition on both sides and range from 4:1 in tanks and 2:1 in infantry to 8:1 in division-size combat formations at the outset of the Soviet offensive. Manstein, however, began receiving reinforcements almost immediately, including the newly formed SS Panzer Corps.

7. Summarized from Carell, *Scorched Earth,* 173–76; and John Erickson, *The Road to Berlin* (Boulder, Colo.: Westview Press, 1983), 44–48.

8. Earl F. Ziemke, *Stalingrad to Berlin: The German Defeat in the East* (Washington, D.C.: U.S. Army Center of Military History, 1968), 87–91.

9. For Manstein's analysis of Hitler as supreme commander, see Erich von Manstein, *Lost Victories,* trans. Anthony Powell (Novato, Calif.: Presidio Press, 1982), 273–88.

10. Heinz Guderian, *Panzer Leader,* trans. Constantine Fitzgibbon (New York: E. P. Dutton, 1952), 302.

11. Field Marshal Lord Carver, "Manstein," in *Hitler's Generals*, ed. Corelli Barnett (New York: Grove Weidenfeld, 1989), 224–25; Timothy A. Wray, *Standing Fast: German Defensive Doctrine on the Russian Front During World War II, Prewar to March 1943*, Research Survey no. 5 (Fort Leavenworth, Kans.: Combat Studies Institute, 1986), 163.

12. Carell, *Scorched Earth*, 180–81.

13. Carver, "Manstein," 224; Manstein, *Lost Victories*, 382–83.

14. Ziemke, *Stalingrad to Berlin*, 91.

15. Ibid., 92; Weinberg, *A World at Arms*, 457.

16. Gen. Frederick Schulz, "Reverses on the Southern Wing, 1942–1943," MS T-15, Foreign Military Studies, Historical Division, U.S. Army, Europe: U.S. Army Military History Institute, Carlisle Barracks, Pa., 78; Carell, *Scorched Earth*, 185–86.

17. Carell, *Scorched Earth*, 183–86.

18. Ibid., 177, 185; Friedrich W. von Mellenthin, *Panzer Battles*, trans. H. Betzler (New York: Ballantine Books, 1971), 252.

19. Ziemke, *Stalingrad to Berlin*, 91.

20. David M. Glantz, *The Role of Intelligence in Soviet Military Strategy in World War II* (Novato, Calif.: Presidio Press, 1990), 81–82.

21. Erickson, *Road to Berlin*, 48–50.

22. Carell, *Scorched Earth*, 191.

23. Ziemke, *Stalingrad to Berlin*, 94.

24. Ibid., 94; Erickson, *Road to Berlin*, 51; James E. Sikes, "Kharkov and Sinai: A Study in Operational Design" (unpublished paper, School of Advanced Military Studies, Fort Leavenworth, Kans., 29 Apr. 1998), 15.

25. Erickson, *Road to Berlin*, 51.

26. Ibid., 53; Glantz and House, *When Titans Clashed*, 147.

27. Erickson, *Road to Berlin*, 53–54.

28. Ibid., 54; David M. Glantz, *From the Don to the Dnepr: Soviet Offensive Operations, December 1942–August 1943* (Portland, Ore.: F. Cass, 1991), 194–98.

29. Glantz and House, *When Titans Clashed*, 147.

30. Ibid., 147; Ziemke, *Stalingrad to Berlin*, 97.

31. Mellenthin, *Panzer Battles*, 253.

32. Martin van Creveld, *Airpower and Maneuver Warfare* (Maxwell Air Force Base, Ala.: Air University Press, 1994), 10–11; Erickson,

Road to Berlin, 51, 53; Ziemke, *Stalingrad to Berlin,* 93; Glantz and House, *When Titans Clashed,* 144.

33. The action of the 15th Infantry Division at Senelnikovo provides an example. See Carell, *Scorched Earth,* 186–87. See also Mellenthin, *Panzer Battles,* 254.

34. Manstein's order to the Fourth Panzer Army was representative: "The Soviet Sixth Army, now racing towards Dnepropetrovsk through the gap between First Panzer Army and Army Detachment Kempf, is to be defeated" (Carell, *Scorched Earth,* 191).

35. Manstein, *Lost Victories,* 441.

36. Wray, *Standing Fast,* 159–60.

37. Glantz and House, *When Titans Clashed,* 103; Ziemke, *Stalingrad to Berlin,* 501. See also Charles Messenger, *The Art of Blitzkrieg* (London: Ian Allan, 1991), 204–205.

38. Mellenthin, *Panzer Battles,* 254; Sikes, "Kharkov and Sinai," 14.

39. Erickson, *Road to Berlin,* 46, 50.

40. Clausewitz, *On War,* 526, 546.

41. Ziemke, *Stalingrad to Berlin,* 91; Glantz, *From the Don to the Dnepr,* 158; Glantz, *The Role of Intelligence in Soviet Military Strategy in World War II,* 69.

42. Clausewitz, *On War,* 384, 528. For extensive discussion of the concept of culmination as it relates to this campaign, see Bruce Meisner, "The Culminating Point—A Viable Operational Concept or Some Theoretical Nonsense?", unpublished paper, School of Advanced Military Studies, Fort Leavenworth, Kansas, 31 Mar. 1986.

43. Erickson, *Road to Berlin,* 47; Carell, *Scorched Earth,* 81–82.

44. Carell, *Scorched Earth,* 190.

45. Clausewitz, *On War,* 572.

46. Glantz, *Role of Intelligence,* 69.

47. Ibid., 71.

48. Ibid., 70, 81, 186; Carell, *Scorched Earth,* 191–92.

49. Sikes, "Kharkov and Sinai," 16.

50. Glantz and House, *When Titans Clashed,* 122.

51. Messenger, *Art of Blitzkrieg,* 211–12.

52. Clausewitz, *On War,* 156.

"By Their Deeds Alone": The 4th Armored Division at Nancy-Arracourt

They shall be known by their deeds alone.[1]
—Maj. Gen. John S. Wood,
commander, 4th Armored Division

The Allied breakout from Normandy in August 1944 heralded the flight of German forces across France in one of the most stunning pursuits in history. As hastily assembled *kampfgruppen* struggled to stem the advance, Allied forces battled both the enemy and the tyranny of logistics in their attempt to breach the West Wall and end the war in 1944. These operations showcased the capabilities of the most maneuverable ground force in World War II—the Army of the United States. While the building blocks of the army consisted of standard, albeit highly mobile, infantry divisions, the fifteen armored divisions in the European theater of operations were the cutting edge of American ground forces there. Of these powerful combined-arms organizations, the 4th Armored Division was among the best. One of its finest operations was conducted when the division fought to breach the Moselle River and encircle the ancient city of Nancy, a little-known battle overshadowed by the Allied airborne operation in Holland that took place concurrently.

In 1944, the 4th Armored Division was nearly eleven thousand men strong and organized into two combat commands and a reserve command, which could be task organized depending on the tactical situation. The division consisted of three tank battalions, three armored infantry battalions, three armored artillery battalions, an armored reconnaissance battalion, an engineer combat battalion, a maintenance battalion, and a medical battalion. Major weapons included 263 tanks and fifty-four self-propelled 105mm artillery pieces. The U.S. Army's official historian describes the armored division of 1944 as a "federation of thirteen battalions led by a major general."[2] Indeed, the organization was quite elastic. Each battalion was self-contained, relying on its own supply and service organization for attachment and detachment across the battlefield. The two combat commands (Combat Command A [CCA] and Combat Command B [CCB]) and the much smaller Reserve Command, headquarters with officers and supporting staff but no organic combat elements, allowed the division commander to task organize as the situation dictated.[3] The commander of Army Ground Forces, Lt. Gen. Lesley J. McNair, intended commanders to use the newly created armored divisions almost exclusively in bold offensive action deep in enemy rear areas, a view echoed in army doctrinal literature.

The commander of the 4th Armored Division was Maj. Gen. John S. Wood. Wood was a 1912 graduate of West Point, where he earned the nickname "P" (for "Professor") for his generous assistance in tutoring classmates. He served with the 3d and 96th Divisions in France during World War I. He graduated with honors from the Command and General Staff School at Fort Leavenworth, Kansas, in 1924 and spent two years at the *École Supérieure de Guerre* in Paris between 1929 and 1931. His interwar career included a year as assistant to the commandant of the U.S. Military Academy and five years as professor of military science and tactics at Culver Military Academy. In 1939 and 1940, Wood served as the Third Army chief of staff in Atlanta. He served as artillery officer of the 1st Infantry Division, commander of the 2d Armored Division Artillery, and as commander of CCA, 5th Armored Division before taking command of the 4th Armored Division at Pine Camp, New York, in 1942. Wood was an aggressive leader who commanded from the front. He preferred to use his division on deep strikes rather than engaging enemy forces head-on. After the war, British military historian Basil H. Liddell Hart called Wood "the Rommel of the American armored forces."[4]

The commander of CCA was Col. Bruce C. Clarke. Clarke represented a younger generation of officers who emerged during the war. He served as an enlisted soldier with the Coast Artillery during World War I, graduated in the top 15 percent of the West Point class of 1925, received a civil engineering degree from Cornell University in 1927, and a bachelor of law degree from La Salle University in 1936. Clarke understood the importance of combined-arms operations, good staff work, and leadership. He served as the commander of the division's engineer battalion and was the division chief of staff prior to assuming command of CCA in November 1943.

The commander of CCB was Brig. Gen. Holmes A. Dager. An infantry officer, he enlisted in the New Jersey National Guard in 1916 and earned a regular army commission the next year. He fought in the Meuse-Argonne offensive during World War I with the 51st Infantry Regiment, and earned a Silver Star for gallantry in action. He was a graduate of the Command and General Staff School (1931) and the Army War College (1936).[5]

Although this combination of leaders proved effective in combat, Clarke and Dager disliked each other intensely, which made for a great deal of competition between the two combat commands.[6] "He rose on our reputation and we were good in spite of him," Clarke would say of Dager in later years.[7] There was a power struggle within the division between Dager's "infantry crowd" and Clarke's "armored force crowd," presided over by Wood, who had a loose command style.[8]

The 4th Armored Ramps Up

The 4th Armored Division received what many units did not: adequate time to prepare for war. Activated in 1941, the division was fortunate to receive three years of training under good leadership before deploying to France in July 1944. This long period of preparation enabled the division's subordinate units to form cohesive teams and undergo extensive training in tactics, techniques, procedures, and the maintenance and handling of complicated equipment. The division's leadership, especially the many young battalion commanders, developed effective command and control techniques for fast-moving, mobile operations. The division also had a chance to remove incompetent leaders from their positions before entering combat. Two of the most valuable periods of preparation were the 1942 Tennessee maneuvers and the time spent at the Desert Training Center in California in 1943. These periods enabled the division to practice the fast, mobile operations they would use in combat in France.

In the desert, the division developed an innovative form of training that saved many lives in combat. Crews loaded their tanks with machine-gun ammunition, "buttoned up" by closing the hatches, and stalked each other in the open desert under the control of officer evaluators. To score a "kill," a crew had to hit the other tank with a machine-gun burst. A thorough after-action review in which the participants evaluated their performance followed each exercise. Except for an occasional shattered periscope, the live-fire training caused little damage and no casualties. This training kept the soldiers interested, for it was realistic. The enemy could appear from any direction. There were no arguments over winners or losers. After a few weeks, the division progressed from tank-versus-tank duels to platoon-versus-platoon fights and company-versus-company battles. Without modern training devices, the 4th Armored Division had developed a simple method to replicate a realistic battlefield.[9]

By the second anniversary of its activation, the division was ready for combat and had learned the three fundamentals of armored warfare: shooting, moving, and communicating. The most important factors in the division's development were good leadership, personnel stability, and excellent training. After a stopover at Camp Bowie, Texas, the division embarked for Great Britain in December 1943. Once there, the troops drew new equipment and continued intensive training in small-unit tactics and maneuver on Salisbury Plain—exercises that honed their skills prior to the division's deployment to France in July 1944.

Patton's Spearhead

In Normandy, the success of Operation Cobra opened a hole in the German lines through which the 4th Armored Division rapidly poured. The division seized the key city of Avranches on 31 July and opened a gateway to the interior of France. The next day, the division was placed under the control of Lt. Gen. George S. Patton's Third Army. Wood chafed at orders that sent his unit into the heart of Brittany in accordance with plans written in England before D day. He was convinced the decisive battle would occur to the east, toward Paris. His superiors persisted, however, and the 4th Armored Division attacked south and west. After advancing to Lorient and Nantes, on 13 August Patton reassigned the 4th Armored Division to XII Corps and ordered it to prepare for an attack toward Orleans. The division's units moved swiftly east and soon ran off their maps. "On the crest of a mounting wave of optimism the 4th Armored Division turned eastward and drove out of Brittany in search of further opportunities," wrote the official army historian, "its commander sure at last he was heading in the right direction."[10]

The 4th Armored Division led a surging Third Army across France at breakneck speed. These were days of glory for the division, with advances measured in dozens of miles each day. The division bounded the Seine, Marne, and Meuse Rivers before fuel supplies dried up on 1 September because the supreme commander of Allied forces in Europe, Gen. Dwight D. Eisenhower, had diverted priority to the British 21st Army Group to the north.[11] For ten days the 4th Armored Division sat astride the Meuse and watched the opportunity to reach the German border disappear. Units conducted intensive maintenance on men and machines in preparation for an advance to the Moselle when supplies permitted a resumption of the attack. The vehicles needed the maintenance: Most combat vehicles had logged fifteen hundred miles since landing on Utah Beach, and supply vehicles had logged more than three thousand miles.[12] The quartermaster did his part to keep morale high. On 3 September he dispatched five truckloads of cognac from Chartres for general troop distribution, and on 10 September he issued two cigars to each man in the division.[13]

The brief operational pause allowed the Wehrmacht an opportunity to stabilize the front in the West. Moving quickly, the Germans transferred the 3d and 15th *Panzergrenadier* Divisions from Italy to Lorraine. Those two capable divisions, along with the 553d *Volksgrenadier* Division, now barred the way across the Moselle. The

3d *Panzergrenadier* Division, commanded by *Generalmajor* Hans Hecker, was an experienced division at nearly full strength. It had a powerful artillery regiment, but initially lacked its organic tank and engineer battalions due to their delay in movement from Italy. An attempt by the 80th Infantry Division's 317th Infantry Regiment to conduct a hasty crossing of the Moselle north of Nancy at Pont-à-Mousson on 5–6 September was repulsed by the 3d *Panzergrenadier* Division with heavy casualties. With the enemy prepared to fight for the eastern bank, XII Corps would have to battle its way across the river in a more deliberate manner.[14] The new XII Corps's plan entailed a double envelopment of Nancy, with the 35th Infantry Division and CCB, 4th Armored Division, crossing the Moselle south of Nancy while the 80th Infantry Division continued its attack to cross the river to the north. The 4th Armored Division's CCA was in corps reserve, prepared to exploit success on either flank.[15]

On 11 September, the 137th Infantry Regiment, 35th Infantry Division, gained a bridgehead across the Moselle. Twenty miles south of Nancy near Bayon, CCB also crossed the river, but in a more creative and innovative manner. A platoon from the 8th Tank Battalion led by 1st Lt. William C. Marshall used its tank main guns to blast the canal running parallel to and west of the river until its banks collapsed. The men threw railroad ties and rails on top of the dirt to provide traction. Marshall gunned his tank over the canal, and then towed the remainder of his platoon across when they mired in the mud on the canal bottom. The platoon forded the four separate streams that comprise the Moselle south of Nancy and wreaked havoc among the German infantry defending the far side, a feat for which Lieutenant Marshall was awarded the Distinguished Service Cross.[16] During the night and following morning, engineers from the 24th Armored Engineer Battalion installed tactical bridges and the remainder of CCB, with the 2d Battalion, 320th Infantry, attached, moved across the river. After repulsing a counterattack by elements of the 15th *Panzergrenadier* Division, CCB exploited northeast. By 14 September, Dager's troops had crossed the Meurthe River and reached the Marne-Rhin Canal east of Nancy, where they stalled due to a shortage of bridging assets, which had been used up on the numerous canals and streams to their rear.[17]

On 12 September the 80th Infantry Division resumed its attack, with the 317th Infantry Regiment, now supported by nine battalions of field artillery, seizing a bridgehead north of Nancy at Dieulouard. The 318th Infantry Regiment soon reinforced the bridgehead, and both regiments dug in and awaited the doctrinal German counterattack. The inevitable reaction came at 0100 on 13 September, when a battalion of the 29th *Panzergrenadier* Regiment supported by a company of assault guns attacked the northern flank of the bridgehead. Another, more powerful thrust by two infantry battalions supported by a tank company soon followed the initial attack. The counterattacks were nearly successful, coming within a hundred meters of the heavy assault bridges across the river before losing momentum as the sun came up.[18]

The Shortest Way Home

At the moment of decision on the morning of 13 September, when the German counterattack seemed capable of regaining the line of the Moselle, Major General Wood stood on the west bank discussing the situation with leaders of the 80th Infantry Division and CCA. Major General Manton Eddy, the XII Corps commander, arrived to join the extemporaneous council of war. Eddy expressed his concern that the German counterattack had reduced the bridgehead too much for CCA to cross the river and deploy on the east bank. He then asked Colonel Clarke what he wanted to do. "We can't do much fighting on this side of the river," Clarke replied. Clarke turned to Lt. Col. Creighton W. Abrams, commander of the 37th Tank Battalion (and a future army chief of staff), to ask his opinion. Pointing across the river, Abrams said, "Colonel, that is the shortest way home." Eddy and Wood agreed, and CCA was ordered to cross the Moselle.[19]

Combat Command A, with the tank-heavy Task Force Abrams leading followed by the infantry-heavy Task Force Jacques, wasted no time in exploiting the moment. Its armored columns entered the shallow bridgehead at daylight on 13 September, sliced into retreating enemy formations, blasted through the German perimeter defenses, and advanced twenty miles to reach the high ground west

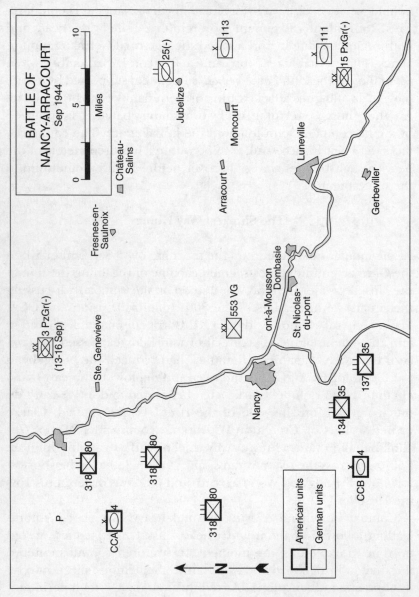

BATTLE OF
NANCY-ARRACOURT
Sep 1944

Miles

0   5   10

Château-
Salins

Fresnes-en-
Saulnoix

Ste. Genevieve

Jubelize

25(-)

113

111

15 PxGr(-)

Moncourt

Arracourt

Luneville

Gerbeviller

3 PzGr(-)
(13-16 Sep)

553 VG

ont-à-Mousson
Dombasie

St. Nicolas-
du-pont

Nancy

318   80

318   80

318   80

134   35

137   35

CCA   4

CCB   4

American units

German units

N

of Château-Salins by nightfall. Efforts by small German detachments to block the advance were futile. The 4th Armored Division Artillery and CCA's logistical tail (loaded with a week's worth of supplies) tucked themselves closely behind the combat elements and moved in the void created by the violent armored advance. The next day, the force attacked south, seized Arracourt, overran the rear of the 15th Panzergrenadier Division, cut the German lines of communication to Nancy, and linked up with reconnaissance elements from CCB to the south.

For three days, CCA fought isolated behind enemy lines. Every night the combat command would form a defensive laager with 360-degree security. The men of CCA bagged hundreds of German prisoners who wandered unawares into their positions. One particularly valuable acquisition was the capture of a truckload of German maps, which were more accurate than American maps and highly prized by the 4th Armored Division soldiers. By 15 September, Wood's men were in a strong position to the east of Nancy, astride the German lines of communication and well positioned for continued operations. In its wake, the division left a swath of destruction, accounting for 1,269 prisoners, fifty armored vehicles, twenty-seven artillery pieces, and more than four hundred other vehicles, while suffering only sixteen killed, thirty-five wounded, and the loss of seven tanks.[20]

German doctrine mandated immediate counterattacks against enemy penetrations. The counterattack toward the American bridges in the Dieulouard sector on the morning of 13 September was a precursor to a larger and more dangerous attack at dawn two days later. This operation was conducted by five infantry battalions pulled from various units under the control of the 3d *Panzergrenadier* Division, supported by artillery and up to forty tanks and assault guns.[21] The attack very nearly succeeded. In the southern portion of the bridgehead, the German assault forced the 3d Battalion, 317th Infantry, back about a thousand meters before being broken by the massed fire of four American artillery battalions. In the northern portion of the bridgehead, German forces drove toward the Moselle, isolating an American battalion on Mousson Hill and retaking the key town of Saint-Geneviève. In the center, however, the 1st and 2d Battalions, 317th Infantry, held the decisive terrain of Hill 382 against repeated enemy assaults.[22]

The turning point in the battle came on the morning of 16 September. The 115th *Panzergrenadier* Regiment, 15th *Panzergrenadier* Division, which had arrived the previous day, attacked the northern portion of the bridgehead in a last attempt to seize the American bridges. Relief for the defenders was to come from a surprising direction. The previous day, Maj. Gen. Horace L. McBride, commander of the 80th Infantry Division, had prevailed on Major General Eddy to order the release of the 1st Battalion, 318th Infantry, which had been attached to CCA during its attack. Colonel Clarke responded by dispatching the infantry to the rear, escorted by a company of medium tanks from the 35th Tank Battalion. During the night, the force fought its way west toward the bridgehead. When radio contact was made with the 80th Division's headquarters in the morning, McBride ordered the column to attack and retake Saint-Geneviève from the east. Caught by surprise from an unexpected direction, the Germans withdrew with the loss of 150 prisoners. The 1st Battalion continued its attack to envelop another German force near Loisy; once again, the Germans broke and withdrew when confronted with an unanticipated attack on an exposed flank. The German counterattack had failed to dislodge the 80th Infantry Division from the key terrain on the battlefield.[23]

To ease the pressure on the 80th Infantry Division, Eddy ordered CCB to attack north toward Nomény on 16 September. Dager's command had managed to cross the Marne-Rhin Canal the previous night, which put both CCA and CCB north of the last significant water barrier in the area. The Reserve Command, seldom used by Wood for combat operations, moved to Lunéville to take up positions alongside the 42d Cavalry Squadron, 2d Cavalry Group, which protected XII Corps's southeastern flank. Energized by the 4th Armored Division's deep strike into the enemy's rear, Patton prepared orders at Third Army headquarters that would send XII Corps attacking northeast toward the Rhine at Darmstadt.

While XII Corps occupied Nancy, continued its attack against the 553d *Volksgrenadier* and 3d *Panzergrenadier* Divisions, and expanded the bridgehead over the Moselle, the German Fifth Panzer Army prepared to counterattack with the 15th *Panzergrenadier* Division and the 111th and 113th Panzer Brigades. The panzer brigades were brand-new formations, organized on Hitler's orders at the beginning of September. They lacked trained staffs, engineers, and mechanics. The young panzer soldiers, inexperienced and hastily trained, lacked the combat skills they would require to face Wood's veteran division. Morale and esprit de corps were weak at best, and discipline was maintained through harsh measures, including the threat of execution.[24] During the two-week battle around Nancy, differences in unit training and cohesiveness would tip the scales in favor of the 4th Armored Division. Additionally, there was very little artillery available to support the counterattack, and promised support from the *Luftwaffe* never materialized.

The brigade commanders, *Oberst* Heinrich-Walter Bronsart von Schellendorf of the 111th Panzer Brigade and *Oberst* Eric Freiherr von Seckendorff of the 113th Panzer Brigade, were both seasoned armor commanders, veterans of the eastern front and recipients of the Knight's Cross. They were new to warfare in the West, however. Neither had experienced the immense power of the American army on the ground and in the air. Both would die east of Nancy while leading their troops in battle.[25]

To help even the odds, each panzer brigade contained a battalion of brand-new Mark V Panther tanks along with a battalion of Mark IVH tanks, an infantry regiment with one battalion in half-tracked vehicles and one in trucks, an antitank company, and a reconnaissance company. The Panther tank, with its high-velocity, long-barreled 75L71 cannon and thick, well-sloped frontal armor, was the finest tank fielded in World War II and was vastly superior to American armored vehicles. The Mark IVH tank and the American M4 Sherman medium tank were roughly equivalent, but even these older German tanks brandished a powerful 75L48 cannon that could outrange the short-barreled 75mm gun on the Sherman.

The M4A3 Sherman tank used by the 4th Armored Division was agile and mechanically reliable, but overmatched by the Panther both in terms of armor protection and firepower. To destroy a Panther, Sherman crews had to maneuver to a flank and hit it in its more vulnerable side armor or fire at extremely close range (less than a hundred yards) to penetrate the front of the turret. A Panther could easily destroy a Sherman at ranges out to two thousand yards or more.[26]

The Sherman was not designed to fight enemy tanks—that was the purpose of the tank destroyers. The M18 Hellcat tank destroyer used by American forces at Nancy-Arracourt had a high-velocity 76mm gun, but its thin armor and lack of overhead armor protection due to its open-turret design made the tank destroyer vulnerable to every antitank weapon in the German arsenal. Nevertheless, the M18 could engage and destroy enemy tanks, including Panthers, at much longer ranges than the undergunned Sherman.[27]

The German counterattack began on the morning of 18 September with a combined assault by elements of the 15th *Panzergrenadier* Division and the 111th Panzer Brigade that forced the 4th Armored Division's Reserve Command and the 42d Cavalry Squadron to withdraw into the northern portion of Lunéville. Major General Eddy responded to this threat by sending CCB, 6th Armored Division, to the vicinity, while Major General Wood reinforced his Reserve Command with a task force from CCA that consisted of a tank company, an armored infantry company, a platoon of tank destroyers, and a battery of armored field artillery. Tank destroyers from the 704th Tank Destroyer Battalion held the 111th Panzer Brigade at bay by destroying several Panthers at close range. The armored artillery battalions supporting the two combat commands, reinforced by the guns of XII Corps artillery, fired in support of the American defenders. Together, these forces compelled *General der Panzertruppen* Hasso von Manteuffel to order the withdrawal of the German forces from Lunéville that night.[28]

To continue the counterattack on 19 September, Manteuffel revised his plan of operations. The 15th *Panzergrenadier* Division would revert to the defensive and hold the area between the Marne-Rhin Canal and the Meurthe River, centered on Lunéville. The 111th Panzer Brigade would cross to the north of the canal and attack in conjunction with the 113th Panzer Brigade, which was assembling at Bourdonnay, about nine miles east of Arracourt. The two panzer brigades would attack directly west to Champenoux to relieve the 553d *Volksgrenadier* Division, which was fighting for its existence against the assaults of the U.S. 35th Infantry Division. The attack would begin precisely at 0600, whether the forces were ready or not.

Clarke Holds Arracourt

The Germans had very little intelligence due to their inability to penetrate the American counterreconnaissance screen, both on the ground and in the air. The German commanders' lack of knowledge concerning the composition and disposition of American units, coupled with their piecemeal commitment of available forces, would hurt them in the upcoming battle. These circumstances would present the 4th Armored Division's CCA with an opportunity to seize the initiative as it defended the Nancy bridgehead and the flank of the 35th Infantry Division against the enemy onslaught.[29]

The 4th Armored Division, poised to continue its attack to the northeast, did not suspect a major counterattack into its flank. Combat Command B was positioned near Fresnes-en-Saulnois in the north, heavily engaged with entrenched German forces in Château-Salins. The Reserve Command guarded the division's southern flank in Lunéville. Combat Command A was spread over a wide area stretching nearly to Château-Salins in the north and the Marne-Rhin Canal in the south. Due to the movement of forces south to support the Reserve Command on 18 September, Colonel Clarke defended Arracourt with a small force consisting of two companies of Sherman tanks, one company of M5 Stuart light tanks equipped with 37mm main guns, an armored infantry battalion, an engineer combat battalion, two platoons of M18 Hellcat tank destroyers, and three artillery battalions. The heavy artillery component would give CCA a decided advantage over its opponents, who operated nearly bereft of fire support during the battle.[30]

The Fifth Panzer Army struck CCA at Arracourt on the morning of 19 September and precipitated one of the largest armored engagements in the West since D day. The 113th Panzer Brigade, with nearly eighty tanks, including three dozen Panthers in the van, attacked in a dense fog. Although screened from American airpower, the Germans could not exploit the superior range advantage of their high-velocity tank cannon due to poor observation. The strength of the Panther was its ability to engage and destroy targets at long range, but most engagements during the morning hours took place at less than 150 meters due to the limited visibility. In the rapid and surprised combat that ensued, the 4th Armored Division's superior crew training more than compensated for the Panther's superiority—and for the fact that the Germans enjoyed nearly a two-to-one superiority in tank strength.

The first contact with the attacking German forces occurred shortly after dawn as SSgt. Edward P. Mallon's light tank platoon was screening Moncourt. No match for the more heavily armed and armored Panthers, Mallon ordered his platoon to withdraw to the northwest while maintaining contact with the German column. Warned by Mallon and by additional reports from listening posts in front of their positions, Capt. Kenneth R. Lamison's C Company, 37th Tank Battalion, waited alertly in hide positions. Two Shermans destroyed the first three Panthers when they appeared out of the fog at a range of seventy-five yards. The remainder of the enemy column withdrew toward Arracourt.[31]

Lamison reacted quickly to the situation. Ordering one of his platoons to follow, he raced south on a parallel course to the retreating enemy and positioned his tanks on a commanding ridge to ambush the enemy column as it appeared again out of the fog. The American tankers destroyed five Panthers with their initial salvo, ducked behind the ridge, and then reappeared and destroyed the remaining three German tanks.[32]

Around 0730, the 37th Tank Battalion's liaison officer, Capt. William A. Dwight, drove down a road east of Arracourt and ran into a German tank column. He was able to escape in the fog and return to CCA headquarters, where Clarke rapidly dispatched a platoon of tank destroyers under Dwight's control to support Abrams's forces at Lezey. The tank destroyers made contact with a German column three miles east of Arracourt. They deployed in a small depression and opened fire at a hundred yards, destroying seven tanks for the loss of three tank destroyers. Later in the morning, another platoon of tank destroyers knocked out eight Panthers only two miles from Arracourt and forced the remainder of the German column to withdraw.[33]

B Company, 37th Tank Battalion, reached Arracourt at about 1100 after marching from its assembly area near Chambrey, several miles to the northwest. Another German column soon appeared out of the fog, and B Company and guns from the 66th Armored Field Artillery Battalion, firing volleys at a range of 650 yards, beat the enemy back after tanks had advanced to within four hundred yards of the CCA command post.[34]

A short time later, one of the most bizarre events of the battle took place. Wood's pilot, Maj. Charles Carpenter, had his L-4 liaison plane rigged with six bazooka antitank rocket launchers underneath the wings, which could be fired individually or in volley with a trigger in the cockpit. Flying over the battlefield near noon, Carpenter noticed a couple of German tanks that had overrun the CCA water point. He dove on the tanks and fired his bazookas, but missed. Undaunted, he dove at the tanks again, this time at an eighty-degree angle. He knocked out both tanks, an exploit that helped to earn Carpenter the nickname "Bazooka Charlie."[35]

When the counterattack began, Eddy was in Lunéville with the commander of the 4th Armored Division's Reserve Command Major William L. Hunter, executive officer of the 37th Tank Battalion and commander of the task force sent to Lunéville the day before, interrupted with the news of the enemy attacks east of Arracourt. Eddy quickly agreed to return A Company, 37th Tank Battalion, back to CCA control. Hunter and A Company arrived back at CCA headquarters that afternoon, and Clarke ordered Hunter to lead a counterattack with the 37th Tank Battalion's A and B Companies. The two companies swept through Réchicourt and into the enemy's flank, where they destroyed nine tanks at a cost of three Shermans. Combat Command A ended the day by clearing enemy infantry from the battlefield.[36]

Poorly coordinated attacks by German tank companies supported by platoons of *panzergrenadiers* failed to penetrate the CCA defenses. German thrusts separated in time and space allowed American commanders to shift their scarce resources around the battlefield to meet each new threat as it developed. These officers—

lieutenants, captains, and majors—skillfully maneuvered their units around the flanks of the German brigade by using the ridges and small towns in the area to shield their moves as they gained a positional advantage over enemy forces and destroyed them with direct and indirect fire. Accurate and sustained artillery fire hammered away at enemy columns as they appeared out of the fog. By the end of the day, CCA had defeated the 113th Panzer Brigade and destroyed forty-three enemy tanks at a cost of only five friendly tanks and three tank destroyers.[37] The victory was so decisive that Patton, who had rushed to Arracourt during the day, decided that the XII Corps offensive to the Rhine could commence as scheduled the next day.[38]

While the 113th Panzer Brigade fought its battle isolated from outside support, the movement of the 111th Panzer Brigade to the north of the Marne-Rhin Canal turned into a nightmare for its commander. The brigade was supposed to have linked up with its sister unit in the early morning hours, but a French farmer misdirected the march column in the darkness. Forced to continue its movement in daylight, the 111th Panzer Brigade suffered attacks by XIX Tactical Air Command P-47 fighter-bombers that swooped in on the exposed unit and destroyed numerous vehicles. The weakened force did not link up with the 113th Panzer Brigade until late afternoon. By that time, the battle had been decided.[39]

Patton, Eddy, and Wood considered the action over by the evening of 19 September. The next morning, CCA began its previously planned attack to the northeast in conjunction with an attack by CCB in the vicinity of Château-Salins. The Reserve Command and the 35th Infantry Division's 320th Infantry Regiment moved north to secure Arracourt. Meanwhile, under strict orders from Army Group G to continue the counterattack, General Manteuffel pressed the LVIII Panzer Corps to continue its assault. The sum total of this effort amounted to a sortie by eight Panther tanks toward Arracourt, but this movement was enough to convince Major General Wood to turn CCA around to deal with the renewed threat. A determined stand by the 191st Field Artillery Battalion's 155mm howitzer crews, shooting over open sights, coupled with action by tanks and tank destroyers of the rear guard, succeeded in destroy-

ing all eight enemy tanks before the bulk of CCA returned. Nevertheless, CCA continued to sweep the area clear of German forces.[40]

By midafternoon, Colonel Clarke's forces had moved back to
clear the area east of Arracourt. Lieutenant Colonel Abrams led
three Sherman tank companies and two armored infantry companies in a thrust south from Lezey. His force was met by a group of
Mark IV tanks and 88mm antitank guns led by *Hauptmann* Junghannis from the 111th Panzer Brigade. The two forces clashed
throughout the afternoon in a bitter battle with the loss of roughly
a dozen tanks on each side.[41]

On 21 September, CCA continued its attack south to the Marne-
Rhin Canal against negligible enemy opposition. Badly in need of
rest and maintenance after nearly ten days of continuous action,
the 4th Armored Division prepared to pause for a day before re-
suming its attack to the northeast. German operations intervened
to ruin the impromptu work holiday. Shrouded by fog and reinforced by the lead elements of the 11th Panzer Division, the 111th
Panzer Brigade attacked from the northeast on the morning of the
twenty-second. The German attack hit the 25th Cavalry Squadron's
screen line north of Juvelize. Although the cavalry's light tanks and
armored cars could do little to slow the German armored assault, a
company from the 704th Tank Destroyer Battalion, operating from
hull-down positions with the cavalry, succeeded in destroying three
enemy tanks and drove the remainder back to the northeast. As the
sun burned away the morning fog, fighter-bombers descended
upon the withdrawing enemy while Abrams led his task force in a
counterattack that destroyed fourteen tanks and killed *Oberst* Schellendorf. By the end of the day, only seven tanks and eighty men remained in the 111th Panzer Brigade.[42]

German counterattacks against the Nancy bridgehead continued
for another week, but the destruction of the 111th and 113th
Panzer Brigades ended any real hope of a major breakthrough to
the beleaguered 553d *Volksgrenadier* Division. Although the Allied
logistical situation prevented a sustained Third Army drive to the
Rhine, the operations conducted in September 1944 brought
American forces across several major river barriers and positioned
them for a continued advance when supplies once again allowed

major offensive operations in November. The 4th Armored Division distinguished itself by its use of maneuver to gain a positional advantage over enemy forces and then destroy them with massed fires from tanks, tank destroyers, artillery, and fighter-bombers. During the period 19–22 September, CCA lost twenty-one tanks and suffered twenty-five killed and eighty-eight wounded, but was still a functioning organization capable of offensive action. By contrast, its German counterparts, the two panzer brigades, had ceased to exist.

The German counterattack, though largely ineffective, coincided with a worsening Allied supply situation and halted XII Corps's offensive beyond Nancy. In the pause that followed, the German high command pieced together a more effective defensive line. The heady pursuit across France was over. On 12 October the 26th Infantry Division went into the line and the 4th Armored Division moved to an assembly area in the vicinity of Nancy to rest and refit for the first time since it had landed in France.

The 4th Armored Counts Coup

Between 19 and 30 September, the 4th Armored Division destroyed 281 enemy tanks, 67 artillery pieces, 59 other armored vehicles, 514 wheeled vehicles, captured over three thousand prisoners, and killed an estimated 3,040 enemy soldiers.[43] The division had fought and defeated all or portions of the 15th *Panzergrenadier*, 11th Panzer, 553d *Volksgrenadier*, and 559th *Volksgrenadier* Divisions, and the 111th and 113th Panzer Brigades. During the entire month of September, 4th Armored Division casualties numbered 225 killed, 648 wounded, 74 missing, and forty-eight tanks destroyed.[44] This loss ratio of more than five to one in the Americans' favor showcased the division's superb combat effectiveness and attests to its superiority over its Wehrmacht foes.

One of the major reasons for the division's victory at Nancy-Arracourt was superior command and control. Air superiority enabled American commanders to control their units from the air. "I spent a lot of time moving my columns across France by flying overhead [*sic*] the column and talking to the leading company commander," recalled Bruce Clarke in an interview years later. "I led Abrams into Arracourt at the time when he captured the German Corps [*sic*] . . . I was over his head leading them in."[45] Major General Wood allowed his subordinate commanders a great deal of latitude. His commands were almost always oral, mission-type orders that allowed his subordinates to exercise initiative in accomplishing their tasks. "We were not given to writing in the Fourth Armored Division," Wood later mused. "Most of my time was spent in my jeep or plane, and my orders were issued there. That sort of business would be too bad at Leavenworth—and it is tough on the historians—but it seemed to work in battle."[46]

German commanders, on the other hand, worked within a rigid framework of orders emanating from Hitler down to division level.[47] At Arracourt, American commanders were more flexible than their German counterparts, even at the small-unit level. This mental agility kept the 4th Armored Division ahead of its German opponents in the decision cycle and forced the enemy to respond piecemeal to each new tactical development.

The type of command and control platforms used by senior leaders matters a great deal in armored warfare. A shortage of tanks forced the commanders of both the 111th and 113th Panzer Brigades to operate from the less survivable environs of a half-tracked command vehicle. Not surprisingly, the conspicuous appearance of these antennae-laden vehicles among dozens of tanks drew fire and resulted in the death of both commanders. Abrams operated from a Sherman tank and survived, as did Clarke in his aircraft overhead.

The 4th Armored Division dominated the battle for information superiority. Air supremacy was a major factor. Although U.S. units routinely received reports from aerial observers when the weather allowed, German units had to rely solely on their eyes and ears on the ground. The Germans made up for this shortfall somewhat through radio intercepts, taking advantage of the notoriously poor radio discipline practiced by American forces. Nevertheless, the 4th Armored Division won the reconnaissance/counterreconnaissance battle on the ground as well as in the air. Scouts tracked the movement of enemy vehicles in the fog-shrouded hills and gathered information that enabled American commanders to outmaneuver enemy columns, gain a positional advantage on their flank, and then destroy them with fire. German commanders, on the other hand, invariably operated in the blind, with little tactical intelligence on which to act. They lacked a feel for the battlefield when it mattered most.

If the operations of the 4th Armored Division at Nancy-Arracourt proved anything, it is that excellent training and sound doctrine are as important as technologically advanced equipment. Time and again in the battle around Arracourt, well-trained American tank and tank destroyer crews in their inferior vehicles outmaneuvered and outshot their opponents manning the superior Panther tanks. The victory at Nancy-Arracourt was also a triumph for the American mobilization system and a validation of the years of training the 4th Armored Division underwent prior to its commitment in battle.

Training and doctrine were the foundation for success, but improvisation and application on the battlefield were the keys to victory. American tanks were not meant to fight enemy tanks according to Armored Force doctrine, yet at Arracourt and elsewhere in Europe, GIs continually found themselves in situations that forced them to fight enemy tanks in close combat. American crews improvised to defeat superior enemy vehicles. One technique was to use white phosphorous rounds against enemy tanks. The burning white phosphorous would blind enemy crews with a dense smoke screen and sometimes forced them to evacuate their vehicles by seeping into cracks in the hatches. American tank crews could then close in for a killing shot with armor-piercing ammunition.[48] The lesson is clear: Technology alone will not win battles; victory also depends on the bravery and skill of the soldiers who fight and the leaders who command.

The ability to maneuver was of critical importance to the 4th Armored Division in its operations. The division's superior ability to maneuver enabled the positioning of soldiers and weapons on key terrain to destroy opposing forces with massed direct and indirect fires. Artillery, the "King of Battle," also played its customary key role in the combined-arms victory—as it would throughout the campaign for France and Germany in 1944 and 1945. The *Wehrmacht,* which suffered from acute ammunition shortages in the West in September 1944, could match neither the accuracy nor the volume of fires placed by American forces on enemy units in their path.

That having been said, the 4th Armored Division's success in combat had as much to do with speed and shock as firepower. "Warfare is mental, not physical," Clarke told a war correspondent after Arracourt. "When you upset the enemy you have him licked, particularly the German. He is big and slow to react, and if you cut his communications and lines of contact he will just take to the woods. But if you give him time to sit down and get out the rule book, he is tough as hell."[49]

Air superiority was a necessary precondition for the battle of maneuver waged by the 4th Armored Division. Airpower gave freedom of movement to U.S. units while denying the same to enemy forces. On 19 September, the crucial day of the battle at Arracourt, the 111th Panzer Brigade failed to appear on the battlefield until too late due in part to the effects of airpower, while 4th Armored Division reinforcements from Lunéville arrived in time to play a significant role in the battle. Writing about the battles around Nancy after the war, the chief of staff of Army Group G, Maj. Gen. Friedrich W. Von Mellenthin, stated, "It was clear that American air power put our panzers at a hopeless disadvantage, and that normal principles of armored warfare did not apply in this theater."[50] The operative word is *normal*. A veteran of the eastern front, Von Mellenthin had maneuvered German panzer divisions with relative freedom from enemy aircraft until his transfer to France in September 1944. Allied air supremacy in the West forced German units to move at night and hide during the day. Logistics became difficult and most German units lacked necessary supplies and spare parts to function efficiently. An army without control of the air attempts to maneuver at its peril.

A final point: The 4th Armored Division succeeded because it was a self-contained unit combining armor, armored infantry, tank destroyers, artillery, engineers, and the logistical organizations necessary for independent functioning on the battlefield. This point is crucial for successful maneuver and one cannot stress it in bold enough terms. Divisions must be self-contained combined-arms organizations in order to fight independent battles of maneuver. The more we tie divisions to higher echelons for supplies and support, the more constraining will be the tether that restricts their capabilities on the battlefield, thereby diminishing the speed and shock that makes them decisive instruments in combat.

The 4th Armored Division outmaneuvered and outshot the enemy at Nancy-Arracourt, but the division planted the seeds of victory in its three years of training prior to the battle. From the Tennessee maneuvers in 1942 through the battle for the Nancy bridgehead and beyond, the division was a cohesive team that lived, trained, and fought together. Personnel stability allowed the division to coalesce as an organization, to develop an implicit trust in its capabilities, and to internalize its standard operating procedures. Major General Wood could use oral, mission-type orders because his subordinate commanders had been with him for two years and understood his intent in shaping the battlefield. The battalion commanders worked well together. The normal mode of operation was in combined-arms task forces consisting of tanks, armored infantry, tank destroyers, field artillery, and engineers. Without the intimate association and trust among the battalion commanders of the division, this method of operation would have failed. By working together as a team, the division's leaders transformed the "federation of thirteen battalions led by a major general" into something greater than the sum of its parts.

The 4th Armored Division's blend of mobility and firepower proved a winning combination that contributed greatly to the Allied victory in World War II. The men of the division richly deserved the Presidential Unit Citation given to them collectively at the end of the war. They had shown, by their deeds alone, what one of the best American divisions in World War II could do to its enemies on the field of battle—even when outnumbered.

Notes

1. Major General John S. Wood's answer to a reporter who asked him during the Tennessee maneuvers in 1942 what nickname the 4th Armored Division would adopt.

2. Kent Roberts Greenfield, Robert R. Palmer, and Bell I. Wiley, *The Organization of Ground Combat Troops* (Washington: Office of the Chief of Military History, 1947), 9.

3. Unlike other armored divisions, the 4th Armored Division did not call its Reserve Command "CCR." The intention was to rotate battalions through the Reserve Command for rest rather than use it as another combat element. The 4th Armored Division used the Reserve Command in combat only on rare occasions, such as in the battle of the Nancy bridgehead and in the drive to relieve Bastogne in December 1944. Likewise, CCA and CCB did not have a fixed structure as in some other divisions.

4. Christopher R. Gabel, *The 4th Armored Division in the Encirclement of Nancy* (Fort Leavenworth, Kans.: Combat Studies Institute, 1986), 5.

5. Biographical data on 4th Armored Division commanders, file 604-0.1, box 15175, Record Group (RG) 407, National Archives and Records Administration, College Park, Md. (hereafter NARA).

6. Bruce C. Clarke, interview by John Albright, Oral History, 13 May 1972, Bruce Cooper Clarke Papers, U.S. Army Military History Institute, Carlisle Barracks, Pa. (hereafter USAMHI), 41.

7. Ibid., 105.

8. Ibid., 119.

9. Maj. C. P. Miller, "Tank-vs-Tank Combat Training," *Armored Cavalry Journal* 55, no. 4 (July–Aug. 1946): 29–30.

10. Martin Blumenson, *Breakout and Pursuit* (Washington: Office of the Chief of Military History, 1961), 368.

11. Charles B. MacDonald, *The Siegfried Line Campaign* (Washington: Center of Military History, 1963), 9–10.

12. Headquarters, 4th Armored Division, "After-Action Report for the Period 17 July to 31 August 1944," 24 Oct. 1944, and "Combat History, 17 July 1944–9 May 1945," file 604-0.3, box 15175, RG 407, NARA.

13. Headquarters, 4th Armored Division, "Quartermaster Report of Operations, 22 Dec. 43–22 Dec. 44," entries for 3 and 10 Sept. 1944, file 604-30, box 15267, RG 407, NARA.

14. Hugh M. Cole, *The Lorraine Campaign* (Washington: Office of the Chief of Military History, 1950), 57–65.

15. Ibid., 70.

16. Kenneth Koyen, *The Fourth Armored Division from the Beach to Bavaria* (Munich: Herder Druck, 1946), 51–52.

17. Cole, *Lorraine Campaign*, 71–74, 89.

18. Ibid., 80–84.

19. Lewis Sorley, *Thunderbolt, From the Battle of the Bulge to Vietnam and Beyond: General Creighton Abrams and the Army of His Times* (New York: Simon and Schuster, 1992), 58.

20. Headquarters, 4th Armored Division, "After Action Report for September and October, 1944," 12 Nov. 1944, file 604-0.3, box 15175, RG 407, NARA.

21. Cole, *Lorraine Campaign*, 100.

22. Ibid., 101–02.

23. Ibid., 103–04.

24. *General der Panzertruppen* Horst Stumpff, "Panzer Brigades 111-113," MS.B251, USAEUR, USAMHI, 2; Richard H. Barnes, "Arracourt—September 1944" (master's thesis, U.S. Army Command and General Staff College, Fort Leavenworth, Kans., 1982), 159.

25. Gregory M. Smith, "Quality Factors at Arracourt: Leadership, Training, Organization and Tactics," *Strategy and Tactics*, summer 1990, 44–49.

26. R. P. Hunnicutt, *Sherman: A History of the American Medium Tank* (Novato, Calif.: Presidio, 1978); Albin F. Irzyk, "Tank versus Tank," *Military Review* XXV, no. 10 (Jan. 1946): 11–16; I. D. White, "A Report on United States vs. German Armor," prepared for General of the Army Dwight D. Eisenhower, 20 Mar. 1945, USAMHI; F. M. Senger und Etterlin, *German Tanks of World War II* (Harrisburg: Stackpole, 1969).

27. Charles M. Baily, *Faint Praise: American Tanks and Tank Destroyers during World War II* (Hamden, Conn.: Archon, 1983).

28. Cole, *Lorraine Campaign*, 221; Headquarters, 4th Armored Division, "Combat History," entry for 18 Sept. 1944; Headquarters,

704th Tank Battalion, After-Action Report, Sept. 1944, file TD Bn-704-0.3, box 23716, RG 407, NARA.

29. Cole, *Lorraine Campaign*, 222.

30. Ibid., 223.

31. 37th Tank Battalion Diary, 19 Sept. 1944, file 604-TK(37)-0.2, box 15309, RG 407, NARA. Staff Sergeant Mallon was awarded a battlefield commission on 14 October 1944.

32. Army historical interview with Capt. Kenneth R. Lamison, combat interviews file, box 24092, RG 407, NARA. Captain Lamison was awarded the Silver Star for his actions.

33. Army historical interview with Lt. Col. Hal Pattison, executive officer of CCA, and interview with Capt. William A. Dwight, combat interviews file, box 24092, RG 407, NARA. Captain Dwight was awarded the Silver Star for directing the fires of the tank destroyers during the battle.

34. CCA, 4th Armored Division, *The Nancy Bridgehead* (Fort Knox: U.S. Army Armor School, 1949), 18.

35. Pattison interview; Wes Gallagher, "Tiger Jack's Spearheads," *Liberty Magazine*, 10 February 1945.

36. Pattison interview; A and B Company interviews, combat interviews file, box 24092, RG 407, NARA.

37. Headquarters, 4th Armored Division, "Combat History," entry for 19 Sept. 1944; 37th Tank Battalion Diary, 19 Sept. 1944.

38. Cole, *Lorraine Campaign*, 225.

39. "War Diary #4," 19 Sept. 1944, in *58th Panzer Corps Reports* (Fort Knox: U.S. Army Armor School, 1986).

40. Cole, *Lorraine Campaign*, 226–28.

41. Ibid. Lieutenant Colonel Abrams received the Distinguished Service Cross for bravery in this action; *Hauptmann* Junghannis and his detachment were cited in dispatches for their courage.

42. Ibid., 230–32; *Generalmajor* Friedrich W. Von Mellenthin, *Panzer Battles* (Norman: University of Oklahoma Press, 1956; reprint, New York: Ballantine, 1980), 378. The next day the commander of the 113th Panzer Brigade was killed by a P-47.

43. Headquarters, 4th Armored Division, "After Action Report for September and October, 1944," 2.

44. Headquarters, 4th Armored Division, "Combat History," September 1944.

45. Clarke interview, 75.

46. Maj. Gen. John S. Wood to Hugh M. Cole, 9 Sept. 1946, file 2-3.7CB4, box 187, RG 407, NARA.

47. Barnes, "Arracourt—September 1944," 153, 162.

48. Clarke interview, 63; United States Forces European Theater, General Board Report, Armored Forces, Study no. 53, "Tank Gunnery," 42.

49. Gallagher, "Tiger Jack's Spearheads."

50. Mellenthin, *Panzer Battles,* 380.

Soldiers of Gideon: The Defense of the Golan, October 1973

And I heard the voice of the Lord, saying "whom shall we send? And who will go for us?" And I answered, "here am I, Lord. Send me!"

—Isaiah 6:8

Dawn broke crisply over the Golan Heights on 6 October 1973 as the nation of Israel observed the solemn ceremonies of Yom Kippur, the ancient "Day of Atonement." From the heights of Mount Hermon, Israeli observers looking eastward could see almost to Damascus itself. What they did not see, masked behind the slopes and ridges of the Golan, was the Syrian army, rumbling toward the border in long, undulating tank columns, exuberant at the prospect of final victory over the Zionists. At home in bed, a freckled, blond reservist named Zvi "Zwicka" Greengold woke that day with little concern beyond how to spend his leave time.

Later in the day Lieutenant Greengold was stunned to hear reports of the massive Arab attack. Anxious to fight, the young officer hitchhiked to the Israeli headquarters at Nafekh and begged the operations officer there for troops to lead. Instead, he was sent off to recover casualties and damaged tanks dragged from the front. Soon he was put in charge of a makeshift platoon of two hastily repaired tanks and told to head south along the Tapline Road to join up with the Barak Brigade at the front. His tiny command was dubbed "Zwicka Force."

Over the next twenty-four hours, Lieutenant Greengold fought against an advancing Syrian armored brigade, at times with nothing more than his own tank. During the night, he maneuvered deftly between advancing enemy units, using the terrain to mask his sudden appearances in the midst of Syrian tank columns. Surviving the destruction of his own tank, he leaped out, wounded and burning, rolled in the dirt to put out the flames, and commandeered another tank to continue the fight. Outnumbered fifty to one during most of the night, Zwicka succeeded in destroying at least twenty enemy tanks himself while he disrupted and defeated several advancing columns. Zwicka's obstinate defense convinced the Syrians that they were up against a formidable Israeli tank force, delaying their advance during the critical hours of that first night. In the early hours of the war, when the fate of Israel hung in the balance, Zwicka and many others like him battled with a determination and skill that bought the time so desperately needed to bring up reinforcements and save the front.

Balance of Forces

The Syrian army attacked at 1400 on 6 October 1973. For the push to the Jordan River, the Syrians massed three infantry divisions—from north to south the 7th, 9th, and 5th—deployed along the "Purple Line" that had separated the Syrians and Israelis since the 1967 war. Behind them were two armored divisions—the 3d camped near Katana, and the 1st near Kiswe. Reinforcing these divisions were several independent tank brigades.

Each of the infantry divisions had two infantry brigades, a tank brigade, and a mechanized brigade, with 160 tanks per infantry division. The armored divisions had another 230 tanks each. These five divisions, along with the independent brigades and smaller units in the area of operations, totaled about 1,500 tanks. Supporting the maneuver forces, the Syrians had approximately one thousand guns and mortars, as well as an array of surface-to-air missiles with which they hoped to hold the Israeli air forces at bay.

Against this tidal wave of armor, the Israelis initially mustered only two armored brigades: the 7th in the north and the 188th or "Barak" Brigade in the south. Together they totaled 177 tanks, many of them spread out in platoon defensive positions along the Purple Line. In tanks alone, the Syrians outnumbered the Israelis almost

ten to one. The Israeli Defense Forces (IDF) had about sixty artillery pieces in support and a handful of air defense missiles, including American-made Hawk missiles.

The Yom Kippur War pitted the Israelis' American, British, and
French weapons against the Arabs' Soviet-made equipment. The
IDF employed American M60 Patton tanks and British Centurions,
both equipped with 105mm main guns. The Syrians had T-54 and
T-55 tanks with 100mm guns, and some of the elite tank brigades
had the latest in Soviet tank technology: the T-62 with a smoothbore
115mm main gun. Soviet tanks, designed for a high-tempo war
of movement in the north German plain, were fast and agile.
Equipped with the latest Soviet night-fighting optics, they were capable of continuous warfare around the clock. They suffered, however, from being cramped inside, and they also had one dangerous
design flaw: Their main gun rounds were stored in the turret, which
frequently resulted in fiery explosions when the turret was hit, even
if the armor was not penetrated.

Still, the Syrian armor was capable and lethal when employed
properly, and what it lacked in quality, it more than made up in
quantity. But the most telling technological advantage went to the
Israeli armor, because the American Patton tanks and the British
Centurions were carrying 105mm guns, which had a five-hundred-
yard range advantage over their Soviet counterparts. Equipped with
superior fire-control systems as well, Israeli crews could pick off the
Soviets at greater ranges. Syrian commanders knew that to win they
would have to close the range quickly.

A Failed Strategy

The Israeli outlook on warfare was conditioned by their startling
successes in the 1967 war. As a result, the IDF counted on two key
components for victory: aircraft and tanks.[1] With limited budgets,
the Israelis calculated that the most prudent and effective invest-
ments were in fighter-bombers and modernized tanks. This re-
sourcing decision reflected their conception of strategy in the event
of an Arab attack: The air force would quickly gain air superiority
and stop the initial enemy attacks while the tank forces mobilized

for a decisive counterattack. (This conception is not unlike that of many U.S. Air Force proponents today.) Events would prove this strategy badly flawed.[2]

If air superiority were simply a matter of shooting down enemy aircraft, then the IDF should have succeeded handily. The Israeli air force employed American-made F-4 Phantoms, A-4 Skyhawks, and French Mirages. The Syrians had Soviet-designed MiG-17s, MiG-21s, and the latest Soviet fighter-bomber, the MiG-23. Plane for plane, crew for crew, the Israeli air forces were superior, although the MiG-23—available only in limited quantities to the Syrians—was a match for American aircraft. Three weeks before the war broke out, an Israeli air patrol encountered Syrian aircraft over the eastern Mediterranean Sea, and a dogfight ensued. Thirteen Syrian MiGs were shot down for the cost of only one Israeli plane.[3] Clearly, the Israelis had an advantage in technology and training. All else being equal, the IDF should have been able to rule the skies almost from the start.

But all else was not equal. The Syrians, along with their Arab allies, had learned hard lessons in 1967. Calculating correctly that they could not win the air-to-air battle, they instead invested heavily in Soviet-designed surface-to-air missiles (SAMs). The Arab armies that attacked in October 1973 advanced under an umbrella of state-of-the-art air defense missiles. The result was that the Israeli air force could not operate to full effect in support of the ground forces, and thus could not stop the initial onslaughts alone. The simultaneous attack on two fronts also hindered the use of massed airpower. One pillar of Israeli national strategy had collapsed.

As for the other—the tank—it too ran into a wall of missiles.[4] Ever since the 1967 war, the Arabs had fielded a daunting array of antitank missiles like the wire-guided Sagger. In the hands of trained infantrymen, these missiles could destroy a tank at three thousand meters (well beyond the maximum effective range of the tank's main gun). When combined with rocket-propelled antitank grenades (RPGs), which were effective against tanks at up to five hundred meters, the Syrian infantry had become much more deadly. These new missiles and short-range antitank weapons took a greater toll on Israeli armor in the Sinai than they did in the Golan Heights, but on both fronts they proved to be an unexpected setback.

The Israelis also had to contend with a fundamental shift in their security strategy. In 1967, the lack of territorial depth and the dangerous proximity of Arab armies—the Egyptians in the Sinai, the Jordanians in and near Jerusalem (as well as on the hills overlooking Tel Aviv), and the Syrians on the escarpments along the Jordan River—compelled Israel to adopt a first-strike strategy. The 1967 war thus began with a devastating campaign of air strikes against Arab forces, including their air forces, which the Israelis virtually annihilated on the first day. Although these preemptive attacks were remarkably effective, Israel paid the political price and had to bear the image of the aggressor. At the conclusion of the fighting in 1967, however, Israel gained strategic depth in the Sinai, the Golan Heights, and the West Bank. This newly acquired breathing space gave rise to a new national strategy.

With the threat of immediate attack into the heartland removed, the Israelis gained the strategic option of allowing the Arabs to make the first move in the next conflict. Even if surprised, the IDF would have enough time to mobilize combat power and mount a counterattack against sudden Arab aggression before the enemy could get within striking distance of the interior. Thus the Israeli leadership, both political and military, entered the Yom Kippur War expecting the Arabs to strike first. Then the IDF would retaliate with airpower and tanks to restore the situation.

In order to make such a strategy work, the IDF counted on timely intelligence to provide strategic warning. However, as often happens in modern warfare, planners had convinced themselves that gathering intelligence was primarily a *technical* problem, forgetting its inherently political character. If there are compelling political reasons to disbelieve the indicators, then no degree of intelligence collection can be effective. Following Maj. Gen. David Elazar's incorrect prediction (based upon intelligence reports) that the Egyptians would attack in May 1973, Israeli leaders gave less weight to the warnings that an attack was imminent.

So it was that Israeli strategy, fundamentally flawed in each of its components, led to a near disaster when Syrian armor rolled up the eastern slopes of the Golan, even as hundreds of Egyptian tanks surged across the Suez Canal and flowed into Sinai.

Initial Dispositions

The initial tactical situation in the Golan Heights area presented unique challenges to both the Syrian attackers and Israeli defenders. The two opposing armies occupied positions along the Purple Line, with barely a mile separating the combatants. For the Israelis, this proximity to the attacker's start line meant there would be no room to develop a security zone to detect, delay, and disrupt attacking formations prior to their arrival in the main battle area. Instead, the senior Israeli commander on the northern front, Maj. Gen. Yitzhak Hofi, would have his main forces in the thick of the fighting from the start. With little or no room to fall back, an "elastic" defense or defense in depth was out of the question. Israeli tankers were faced with a stark choice: They could conquer, or they could die.

For the Soviet-equipped Syrians, the close proximity of the Israeli main defense line and the character of their army required a modification of classic Soviet doctrine. Soviet offensive tactics center on the concept of echelons, with small, independent combined-arms teams moving in advance of the main body. These teams range in size from two-vehicle patrols to battalions, and their mission is to conduct extensive reconnaissance in support of each level of fighting unit.

Typically, an attack would feature small regimental recon teams, followed by a platoon-size combat recon patrol, followed by a forward security element of about company size. Finally, an advance guard battalion precedes the lead regiments of the main body. Often, Soviet commanders would send out forward detachments as well—company- or battalion-size units typically tasked with seizing a critical piece of terrain. Each of these advance units assists the commander in determining the most vulnerable aspects of the defense, and they provide critically needed last-minute information for targeting and maneuver. With the advantages that such extensive re-

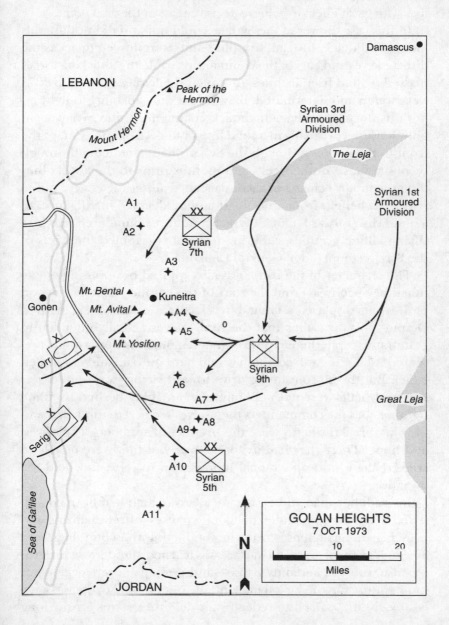

Damascus

LEBANON

▲ Peak of the Hermon

Mount Hermon

Syrian 3rd Armoured Division

The Leja

Syrian 1st Armoured Division

A1 ✦
A2 ✦

XX
Syrian 7th

A3 ✦

Mt. Bental ▲

Gonen ●

● Kuneitra

Mt. Avital ▲

A4 ✦

0

A5 ✦

▲ Mt. Yosifon

X
Orr

Syrian 9th
XX

A6 ✦

A7 ✦

Great Leja

X
Sarig

A8 ✦
A9 ✦

A10 ✦
XX
Syrian 5th

Sea of Galilee

A11 ✦

N

GOLAN HEIGHTS
7 OCT 1973

10   20

Miles

JORDAN

connaissance provides, the Soviet commander could vector his attack with great effect to achieve decisive mass at the vital point.

In this case, however, the Syrians could not and did not use this method of attack. Instead, frontline units were forced to act as the directed eyes and ears of the commander, while the attacking forces massed behind friendly lines. Although the Syrian soldiers in 1973 were tough and determined, they lacked the capability to fight using this doctrine. When the attack commenced, the Syrian main body advanced virtually in a solid line of tanks from one end of the front to the other.[5] Although the Syrians had conducted thorough reconnaissance in the weeks and months prior to the attack, they did not employ echeloned reconnaissance *during* the attack, and so could not benefit from crucial last-minute detailed intelligence. In a blind rush forward, much of the Syrian force blundered into horrifying killing grounds, suffering losses that crippled the plans of the Syrian commander, General Chakour.

The character of the battle was also colored by opposing operational perspectives. From the start of the conflict, Arab leaders on both fronts displayed a limited proclivity for *operational* maneuver. Despite postwar claims that the Arabs never actually intended to penetrate deeply, there is little doubt that, had the opportunity presented itself, the Arab coalition would have overrun and eradicated Israel. But the all-consuming drive toward victory was wholly lacking. Arab staffs were not well trained in anything beyond frontline fighting, and the commanders themselves seemed to think that war-winning breakthroughs were the product of numbers, explosives, and hope. These they had in abundance, but they were unable to convert them into operational momentum to seize and hold the initiative.

Instead, Egyptian and Syrian war plans (which had been coordinated in advance) included deliberate pauses for reorganizing and bringing up air defenses prior to conducting the coup de grace.[6] The old lesson of armored warfare was learned anew: If you plan for a pause, you will certainly pause—and perhaps never regain your momentum. On the Egyptian front, the operational pause was a necessity given the need to redeploy air defense systems for the long march across Sinai. There was no such need on the Golan Heights, for once across the relatively narrow highland plateau the Syrians would break into northern Israel.

The Israelis, on the other hand, thought in terms of depth from the start of the conflict and were dismayed by their early setbacks in achieving it. General Hofi had Damascus on his mind, and his tank crews scrawled it on the hulls of their tanks. From the start of the campaign, Israeli leaders intended to press toward Damascus and use it like a pressure point to force Syrian capitulation. Although they never reached the Syrian capital, their instinctive grasp of operational maneuver helped to wrest the initiative from the Syrian attackers, whose thinking generally progressed no farther than the range of their tank guns.

A modern armed force can, with determination and imagination, overcome technological weaknesses, strategic setbacks, and logistical constraints. But no army can grow beyond its own leadership culture. Soldiers sometimes fall short of the level of competence of their leaders, but they never exceed it. Israeli leaders from platoon to front (roughly equivalent to a U.S. corps) level were, as a rule, competent, brave, and capable of independent action. Syrian tactical leaders often showed individual toughness and courage, but they suffered from a political environment that failed to foster initiative and trust. Israeli commanders were a close-knit community, born and bred in battle. They also had the best of all reasons to fight, for their failure would mean not only defeat but also national extinction. As a result, their soldiers fought as a cohesive team, even in the face of horrendous casualties.

For the Syrians, the command culture was very different. A wide gap separated officers and soldiers. In keeping with the doctrine of their Soviet sponsors, Syrian commanders frowned on independent decision making in battle and practiced an extreme form of centralized control. When things began to go wrong, the tendency was to hew ever more closely to the plan. This inability to adapt on the move in accordance with the tactical situation led to failure time and again. As the battle wore on, the distrust and despair of a failed chain of command gave rise to suicides, mutinies, and firing squads.

Though the Syrians had real advantages in mass, firepower, and initiative, these were squandered by poor leadership and badly flawed command and control.

Fighting in Time

The physical and psychological dimensions of the battle for the Golan Heights were crucial, but its temporal aspects were perhaps even more important. The mere twenty miles or less that separated the Syrians from the escarpment leading into Galilee meant that a serious breakthrough along the front could translate into strategic disaster in a matter of hours. On the other hand, the mobilization of Israeli reserves and their movement to the battle area would restore the balance of combat power within seventy-two hours or so. Hence, there would be a window of opportunity—no more than three days at the most—during which the Syrians must make the most of their numerical advantage.

Syrian plans anticipated the total defeat of the Israelis in the Golan Heights by Monday morning, 8 October. In the event, they actually reached the zenith of their success during the course of that Monday, and the outcome hung in the balance through Tuesday. By Wednesday, 10 October, there were no operational Syrian tanks left west of the Purple Line, and the initiative had swung irretrievably to the Israelis. By the narrowest of margins, the IDF defenders foiled the Syrian timing long enough to mobilize.

The battle that resulted was framed by this competition for time. On the Syrian side, the timing of the attack to correspond with Yom Kippur produced tangible results. Many Israeli soldiers were on leave or otherwise distracted by the holiday, which called for fasting as part of worship. When the last-minute intelligence indicators began to paint a clear picture of imminent attack, Israeli leaders did not want to act for fear of disrupting the holiday. However, as in a chess game, where every move gains something and loses something, the timing of the attack also had its drawbacks. When the Israelis finally did order full-scale mobilization, the soldiers rushing to the front found the streets empty of civilian traffic, which would otherwise have been a major obstacle to deployment.

The decision to commence the attack at 1400 was driven by several considerations.[7] On the Egyptian side, it was necessary to attack after the sun had risen past the point where it would interfere with the attackers' ability to see and shoot. On the Syrian side, a midafternoon attack would give the attackers enough time to attain their first-day objectives, while at the same time avoiding an Israeli counterstrike by air. But by sunrise on Yom Kippur, all Israeli commanders knew that the war would commence that day, and the decision to delay until 1400 gave those commanders time to get their troops ready.

The Israeli mobilization effort reinforced the 75,000 active-duty soldiers of the Israeli Defense Forces to 275,000 in less than three days. In fact, many units were ready for combat in less than half that time. This Herculean performance was the result of careful planning and hard work in the years and months prior to the war. In the course of the previous winter, Gen. Rafael "Raful" Eitan, the local *ugda* or division commander, had urged the upgrading of the roads that served the IDF in the Golan Heights. He also recommended moving the mobilization sites of the units designated to reinforce the Heights closer to the sector. These improvements, along with the rigorous administration and training that underpinned the mobilization system, halved the response time when the war broke out.

On 26 September, the Israeli General Staff, alerted by Syrian troop dispositions that clearly indicated imminent attack, ordered the 7th Armored Brigade to send selected elements to the Golan Heights. However, as the final days played out, the main fighting strength of the brigade was still moving into the Nafekh area. From Rosh Hashanah (27 September) onward, the Israeli soldiers redoubled their efforts to lay mines and dig antitank ditches. By 2 October there was no longer any doubt that an attack was imminent. Three days later, on Friday, 5 October, the Israeli general headquarters put the army on full alert. The next morning, Major General Hofi was informed that war would break out that day and to hold his command in readiness.

The speed of the Syrian advance—the other side of the time equation—was likewise a matter of grave concern to the Israelis. Under Major General Hofi, the commanders on the Heights improved the defenses built along the Purple Line with the intent of channeling the attackers into prepared killing zones. When the actual assault occurred, the Israelis concentrated their fires on engineer vehicles, the key to crossing the Israeli antitank ditches or breaching their minefields.

Soviet doctrine allows for the failure of initial attacks and compensates for that possibility by echeloning. When echeloned attacks work correctly, the defenders have no time to refit between fighting the first echelon and the second. Even if the first attack fails, the second and subsequent attacks should succeed because the attackers are fresh and the defenders are worn out. The Syrians failed to achieve this effect, with the result that although the Israeli defenders were hard pressed, they had time between major engagements to refuel, rearm, and refit.

Modern warfare thus pits the pace of logistical replenishment against the pace of operations. In the Yom Kippur War, the IDF mechanics, medics, fuel handlers, and truck drivers defied Syrian fighting tempo by rapidly refitting the fighting units between battles. In the first critical days there was hardly an Israeli tank in the line that had not been damaged, repaired, and returned to battle. As the opening battles played out, small groups of mechanics repaired shot-up tanks, under fire, without rest or sleep. With incredible poise and resolution, they kept their wrenches turning and helped save a nation.[8]

The Battle Begins

The Syrians attacked promptly at 1400 on 6 October, starting with a massive artillery preparation and air bombardment all along the Israeli positions. Their plan was to attack along the two primary avenues of approach: The supporting attack would develop toward Kuneitra and from there to the Bnot Ya'akov Bridge; the main attack against the Rafid opening and along the Tapline Road toward Nafekh.

The lead Syrian ground combat units hit simultaneously between fortifications A1 and A2, on A3 north of Kuneitra, and near Kudne. Colonel Ben-Shoham, commander of the 188th "Barak" Brigade, directed a reserve tank company from the 4th Battalion to counter-attack. The Israeli armor made short work of the northern thrust, and then turned to reinforce the defense at A3. The Israelis also held off the attackers near Kudne, but the weight of the Syrian numbers began to be felt even after the shock of the initial onslaught had lessened.[9]

Although Major General Hofi had two brigades available in the Golan Heights, the 7th Brigade, under Col. Avigdor "Yanush" Ben-Gal, had only just arrived and was in reserve near Nafekh when the Syrians attacked. It was not until early evening, after the initial attacks, that Hofi decided to commit the 7th Brigade in the northern sector, while assigning the Barak Brigade to the south. Part of the reason for the Israelis' hard-won successes over the next few days was the flexibility of their command system. In splitting the Golan sector into two subsectors, Hofi caused a reorganization of the two brigades. Since Ben-Shoham's battalions were already in the line, the ones north of Kuneitra transferred to Ben-Gal, who in turn lost two of his battalions to Ben-Shoham. These transfers occurred without undue disruption of fighting capability and were a credit to the culture of leadership within the IDF.

As Colonel Ben-Gal took responsibility for his sector, he had his own 1st Battalion defending from the foothills of Mount Hermon southward four miles to Hermonit Hill, including fortifications A1 and A2. In the area of Hermonit, including fortification A3, he placed the 7th Battalion under Lt. Col. Avigdor Kahalani, who later wrote a detailed account of the war from his personal perspective. Hofi had also placed Lieutenant Colonel Yair's 4th Battalion under Ben-Gal's control. It defended the sector from fortification A3 southward to Kuneitra. Throughout the first few days, the brigade and battalion commanders shuffled small remnants of platoons and companies from one sector to another.

Farther south, the Barak Brigade assumed responsibility for the sector stretching from Kuneitra southward to the Yarmak River valley. To cover that area in the opening hours of the fight, Ben-Shoham had his own 3d Battalion under the command of Lieutenant Colonel Oded, and at about 1600 he asked for and received the 2d Battalion from Ben-Gal's 7th Brigade. Meanwhile, on the extreme northern flank of the Golan Heights, Mount Hermon fell to a daring helicopter assault by Syrian commandos. The Israeli observation post (OP) on Mount Hermon was crucial to the defense of the Golan Heights. From it, Israeli observers could see all the way from the Mediterranean Sea in the west to Damascus in the east. The OP also contained radar and other electronic intelligence equipment that could monitor the entire battlefield. Lulled into a sense of impregnability, the fifty-five soldiers defending the position atop Mount Hermon on 6 October were unprepared for the attack by Syrian soldiers airlifted onto the mountain by helicopters. Suddenly surrounded and isolated from support, the defending Israelis clung to the main bunker until dark, when a handful escaped to friendly lines. The OP that had been "the eyes of Israel" was now in Syrian hands.[10]

The Syrian attacks to the south continued despite the initial successes of the Israeli defenders. The 5th and 9th Divisions (commanded by Brig. Gen. Ali Aslan and Col. Hassan Tourmkmani respectively), reinforced with the 1st Armored Division (Col. Tewfiq Jehani) and elements of the 3d Armored Division (Brig. Gen. Mustafa Sharba), conducted the main attack in the south. The 7th Division and the rest of the 3d Armored Division pushed hard in the north. As the Syrian attack developed, General Chakour reinforced the initial successes near Hushniyah, committing both the 9th and 7th Infantry Divisions to the encirclement of Kuneitra, while the 5th Infantry Division thrust through the Rafid opening southwestward toward Ramat Magshimim and northwestward along the Tapline Road.

As darkness fell on the first night, Israeli tanks north of Kuneitra focused on destroying Syrian bridging vehicles in order to slow the Syrian advance across the tank ditch along the Purple Line. The IDF Centurions and Pattons, manned by perhaps the best-trained tank crews in the world, destroyed Syrian tanks by the dozens. But when night came, the Israelis felt their lack of night-fighting equipment as the Syrians pressed on. Short of illumination flares for their artillery, and unable to use their infrared searchlights for fear the Syrian tank crews would spot them, Israeli tank commanders fought almost blindly.[11] Soon the Israeli fortifications were awash in enemy infantry carrying deadly RPG-7s and Sagger missiles. Throughout that first night, IDF commanders called down artillery on their own fortifications to scatter the Syrian infantry, while a handful of tanks maneuvered from position to position to destroy Syrian tanks that advanced too far. Sometime in the early hours of 7 October, after losing more than forty tanks with little to show for their sacrifice, the Syrian first-echelon assault forces withdrew.

To the north and south of Rafid, Israeli fortifications became islands of resistance in a sea of Syrians. Fortification A10 held out for four days as Israeli artillery continually pounded the area while a handful of IDF soldiers inside continued to fight. On 10 October, a relieving force finally cut its way through to rescue the platoon manning the fortification. They found the area littered with Syrian corpses and destroyed tanks. The defenders were miraculously still alive.

Despite the tenacious defense, the Syrians eventually breached the Israeli lines near Rafid and Kudne. Colonel Ben-Shoham put together the anxious reports of the commanders in the front line and determined that at least a brigade of Syrian tanks had penetrated in the south, headed for Nafekh. During the night, a Syrian tank battalion passed through the attacking infantry and headed for Kuneitra. An Israeli force under Capt. "Tiger" Meir intercepted and virtually destroyed the entire tank column in two engagements. In this and similar skirmishes during those first few days, the range advantage of the Israeli 105mm main guns, coupled with superlative crew training and aggressive tactical leadership, saved the day. Still, the situation was rapidly deteriorating in the south, and by early Sunday morning there were only fifteen operational tanks left in the Barak Brigade to face 450 Syrian tanks. By every rule, the Israeli defense must soon crack altogether.

It was during this first night that young Zwicka fought single-handedly against more than fifty enemy tanks. As the night wore on, Zwicka and a handful of other leaders and soldiers fought desperately, with only nervous energy and tired, bloodshot eyes to guide their skilled hands. By his own admission, Zwicka did not at first know that his tank was the last defense between the attacking Syrians and Nafekh—and ultimately the Galilee. As that endless night wore on, the truth dawned on the handful of grim youths. As Zwicka reminisced more than twenty-five years later: "We had no choice but to succeed."[12] In the eerie darkness, these men redeemed a fatally flawed strategy, hoping against hope that help would arrive before the final collapse.

Help, in fact, was on the way. By 2200 on that first night, hastily mobilized tank reserves had begun to ascend the Golan Heights. Because the situation was so desperate, there was no time to organize the newly arrived men and vehicles into a powerful counterattack force. Instead, individual tanks and platoons were intercepted at crossroads and sent to whatever sector was most threatened at the moment.

First light on 7 October revealed the extent of the disaster. The Barak Brigade had suffered almost 90 percent casualties among its leaders alone in less than twenty-four hours, and the Syrians were still advancing. Colonel Ben-Shoham and his staff were cut off from Lieutenant Colonel Oded's battalion and the other remnants of the brigade, still isolated and engaged near the frontier. Oded, commanding the southernmost elements in the brigade sector, pulled his forces back to Tel Faris, thus uncovering the Syrians' most direct route from Rafid to Arik Bridge at the northern tip of the Sea of Galilee.

At this point, the Syrian commanders decided to exploit the breakthrough at Rafid, throwing the 3d Armored Division's mechanized brigade into the breach to add weight to their success. With only twelve tanks remaining, Lieutenant Colonel Oded faced six hundred Syrian tanks advancing both southwestward and northwestward. Besides Oded's tiny force at Tel Faris, Ben-Shoham still had a small force blocking the Tapline Road and his own tank. He moved his command group to join his deputy brigade commander, David Yisraeli, along the Tapline Road. As the two led a spirited defense there, the remnants of the brigade staff back at Nafekh organized the small packets of reserve tanks that began to trickle in and put together a makeshift company that was then sent toward Hushniyah, reinforcing Ben-Shoham's left flank.

As the afternoon progressed, these desperate defenders faced the weight of the Syrian main attack. The forces near Hushniyah eventually collapsed, and the Syrians raced toward Nafekh. General

Eitan, a legendary paratrooper and IDF hero now in tactical command of the division-size forces deployed on the Golan, ordered Colonel Ben-Shoham to withdraw to defend Nafekh. As the brigade commander began to fight his way back, his deputy, Yisraeli, in command of the rear guard, fought tenaciously to delay the Syrian advance. Finally running out of ammunition, Yisraeli ordered his driver to charge the attacking tanks while he fired his machine gun at the attackers. A moment later, a main gun round slammed into Yisraeli's tank, killing him.

Ben-Shoham meanwhile continued toward Nafekh, unaware of his deputy's death. As he passed a knocked-out Syrian tank alongside the road, a crewman suddenly appeared and sprayed the Israeli tank with machine-gun fire, killing the colonel instantly.[13] The Barak Brigade, bereft of its commander and most of its officers, and consisting of scattered teams of isolated tanks, began to retreat. When Major Dov, the intelligence officer, encountered fleeing units along the road to Aleika, he used his own armored personnel carrier to block the road and began to order individual tank crews to stop and face the enemy. Slowly he began to rebuild a small blocking position.

In the north, the 7th Brigade faced the Syrian supporting attack, but the waves of tanks and ferocious bombardments seemed no less intense to the understrength companies attempting to block the advance. Colonel Ben-Gal fought to hold the heights overlooking the Purple Line while at the same time keeping a small reserve. For four days and three nights, the battle continued with up to five major Syrian assaults every twenty-four hours. Before and during each attack, the brigade, battalion, and company commanders balanced fatigue, scarce supplies, and threatened breakthroughs in an effort to withstand the relentless pressure. The components of success in these frantic hours were the superior firepower of the 105mm gun and the iron will of the brigade's leaders. Withdrawal was not an option. There was no place to run.

The historical records shed some light on the Syrian inability to break through despite the weight of their numbers. Two or three tanks working together can suppress, maneuver against, and outflank a single opponent. But without coordination, the skirmish becomes a series of individual tank duels, which the better-trained Israeli crews were quite prepared to win. Likewise, all the components of combined arms were present on the Arab side: infantry equipped with effective tank-killing weapons, modern tanks, and artillery. Furthermore, the Syrians had adequate combat support in the form of mine-clearing tanks and engineers. But again, it was the effective integration of these tools that was lacking. The battle accounts relate the devastating artillery bombardment, the clever maneuver of a tank in a hidden valley, the sudden appearance of Arab infantry on a flank, even the occasional terror of an Arab fighter-bomber on a strafing run. But the art of welding these singular successes into a devastating battle formula seemed to elude the Syrian chain of command. Though not averse to heavy, upfront fighting, they could not synchronize their battlefield power to deliver the decisive blow that would shatter the Israeli defense before help arrived.

As Colonel Ben-Gal looked for a way to pull back his few survivors on Tuesday afternoon, 9 October, Lt. Col. Naty Yossi arrived with a small force of thirteen repaired tanks, crewed mostly by wounded soldiers. Yossi, who had been on his honeymoon in the Himalayas when the war broke out, rushed back to Israel upon hearing the news and arrived in the very nick of time on Tuesday. Reinforced with Yossi's tanks, Ben-Gal ordered a counterattack that surprised and demoralized the Syrians. The Arab attackers broke and fled.

Even while these thin frontline defenses were trying to hold, as early as Monday, 8 October, the IDF's leaders were organizing a counterattack. Major General Moshe Peled's division arrived and began to reinforce the threatened Israeli right flank. Still far outnumbered, Peled's forces slowly turned a piecemeal reinforcement into a series of local counterattacks and eventually into a full-fledged counteroffensive to clear the Syrians from the threatened sector. Throughout the ninth, Peled's forces pushed from El Al toward Juhader, threatening the left flank of Colonel Jehani's 1st Armored Division. By the tenth his forces had survived attempts by Jehani's tanks to break through to the east, and Peled's division had pocketed much of the Syrian 1st Armored Division near Hushniya. Simultaneously, Maj. Gen. Dan Laner's brigades attacked from the direction of Sindiana and Kuzabia, and annihilated the Syrians' cut-off forces. Some four days after the initial Syrian onslaught, the at-tackers had been cleared from the Israeli side of the Purple Line.

Counterattack and Aftermath

At 1100 on Thursday, 11 October, a reconstituted 188th Brigade—all but destroyed two days before—led the counterattack of Major General Eitan's division. Major General Hofi had decided to launch the counteroffensive toward Damascus in the northern sector, pri-marily because it offered the shortest route to the Syrian capital. An army attacking along the northern half of the Golan Heights could anchor its left flank on the mountains to the north. It was a fortu-itous decision, as events would show.

Hofi's plan was for Eitan's division to attack from assembly areas north of Hermonit Hill toward a final objective of Mazrat Beit Jan. To his south, Laner's division would conduct a parallel attack to-ward Maatz Crossroads and Nasej. Hofi was prepared to reinforce success wherever it appeared: If Laner's advance progressed quickly, it would become the main attack; if Eitan's division had greater success, then it would be the main effort. Meanwhile, Peled's division in the south was to hold where it had gained the Purple Line near Rafid.

The attacks in the north both succeeded, with intense but inef-fective resistance from the Syrians. Eitan's forces captured Mazrat Beit Jan by 1700 on 12 October, only thirty hours after the attack commenced. Laner's forces, after initial setbacks, succeeded in tak-ing their objectives also. But on Friday morning, as his lead brigades were pressing on toward Knaker and the Syrians seemed in full flight, Laner suddenly ordered his brigades to halt and regroup on his southern flank. Gazing southward, Laner had been shocked to see several columns of enemy tanks headed toward him. Quickly re-inforced with the 20th Brigade from Peled's division, Laner de-ployed his forces to defend against this new assault.

Thus began the Arabs' last attempt to destroy the Israeli presence on the Golan Heights. For the next five days, until relieved by Peled, Dan Laner fought a tenacious defense against the combined forces of the Syrians and the newly arrived Iraqis and Jordanians. The battles that resulted, especially the actions in and around the Maschara Box, were classic examples of armored warfare at its best and worst.[14] The Israelis, still badly outnumbered, used dynamic maneuver, disciplined fire control, and steely determination to thwart attack after attack. On the Arab side, even the well-trained and experienced Jordanian 40th Armored Brigade could not overcome the lackluster coordination and botched planning of the Syrian high command. Time and again, Jordanian and Iraqi attacks were disjointed and poorly timed. Iraqi artillery inadvertently shelled Jordanian troops, Jordanian tanks failed to attack on schedule, Syrian antiaircraft missiles shot down Iraqi planes, and so on. Still, the IDF was hard pressed as the war wound down toward a cease-fire on 22 October. At the end of the war, the Israelis had cleared the Syrians from the western portion of the Golan Heights and were sitting on newly won territory taken from the erstwhile attackers.

The counterattack and the successful conclusion to the Yom Kippur War were made possible in those first few days when a hopeless task fell to the Israeli defenders along the Purple Line. Despite the constant threat of war, despite a much-vaunted and powerful military tradition, despite a clear advantage in the air, the IDF was ill prepared for the numbers and determination unleashed against it on 6 October. In the final result, Israeli strategy and preparations fell short of the mark, and the brunt of the crisis fell on the shoulders of men like Zwicka Greengold. These bleary-eyed, wounded, and exhausted soldiers had to redeem the failures of ministers and generals with their blood, and in doing so they made history.

The battle for the Golan Heights is a rich trove for the soldier and historian searching for keys to success in war. Why did the attack, mounted in overwhelming strength, fail so badly? Why did the defense, handicapped at every turn, succeed so brilliantly?

The attack failed for a number of reasons that collectively hamstrung the Syrian offensive. The concept of the operation itself was flawed, counting upon misdirected mass rather than echeloned, purposeful combat power. Furthermore, the leaders and soldiers of the Syrian army—tough and determined as they were—lacked the capability to act independently and to integrate the strengths of their combat arms. The Syrians were an army looking for a reason to stop and regroup, and the Israelis obliged them. Ideal defensive terrain, defended by resolute soldiers with outstanding gunnery skills, blunted the forward movement of the Syrian armor at every turn. Finally, Syrian combat leadership, though often desperately courageous, proved amateurish at every level.

The defense succeeded because of a fortunate combination of strategic, tactical, technical, and cultural factors that together staved off defeat long enough to enable victory. The steps taken to increase the IDF presence on the Golan Heights just before the shooting started and the streamlined mobilization process tipped the time balance in the Israelis' favor. The technological advantages of range and fire control in the IDF tanks helped to mitigate the overwhelming numbers of the attackers. Still, the defense would have failed except for the magnificent leadership shown by Israeli commanders and leaders at every level, as well as the remarkable cohesion of units that, by all rights, should have collapsed by the second day.

This desperate campaign, fought against incredible odds on a battlefield that allowed no retreat, remains a shining example of an army that triumphed despite the odds. Like all wars, the 1973 Yom Kippur War saw horrifying violence, destruction, and loss of life. But the very best in human nature also shined through: loyalty, courage, honor, and selfless duty. In October 1973, when a nation's survival hung in the balance, these virtues saved a people.

Notes

1. Zvi Greengold, interview with author, Akko, Israel, 4 June 1998.

2. Chaim Herzog, *The War of Atonement* (Boston: Little, Brown), 1–12.

3. George W. Gawrych, *The 1973 Arab-Israeli War: The Albatross of Decisive Victory* (Fort Leavenworth, Kans.: USACGSC, 1996), 1–8.

4. Herzog, *War of Atonement*, 60.

5. Frank Aker, *October, 1973: The Arab-Israeli War* (Hamden, Conn.: Archon Books, 1985), 35–45.

6. A. J. Barker, *The Yom Kippur War* (New York: Ballantine Books, 1974), 71.

7. Herzog, *War of Atonement*, 286–87.

8. Aker, *October, 1973,* 18.

9. Avigdor Kahalani, *The Heights of Courage* (Westport, Conn.: Greenwood Press, 1984).

10. Herzog, *War of Atonement*, 78.

11. Edgar O'Ballance, *No Victor, No Vanquished: The Yom Kippur War* (San Rafael, Calif.: Presidio Press, 1978), 128–30.

12. Greengold interview.

13. Herzog, *War of Atonement*, 90.

14. Ibid., 136–40.

"Action Front": The 2d Dragoons at 73 Easting

> This story shall the good man teach his son; and Crispin
> Crispian shall ne'er go by, from this day to the ending of the
> world, but we in it shall be remembered . . . we few, we happy
> few, we band of brothers!
>
> —William Shakespeare, *Henry V*

On the picturesque terrain of Grafenwöhr, Germany, the former training ground of Hitler's panzer troops and the Kaiser's Imperial Army before them, Capt. H. R. McMaster briefed his lieutenants on the day's training. McMaster's Eagle Troop would lead the 2d Squadron, 2d Armored Cavalry Regiment (ACR), that day as the squadron practiced a movement to contact, the bread and butter of the cavalry. As McMaster talked, a trooper arrived at a dead run with an urgent message: "The Iraqis have invaded Kuwait!" McMaster turned to his troop and said, "Men, the next operations order I give may be in the sand of the Persian Gulf."[1] The date was 2 August 1990.

For the past year, the 2d ACR had prepared for a Cold War fight against the Warsaw Pact. Now, the regiment would put its men and training to the test, not on the rolling plains of central Europe, but in the open desert of the Arabian peninsula. Six months later it would fight and win the battle of 73 Easting, perhaps the outstanding tactical action of the war, adding another chapter to the long, proud history of the storied "Second Cav."

Prelude to War

When Saddam Hussein launched his massive offensive campaign into Kuwait, Grafenwöhr was abuzz with how Pres. George Bush would react. Would the president send forces from Germany—long the army's highest priority—to deal with the Iraqi invasion? The 2d ACR, the famous "Second Dragoons," led by Col. L. Don Holder, was one of the oldest and most prestigious formations in the U.S. Army. For decades it had guarded the inner German border against Soviet-backed troops in East Germany and Czechoslovakia. In the regiment's motor pools and dayrooms, many cavalrymen speculated that units based in the United States would get the call. As summer deepened into fall, the uncertainty persisted.

Finally, on 8 November 1990, a Pentagon broadcast confirmed the rumors that a large number of troops from Germany would be sent to the Gulf under the command of Lt. Gen. Frederick Franks Jr., the VII Corps commander. Within days, advance parties began to flow into the theater, led by Maj. Gen. Ronald Griffith and Maj. Gen. Paul "Butch" Funk, commanding the 1st and 3d Armored Divisions, accompanied by staff officers from every major unit in the corps.

The 2d Dragoons were on the ground in Saudi Arabia by mid-December, having led the corps in every move from Nürnberg to the Iraqi border. The story of the movement of VII Corps from its *kasernes* in Germany to its attack positions astride the Iraqi border is an epic in itself. With almost 145,000 soldiers, more than forty-five thousand vehicles (including sixty-six hundred tanks), and more than six hundred aircraft, VII Corps by itself could take on and defeat most armies in the world.[2] Throughout the winter, the corps flowed into the theater, married up with its seaborne equipment, and moved forward into tactical assembly areas to begin intensive training and rehearsals.

In February, as air force, navy, and marine fighters and bombers pounded the Iraqi army and its supporting infrastructure, the VII Corps moved forward to its jump-off positions with the 2d ACR in the van. The final attack plan, completed on the eve of battle, called for the 1st Infantry Division to create multiple lanes through the Iraqi obstacle belt, then pass through the British armored division attached to the corps, to be followed by the 1st Cavalry Division. In the west, the 2d ACR would lead the 1st and 3d Armored Divisions around the Iraqi defenses. The corps would then mass for a powerful drive to the east to engage and destroy the Iraqi Republican Guard.

VII Corps Moves Out

When Operation Desert Storm began on 23 February, the regiment led VII Corps across the Iraqi border. General Norman Schwarzkopf had given Franks a simple, direct mission: find, attack, and destroy the armor-heavy Republican Guard. Once past the obstacle belt, Franks's intent was to find and fix the Republican Guard with the cavalry, then strike with three heavy divisions, Griffith's 1st Armored Division ("Old Ironsides"), Funk's 3d Armored Division ("Spearhead"), and Maj. Gen. Thomas Rhame's 1st Infantry Division ("Big Red One"), backed up by two more, the 1st Cavalry Division and the British 1st Armored Division.[3]

One of only three armored cavalry regiments in the U.S. Army, the 2d ACR went to war as a self-contained combined-arms force of terrific striking power and mobility for its size. Its principal combat elements were its three ground squadrons, each organized with three cavalry troops (two tank platoons and two M3 Bradley-equipped scout platoons each), a tank company, and an organic 155mm self-propelled howitzer battery. The regiment was augmented for Desert Storm with three more artillery battalions from the 210th Field Artillery Brigade. The 4th Squadron provided the regiment's attack aviation in the form of highly lethal (but weather dependent) AH64 Apache helicopters. Colonel Holder, the regimental commander, was recognized throughout the army as both intellectually brilliant and a consummate tactician and cavalry commander. Man-for-man and pound-for-pound, the 2d ACR was the most flexible and powerful ground formation in the U.S. Army.

Tasked to clear the zone of attack in front of the powerful tank divisions, the regiment was also expected to identify the outlines of the Republican Guard's main defensive sector. Since only the Republican Guard was equipped with the T-72 tank, Holder knew that the first reports of engagements with the Russian tank would mean

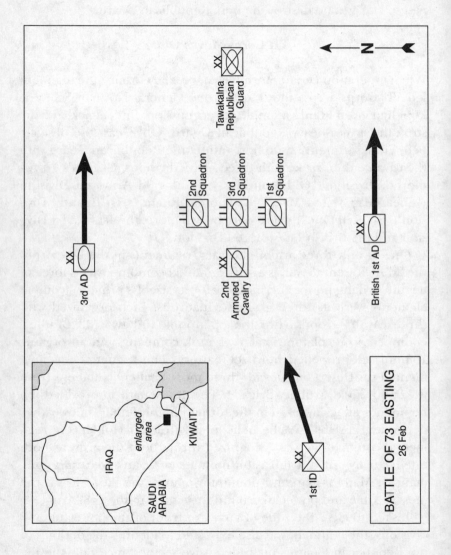

N

3rd AD

2nd Squadron

3rd Squadron

1st Squadron

Tawakalna Republican Guard

2nd Armored Cavalry

British 1st AD

1st ID

IRAQ

SAUDI ARABIA

KIWAIT

enlarged area

BATTLE OF 73 EASTING
26 Feb

he had found the Guard. On G day, 24 February, the regiment moved out in the early afternoon on a forty-kilometer-wide front. Preceded by the attack and scout helicopters of 4th Squadron (heavily reinforced with attack aircraft from the 1st Armored Division), the 1st and 3d Squadrons advanced at a rapid pace, followed by the 2d Squadron. Throughout the day, the 2d Dragoons sliced through Iraqi army units almost as if they were not there, covering forty kilometers in the first two hours and taking hundreds of prisoners. In meeting engagements with obsolete Iraqi T-55 tanks from the Iraqi 26th Infantry Division, the mix of airpower, attack aviation, and the overmatching technology of the M1A1 Abrams tank proved an annihilating combination the Iraqis were powerless to meet.[4]

Pausing that night to rearm and refuel, the regiment continued the advance the next day. Despite the rapid advance, McMaster felt uneasy. There had been little contact with the enemy during the first two days of the ground war, a profoundly unsettling state of affairs for a cavalryman. Now there was talk that the regiment would go into corps reserve as battle loomed with the elite Republican Guard. In his journal for 25 February, a day darkened by storm clouds, McMaster wrote, "The sun had set and the weather changed as if to become consistent with my mood."[5]

That evening it became apparent that the regiment would soon meet the enemy. For the first two days, 1st Lt. T. J. Linzy of Fox Troop had led the way, ten to fifteen kilometers to the front to provide early warning to the ground forces. At approximately 1800 on 25 February, Linzy's platoon began to take light fire from a defensive position east of the 60 Easting, which was then known as the regiment's "Objective Merrill." Without much resistance, Linzy's platoon gained positive control over the bunker complex and began to clear it. At 2300, however, Linzy found himself in an ethical dilemma not covered in service schools:

> Around 2300 my vehicle and two others from my platoon were engaging a bunker complex and a couple of vehicles when we hit an ammunition bunker. The explosion and ensuing fire forced hundreds of the enemy to flee toward us and we began

a big EPW [enemy prisoner of war] exercise. Squadron kept telling us to get off Merrill, because air strikes had been called for the whole of the objective. I called back each time and told them we could evacuate and leave the EPWs exposed to the air strike or we could stay until we could get transport forward from squadron to clear them, which would take several hours. Each time the order came back to get off Merrill now and take the EPWs with us.

For the next five hours, Linzy simultaneously policed up six hundred EPWs and, through constant radio chatter, held off an air strike that would surely obliterate not only the EPWs but much of his lightly armored Bradley scout platoon. For his efforts, Linzy was awarded the Bronze Star for valor, and many of his Bradley commanders received Army Commendation Medals for valor. Of his mission, Linzy said: "1st Platoon Fox performed more like a scout platoon for the squadron than an armored cavalry troop scout platoon. I feel we performed a classic economy of force reconnaissance mission in working forward of the main body and preserving combat strength by eliminating lighter resistance and allowed Eagle and Ghost to take the lead the next day when it became obvious we were about to hit the Republican Guard."[6]

The next morning, surprised at the lack of resistance Linzy had encountered, McMaster was nonetheless encouraged by orders to continue the advance. Strangely, his scouts had detected no Iraqi attempts to probe his positions. Now, as his Abrams main battle tanks and Bradley scout vehicles pounded ahead, Eagle Troop's command net came alive. "Contact, east!" came a shouted radio call. McMaster's scouts reported three Iraqi armored vehicles, known as MT-LBs, lying in wait just ahead.

Racing forward in his M1A1, McMaster saw two Bradleys from Ghost Troop (the friendly unit to his north)—commanded by his West Point classmate, Captain Joseph Sartiano Jr.—destroy two of the three MT-LBs. As the third enemy scout ran, McMaster radioed to his 1st Platoon sergeant, Robert Patterson, "Red 4, this is Black 6, does that MT-LB have my name on it?" "Roger," Patterson replied, "your name's written all over it."[7] Staff Sergeant Craig Koch, Mc-

Master's gunner, laid his crosshairs on the rear of the retreating vehicle. McMaster ordered Koch to fire and almost simultaneously the MT-LB exploded catastrophically, destroyed by a direct hit from an armor-piercing sabot round.

McMaster, recognizing the targets as reconnaissance vehicles, now knew the enemy was close. Somewhere to the east lay a division or more of Iraqi tanks. With VII Corps fully turned to the east, the 2d ACR formed the spearhead of the corps's attack. Behind the regiment, four powerful armored divisions were arrayed from north to south: the 1st and 3d Armored Divisions, the British 1st Armored Division, and the 1st Cavalry Division (the 1st Infantry Division trailed behind the frontline divisions in corps reserve). Holder had deployed the regiment on line, with 2d Squadron on the left flank to the north, 3d Squadron in the center, and 1st Squadron to the south. The 2d Squadron S3, Maj. Douglas A. MacGregor, was not happy with the small frontage assigned to the squadron. He later said, "Having been forced into a 10 kilometer zone, I decided to put two troops forward, reckoning that 5,000 meters was required for troop maneuver, as well as to reduce the density of troops in the zone to avoid fratricide . . . I designated E Troop as the main attack and Ghost Troop as the supporting attack at about 1100 hours."[8]

As Fox Troop moved back and Ghost and Eagle headed forward, the most lethal killer for coalition forces thus far—friendlies engaging friendlies—could have occurred. However, 1st Lt. John Hillen, McGregor's assistant, who was also forward with McGregor in Eagle's formation, said, "We had nine battle drills. To this I credit the fact that we had no fratricide incidents . . . like football, we knew where the pulling guard would be."[9]

Shortly after 1400, a corps order to move east to the 60 Easting (the north to south longitude line) filtered down to McMaster's second in command. First Lieutenant John Gifford, the troop executive officer, was monitoring four different radio nets in the troop command post moving in the rear of Eagle Troop's formation. Gifford, an experienced veteran with three years' service in the regiment, listened closely.

At 1430, Lieutenant General Franks instructed the 2d ACR: "Do

not become decisively engaged; be prepared to pass the First Infantry Division through." Holder subsequently gave the order to
"conduct a movement to contact forward in zone, to the 70 Easting
to find and fix the main body of the Tawakalna Republican Guards
Division."[10] The 2d ACR's forward command post relayed the order,
instructing all units to stop their tanks at the 65 Easting and their
scout vehicles at the 67 Easting. Gifford thought this seemed odd,
since a sudden contact might require McMaster to bring his tanks
forward quickly.

Acknowledging the order, McMaster put his troop in a modified
wedge led by his scouts in their Bradley Fighting Vehicles. A desert
sandstorm had reduced visibility and grounded all supporting attack helicopters. As a result of the poor visibility and unknown enemy situation, McMaster began to parallel a road to help maintain
his easterly bearing. Maps were almost useless at this point. In fact,
despite air force bombing raids that had identified the road earlier
in the war, Holder's ground troops did not even know the road existed or that enemy troops had been spotted along it. "In the corps's
terrain analysis and my own maps, it did not appear," recalled
Holder.[11] In the almost featureless terrain, graphic control measures would prove vital to separating friend from foe, especially in
the driving sandstorm that blanketed the battlefield.

"Tanks, Direct Front!"

Gifford's earlier misgivings now began to be realized. At 1556, Mc-
Master's lead scout platoon, led by 1st Lt. Tim Gauthier, picked up
two surrendering enemy soldiers in a bunker complex to their
north. Just as the Bradley crew turned west to take them back to the
rear, the platoon began to take heavy machine-gun fire from a village to the east.[12] Ironically, before the sandstorm hit, one of the attack aviation troops had seen and fired upon this same village.
Word of this engagement, however, had not made its way down to
the ground troop commanders. McMaster later found out from a
captured enemy brigade commander, Major Muhammad of the
Tawakalna Republican Guard Division, that the Iraqis had a forward
security element in the town armed with 23mm towed cannons,

14.5mm machine guns, and rocket-propelled grenade launchers. McMaster's lead elements now found themselves under intense fire.

Seconds later, Staff Sergeant Harris of the lead scout platoon requested guidance on how to respond to the fire from the village. His commander replied curtly, "Kill them!" McMaster then ordered Lieutenant Gauthier to fire a TOW missile into the center of the town to help focus Eagle Troop's attack.[13] He then ordered his two tank platoons to come on line, "Green, come up on my right, White come up on my left. Village, one round HEAT, village direct front, frontal, at my command, ready, report."

Within minutes the town was ablaze. Eagle Troop continued to move eastward, this time with tanks leading and the scout platoons echeloned to secure the flanks. Despite Gifford's efforts to establish contact with his neighbors to the south, Iron Troop had, in fact, fallen almost five kilometers behind due to contact in its own sector and the need to maintain contact with the 3d Squadron, which lagged even farther behind. Almost simultaneously, Gifford monitored new guidance from the regiment to move up to, but not beyond, the 70 Easting.

McMaster had placed SSgt. Lawrence Magee and a scout section to the north as flank security. Magee now reported an enemy tank in the vicinity of the 70 Easting. Visibility was down to a hundred meters or less. At 1618, McMaster—who was now in the lead vehicle—felt the tank rise as it crested a low ridgeline. When the vehicle began to level off, McMaster's gunner, Sergeant Koch, yelled, "Tanks, direct front!"[14]

Approximately a mile ahead sat eight Iraqi T-72 tanks from the Tawakalna Division of the Republican Guard. Believing that the fast-moving, armor-heavy American force would bypass built-up areas, the Iraqis had placed themselves in a classic reverse-slope defense that would enable them to fire at the exposed underbellies of the American tanks as they crested the ridge. Unknown to the cavalry troopers, the battle of 73 Easting was about to be fought on the Tawakalna's tank training ground, over terrain the enemy knew intimately.

Despite the sudden appearance of Iraqi tanks, which seemed to materialize out of nowhere, three critical elements were in

McMaster's favor. First, the destruction of the enemy reconnaissance screen deprived the Tawakalna of early warning. Second, the
raging sandstorm masked Eagle Troop's approach. Finally, the
American M1A1 tanks had thermal vision sights that clearly highlighted the enemy tanks, whereas the Iraqi tank optics were useless
in foul weather.

To tankers, the first few seconds of an engagement are literally
life and death, and McMaster's crew wasted no time. Sergeant Koch
engaged his laser range finder, which pinpointed the target as being 1,420 meters away. McMaster shouted the command to "Fire,
fire sabot!"—which meant to fire the high-explosive antitank
(HEAT) round already loaded in the main gun, to be followed immediately by a sabot round, a kinetic energy round with a super-
hard, depleted-uranium-tipped penetrator. McMaster later explained that the highly visible HEAT round would mark his target,
allowing Eagle Troop to orient on his fires. The tank recoiled and
the turret filled with acrid smoke from the burnt gunpowder. Mc-
Master later recounted: "I'll remember this vividly, the enemy Tank
Commander was up in the hatch . . . the HEAT round penetrated
the tank, immediately ignited it, and expelled that TC out of the
hatch and he was on fire himself."

McMaster's driver, Pfc. Christopher Hedenskog, hit the accelera-
tor to move through the smoke cloud caused by the discharge of the
round. Hedenskog also knew that he had to keep his tank, and thus
the troop, oriented on the enemy. McMaster was too busy fighting
the troop and giving fire commands to tell his driver which way to
go. With his tank still in the front and still closing, Koch slewed the
turret to the next enemy tank. The surprise was over and that enemy tank was one second ahead of Koch in fixing on him. There was
no time to spare. Fortunately, McMaster's loader, Pvt. Jeffrey Taylor,
had already reloaded the main gun. Koch fired and the Iraqi tank's
turret flipped off like a coin being tossed in the air. Another cata-
strophic kill.

Well within the enemy's range, McMaster's tank now faced two
problems. First, the surviving Iraqi tanks were firing back at a fairly
rapid pace. Second, there appeared to be enemy mines scattered all
over the battlefield. Again, McMaster had no time to verbally direct

Hedenskog around the mines. The young driver also knew that it would be disastrous to stop in front of the enemy vehicles. In fact, Hedenskog later told McMaster, "Hey, sir, just thought you'd like to know, we just drove through a minefield."

Accelerating into the enemy, McMaster called over the troop radio net, "Contact east, eight armored vehicles, Green and White are you with me?" The two tank platoon leaders brought their tanks on line, issued their own platoon fire commands, and destroyed the remaining Iraqi tanks. Eagle Troop's trailing scout platoon, led by 2d Lt. Mike Peschek, spread out behind the tanks, providing suppressive fire against the enemy infantry. By 1622, at a rate of thirty kilometers per hour, the M1A1 tanks had drawn even with the burning hulks of the Iraqi T-72s.

Just then, Peschek's platoon took fire from an Iraqi bunker and an Iraqi 23mm antiaircraft gun. The Bradleys responded by firing two TOW missiles, destroying the vehicle and bunker. However, there were T-72s in support, and the thinly armored Bradley platoon came under intense tank fire. Sergeant Timothy Havermale, one of the Bradley commanders, saw the T-72s and trained his TOWs on the massive tanks. Havermale's vehicle and those around him quickly destroyed several of them before turning their 25mm chain guns onto the dismounted enemy infantry who were firing both small arms and rocket-propelled grenades.

Southwest of the village, Capt. Daniel B. Miller's Iron Troop encountered observation posts (OPs) with dug-in armored vehicles. The Iron Troop fire-support officer first called in artillery fire, but then switched to his organic 4.2-inch mortars to suppress the OPs. As Miller's troop approached the village, which sat astride the seam between Eagle and Iron, Miller's gunners began to identify the silhouettes of Iraqi tanks two miles to the east. Miller formed his troop into a wedge with his tank platoons in the center and the Bradleys on the flanks. He commanded, "Action front, action front, follow me."[15] Miller's troop quickly dispensed with the lightly dug-in T-72s. Just as his scouts crossed the 70 Easting, a counterattacking force of tanks moved in from the southeast. Iron Troop's 4th Platoon, moving in the southern portion of the zone, immediately began to fire and destroyed the counterattacking force in its tracks.

On Miller's southern flank, his Bradley-equipped 1st Platoon also attempted to suppress the counterattacking enemy. One of the Bradleys, commanded by Sfc. Ron Mullinix, suffered an electrical malfunction that disabled the firing system. As Mullinix moved his vehicle into an empty Iraqi revetment, a Bradley from the 3d Squadron to his right mistook Mullinix's vehicle for an Iraqi vehicle and fired a TOW missile at it.

> The missile struck the Bradley turret, ricocheted, and ripped off the driver's hatch. Shrapnel spattered Mullinix in the legs and peppered the back of his driver, Private First Class Gregory Scott. Fire swept through the Bradley, melting the radio and igniting the machine gun ammunition box. Coaxial rounds sprayed the turret. The gunner, Sergeant Kirk Alcorn, had been flung from his hatch by the blast. His face burned and eyelids seared shut, Alcorn crawled across the TOW launcher and leaped to the ground. Scott rolled screaming across the desert, his back and arms afire. Mullinix hobbled over to help beat out the flames and rip off the driver's burning flak jacket. The three wounded soldiers, all of whom would survive, were bundled into the rear of another Bradley to await a medic.[16]

With the troops essentially engaged in their own individual fights to their direct front, the limit of advance (LOA) now became an issue. As a regimental control measure it could help guard against misidentification of friendlies in the swirling sandstorm by helping to keep the fighting squadrons roughly on line. But for the troops and platoons up front in heavy contact, standing still on an arbitrary line within range of enemy tanks was not a viable option. Lieutenant Colonel Steve Robinette, in the regimental tactical operations center (TOC), believed the 2d ACR was gaining and maintaining contact with the enemy in accordance with the corps's mission to "destroy the Republican Guard." Given these circumstances, Robinette told Lt. Tony Ireardi in the 2d Squadron TOC that they were clear to move beyond the LOA of 70 Easting. Unlike graphic control measures in Germany, the limit of advance of the 70 Easting had no geographic significance. It was not a road, a map-defined ridgeline, or a built-up area. As Robinette said, "It was simply a line on the map."[17]

McMaster also knew the importance of the LOA. He had paused at the 71 Easting to develop the situation and realized that would leave him in essentially the same predicament he had been at the 70 Easting: sitting in an enemy engagement area. He ordered his troop forward.

As he approached the next ridge, McMaster saw a coil of seventeen Iraqi T-72s two kilometers to his front. The troop again attacked, closing rapidly to destroy the enemy tanks in just eighteen minutes. At 1640, McMaster called a halt just beyond the 73 Easting to reassess the situation. According to McMaster, "In twenty-three minutes, Eagle Troop had reduced the enemy position to a spectacular array of burning vehicles. . . . I really think the fight was won in about forty-five seconds. After we were able to get off rounds from all nine of our tanks, it was over; the enemy was hit so hard, they could not recover."[18]

At this point the regiment received orders from Franks to consolidate, reorganize, and allow the Big Red One to pass through to carry on the fight against the remaining main body of the Tawakalna Division. While he prepared to execute the passage of lines, McMaster had his 4.2-inch mortar section fire on the dug-in Iraqi forces. "It was really eerie," McMaster later recalled, "the sun was kind of set at this time and there was fairly low cloud cover with the fires reflecting off the low clouds; it was like we were encased in a great red glow."[19] At first light, a tour of the battlefield revealed that Eagle Troop had destroyed more than thirty enemy tanks, approximately twenty personnel carriers and other armored vehicles, and about thirty trucks.[20]

To the north, Captain Sartiano's Ghost Troop fought a battle similar to McMaster's Eagle Troop between the 70 and 73 Eastings in the late afternoon. However, unlike McMaster's fight, Sartiano's lasted until nearly 2200. Like his counterpart in Iron Troop, Sartiano pushed his two Bradley platoons to the flanks and moved the eight tanks to the center. He then ordered, "Troop on line, tanks lead."[21] Sartiano's gunner, Cpl. Frank Wood, soon picked up a large mass in his thermal sight about six hundred meters to the front, but with no clear vehicle contours. As Sartiano ducked inside the turret to observe through the commander's primary site extension, Wood shouted, "Holy shit! Troops! These guys don't have their hands up!" Using his coaxially mounted 7.62mm machine gun, Wood sprayed the enemy troop formation just as he had done countless times in the computer trainer. This time, however, the targets "jerked grotesquely . . . slumped to the ground, struggled to their knees, and pitched forward again."[22] Sartiano had his troop take up a hasty defense at the 73 Easting and used the tactics that he and his men had honed to near perfection in training: firing, repositioning laterally, and firing again.

To the north, Sartiano's Bradley-equipped 1st Platoon was engaging enemy infantry and personnel carriers. One of them had two 73mm rounds hit the turret. The first round grazed off the front slope, prompting the gunner, Sgt. Nels A. Moller, to say, "What was that?" Before anyone could answer, the second round struck right beneath the TOW launcher where Moller sat, killing him instantly. The round continued through the Bradley's troop compartment and wounded another soldier.

For the next several hours, Ghost Troop fought and killed enemy vehicles pouring into their engagement areas. At 1740, an Iraqi company counterattacked from the northeast. Although Sartiano did not get the air support he requested, he was able to reinforce his Bradley platoon by pulling a tank platoon out of the center sector. Combining direct fire with artillery and mortar strikes, Ghost Troop destroyed all fifteen of the enemy vehicles.[23]

At 2000, an enemy force of sixteen vehicles attacked from the southeast. Sartiano's platoons engaged and destroyed them all with deadly accurate tank and TOW shots. Throughout much of the day, the 2d ACR's organic howitzer batteries had been out of range due to the fast-paced movement of the ground troops. MacGregor later commented: "We quickly outran the artillery and the missions had to be check-fired. The notion that combat under these circumstances is a controlled and predictable affair is an illusion, especially against an enemy who shoots back with live ammunition."[24] Now, however, the "King of Battle" made its entrance. From 1730 to 2100, two thousand howitzer rounds and a dozen multiple-launch rocket system (MLRS) rockets dropped 130,000 bomblets in front of the 2d Squadron. Air force bombers also got into the fight as F-16s and A-10s destroyed Iraqi artillery and armored forces east of the 2d Squadron's main battle area.[25]

Of the three-troop battle, Colonel Holder said, "Don't forget this is a small part of the story . . . this was a regimental fight and all the brothers were brave." Almost miraculously, only one dragoon was killed: Sergeant Moller. During a lull in the fighting, Joe Sartiano and the men of Ghost Troop held a battlefield memorial service for him in the troop's tactical assembly area.

Post-Battle Critique

In the aftermath of the battle, America embraced the men who fought at 73 Easting as representatives of an army that had come all the way back from the trauma of Vietnam. The battle was analyzed in detail, glorified by the media, and used as a case study in army service schools. Perhaps predictably, however, as the glow of victory subsided, muted criticism began to surface. Some argued that junior commanders had acted too boldly, even rashly, while others argued that the cavalry and tank divisions should have been handled even more forcefully. Douglas MacGregor, who was present as the 2d Squadron S3, observed:

> On the whole, we never exploited the real combat potential at our disposal in the Regiment, the Corps and the Army and operationally we failed to achieve our strategic objective against the Iraqis. Instead of seeking the optimum positional advantage, the 2d ACR moved too slowly as did the whole unwieldy VII Corps. When the decision to turn the Corps' divisions into the enemy was taken instead of moving north of the enemy, we surrendered the strategic initiative, and created an

opportunity for the enemy to rescue his best troops and equipment.[26]

What of the charge that the troop commanders pressed too far forward, beyond the established limit of advance? From a captain's perspective there seems to have been little choice. Once engaged with enemy main battle tanks at close range, any hesitation or doubt could have resulted in serious losses, especially to the lightly armored Bradley Fighting Vehicles that made up half the strength of the ground troops. Nor were they restrained by positive orders from higher echelons, which presumably were aware of their general location and situation. John Hillen summed it up when he said, "Initially, we fell into a situation where people started to want to fight the plan and not the enemy. Fortunately, H. R. McMaster and others realized that to be successful we had to have a mix of 90 percent speed and 10 percent of the other principles of war. It became clear that people win wars, not machines."

On balance, the weight of the evidence suggests that the battle was what it initially appeared to be: an overwhelmingly successful tactical engagement that showcased the U.S. Army at its best. Amid a host of stellar performances in VII Corps, the 2d Dragoons stood out as masters of mobile warfare. As General Franks later wrote: "For VII Corps, the battle was critical because the 2d ACR not only succeeded in collapsing the security zone of the developing Iraqi defense, but delivered a resounding defeat to the Tawakalna first echelon and kept the Iraqis off balance . . . until we got the 1st Infantry [Division] into the fight."

The battle of 73 Easting continues to be hailed as the model for the many successful ground engagements fought during Desert Storm. Against a poorly trained, irresolute opponent equipped with inferior systems, VII Corps and its vanguard, the 2d ACR, simply crushed the Republican Guard, demolishing everything in their path.

In the hard test of tank-versus-tank combat, the men who fought at 73 Easting proved themselves courageous, aggressive, and worthy of the great traditions of a great army. In the words of one hard-bitten veteran of the eastern front in the Second World War:

"The right moment alone, correctly judged, exploited with lightning speed and prompt action, can produce victory—and despite the fact that these victories may not at times correspond to the exact ideas and wishes of the higher commander, this must be accepted in silence. *Victory is the only thing that matters.*"[27]

Notes

1. Maj. H. R. McMaster, interview with author.

2. Brig. Gen. Robert H. Scales Jr., *Certain Victory: The U.S. Army in the Gulf War* (Washington, D.C.: Brassey's, 1994), 149.

3. Michael Gordon and Lt. Gen. Bernard E. Trainor (Ret.), *The Generals' War: The Inside Story of the Conflict in the Gulf* (Boston: Little, Brown, 1995), 389.

4. Scales, *Certain Victory*, 224.

5. U.S. News & World Report, *Triumph Without Victory: The Unreported History of the Persian Gulf War* (New York: Times Books, 1992), 333.

6. T. J. Linzy, interview with author, 9 Mar. 1999.

7. McMaster interview.

8. Col. Douglas A. MacGregor, E-mail to author, 1 Feb. 1999.

9. John Hillen, interview with author, 16 Mar. 1999.

10. U.S. Army Armor Center, Video, *The Battle of 73 Easting*, A0515-91-0177, Fort Knox, Ky., 1991.

11. Gordon and Trainor, *Generals' War*, 390.

12. U.S. News & World Report, *Triumph Without Victory*, 338.

13. The TOW is a tube-launched, optically sighted, wire-guided (from which the acronym TOW is derived) missile with a high degree of accuracy at extended ranges.

14. U.S. News & World Report, *Triumph Without Victory*, 338.

15. Rick Atkinson, *Crusade: The Untold Story of the Persian Gulf War* (Boston: Houghton Mifflin, 1993), 444.

16. Ibid., 445.

17. Lt. Col. Steve Robinette, interview with author, 18 Dec. 1998.

18. Gen. Fred Franks Jr. (Ret), with Tom Clancy, *Into the Storm: A Study in Command* (New York: G. P. Putnam's Sons, 1997), 337.

19. H. R. McMaster, speech before the Amphibious Warfare School, U.S. Marine Corps, Quantico, Va., 20 Nov. 1998.

20. Franks with Clancy, *Into the Storm*, 358.

21. Atkinson, *Crusade*, 445.

22. Ibid., 446.

23. Ibid., 447.

24. MacGregor to author.

25. Atkinson, *Crusade*, 445.

26. MacGregor to author.

27. Attributed to General Schultz, commanding general of the XLVIII Panzer Corps, cited in FM 71-100, *Division Operations* (Washington, D.C.: Department of the Army, 28 Aug. 1996), 46.

African Holocaust: The Rwandan Civil War

Urge not your peasant millions into gladiatorial war . . .
—John Ruskin, *Crown of Olives*

In the end, the Rwandan Patriotic Front took Kigali, the capital of Rwanda. And, as happened so often in warfare at the close of the twentieth century, by winning the capital they won the war. But it was too late. It was a ghost city they won, a ghost city in a ghost country. Nothing was left: no electrical power, no banks, no currency, no communications system, no infrastructure, no economy, no industry, no agriculture, no hospitals, no schools, no people. At least none you could see. Except the dead.

Lots of dead. More than a half million of them, maybe a million. You couldn't count them, there were so many. They lay everywhere: in the fields, on the roads, at the soccer stadiums, in the churches. The bodies fouled the air and polluted the rivers, leaving nothing clean. Not a corpse remained unmutilated. The livestock were gone, too, eaten or caught up in the endless lines of refugee columns making their way out of the country. Crops lay rotting in the fields, blending their pungent aroma with decomposing corpses.

The survivors were scattered, hiding in the bush, traumatized by the horror of the past one hundred days. The murderers, now shorn of their unbridled power at home and fearful of retribution for their unspeakable crimes, had fled to gather in the teeming death camps in Zaire, Tanzania, and Burundi. Around them they gathered the entire population of displaced Rwandan Hutus, coerced confederates in the killing and in the exodus. Exposed to the elements without food, medical assistance, or shelter, the

refugees died in droves. The hard lava ground around the shores of Lake Kivu kept the survivors from burying their dead. They threw them in the lake instead, pushing the bloated bodies aside only when it was time to draw more drinking water. At Goma in Zaire, the water-ingested cholera killed at the rate of six thousand a day, creating ever more corpses for Kivu and ever more cholera to consume.

But it was a glorious victory. In less than ninety days a rebel army had defeated a larger, better-armed force supported by at least one leading European nation (France) and perhaps another (Belgium). In a series of dashing pincer movements, the foot mobile Rwandan Patriotic Army (RPA), the military arm of the Rwandan Patriotic Front, had slashed across the country in several directions at once, scattering the bulk of the government's troops, the Force Armée Rwandese (FAR), away from the crucial fight for the capital. Closing on Kigali to link up with a lone battalion holding key positions in the center of the city, the RPA battled for six weeks before driving out the FAR, toppling the government, and installing the Rwandan Patriotic Front as the new leadership of Rwanda. It had been a generation's journey for many of them. It was also a journey that ended ninety days too late to deter one of the worst genocides of modern times.

How all of this came about is, to an alarming degree, the story of warfare in the last years of the twentieth century.

Setting the Stage

The Rwanda tragedy belies simple recounting of cause and effect. There is no clear history that leads step by inexorable step to the intentional murder of an entire people. Indeed, there is no pure definition of what constitutes "a people" in this case. What we know is the articulation of events: The state machinery comprised of Hutu elites killed as many of the minority Tutsis and Hutu moderates (defined as those Hutus who would not take part in killing Tutsis) as they could. But the meaning of Hutu and Tutsi is hardly exact. Most Tutsis were herdsmen, with a warrior tradition. Most Hutus were farmers, tied to the land. The two cultures collided sometime in the sixteenth century when the Tutsi people wandered into the region and, despite their fewer numbers, took control of Rwandan society.

Yet the truth is hardly so simple. Over time the two groups intermarried. In this way, children of Hutus became Tutsis, and children of Tutsis became Hutus. And these children also intermarried, mingling generation by generation. Physical archetypes remain: The Hutus are described as stocky, round-faced, dark-skinned, square-jawed, flat-nosed, and thick-lipped; the Tutsis as tall, lanky, lighter-skinned, with thin angular faces. Yet in truth, such descriptions deny reality: Most Rwandans are indistinguishable from each other. Not that that mattered in the recurring Rwandan massacres of the last half of the twentieth century.

The first round of violence erupted in 1959 when the majority Hutus, supported by their former colonial masters, the Belgians, rose against the Tutsi royal house. Estimates of the numbers of Tutsis killed varied from ten thousand to a hundred thousand. The style of killing, up close and personal, by club and by machete, with no victim left intact, was a forerunner of what would come thirty-five years later. Many of the survivors fled for their lives, often the mother leaving the murdered father behind to struggle on alone with her infants on her back and toddlers in tow. It would be these "children of 1959" that would rise to retake Rwanda in 1994.

In neighboring Burundi, wracked by identical Hutu-Tutsi power struggles, the same grim reality prevailed. Alarmed by what they saw happening to their kinsmen in Rwanda, the Tutsi government in Burundi proceeded to slaughter a quarter of a million Hutus in 1972 alone. The killings then and over the years drove many an embittered Hutu into Rwanda to return the favor. In both countries, the cycle of violence continued, broken by spells of peace where the groups lived side by side according to the ancient traditions. But the seeds of destruction were sown. It was Rwanda's grim fate to reap the harvest.

Military Antecedents

The military foundations of the Rwandan Patriotic Army lie in the National Resistance Army of Yuveri Kagate Museveni, a Ugandan who fought against the harsh tyranny of Milton Obote, ultimately taking control of the country in 1986. For more than twenty years, Uganda had suffered horrendously under the successive regimes of Idi Amin Dada and Milton Obote. Obote came first, only to be overthrown by Amin, who was subsequently overthrown by Obote. Between the two of them, hundreds of thousands were killed. Very few of these were soldiers. Whole populations of innocent civilians were slaughtered for tangled and confused political purposes. Caught up in these insane massacres were the Rwandan Tutsis who had fled from the brutality of their own country in earlier times.

When Obote returned to power in 1980, Museveni, a former Minister of Defense, broke away. Joining him in a small group of twenty-seven were some of the future leaders of the Rwandan Patriotic Front, including Fred Rwigyema, Peter Bayingama, and a youngster by the name of Paul Kagame. Museveni was a good teacher, and his subordinates learned well. He taught his followers classic guerrilla tactics and instilled in them an understanding of why they fought, a respect for the villagers among whom they lived, and the practice of paying for food and supplies they obtained from the locals.

Fred Rwigyema was the obvious leader among the Rwandans. A strong and outgoing personality, he both exhorted and inspired the others. Every inch the extrovert, there was little doubt that here was a man of action, one who was intent, among other things, on someday retaking his own country. In stark contrast was the quiet and introverted Paul Kagame. Tall and extremely thin, he did not appear to possess the physical constitution to withstand the hard life of soldiering. Nor did his manner of speaking in low, barely audible whispers promise an authoritative voice one could expect to hear above the din of battle. But his physique belied a physical grace of movement that would stand him in good stead on the march, while his soft-spoken mannerisms only accentuated the gripping intelligence of his words.

On closer inspection, one could see that despite his humble origins he was a leader born for the task, for he had the one trait that would ensure his success: He learned from everything he saw and did. No less than Rwigyema, he wanted above all else to return to Rwanda. In the meantime, they had to learn how to fight.

Uganda's Luwero Triangle would be their university, Rwanda their cathedral.

By 1982, Obote had turned his attention away from Uganda's north where he had laid waste Nile Province (so named for its contiguity to the White Nile) and driven the half-million survivors into a harsh exile over the border into the Sudan. The next target of Obote's attentions was Museveni and his people, for there lay the greatest threat to his dictatorship. Yoweri Museveni was training his guerrilla army, which had swollen in size thanks to the brutal tactics of the Ugandan army, to strike.

Over the next five years, Obote's troops killed as many as five hundred thousand people, many of them Rwandans. Despite his best efforts, however, Obote was eventually beaten. For four brutal years, Museveni and his army fought out of the Luwero Triangle. Then, in 1985, he moved out to open a second front in the west, teaching his Rwandese followers a lesson in the benefits of maneuver warfare. When Milton Obote was overthrown in a coup d'état in July 1985, Museveni was well placed to eventually succeed to power, which meant his chief subordinates would now transition from being a rebel army to one that had to consolidate power. Much of the effort now focused on putting down the factions and ethnic populations that might threaten Obote's successors. The Rwandans were now part of a professional army.

Most important for the future of Rwanda, with Yoweri Museveni's victory in Uganda, the Tutsis of the Rwandan diaspora had been given a unifying organization upon which they could base their hopes for a return to Rwanda. The Rwanda Alliance for National Unity (RANU) had first established itself in 1979 with the fall of Amin. During the struggle against Obote it grew in strength and experience. By the end of these two long conflicts, the Rwandans involved began to make plans for the eventual fight for Rwanda itself. By 1987, RANU had renamed itself the Rwandan Patriotic Front (RPF) under the leadership of the charismatic Major General Fred Rwigyeme.

Comprised mostly of Tutsis, but also including in its ranks and among its leadership moderate Hutus, the RPF offered a battle-hardened and politically savvy nucleus around which to build a structure that could challenge the regime of Rwandan strongman Juvenal Habyarimana, despite his support from France. The nucleus of the Rwandan military elite was, in rank order, Major General Rwigyema, Maj. Peter Bayingama, Major Bunyenyezi, and Maj. Paul Kagame. The first three would be dead by the second day of the campaign to retake Rwanda.

The Campaign

The RPF dates the beginning of the military campaign to retake Rwanda from 1 October 1990. On that date, twenty-five hundred RPF soldiers invaded Rwanda from Uganda. For decades the Tutsis in the diaspora had dreamt of retaking their homeland, but they had only just arrived at a crossroads where they felt it was now or never.

On the positive side, they had secured a relatively stable support base in Uganda. Their leaders were all well-experienced soldiers, having fought and survived against impossible odds during the bloody reign of Obote. RPF units had been able to secure arms and ammunition from the Ugandan army and they were rapidly expanding their forces by drafting young Tutsis into their ranks.

On the negative side, they felt compelled to move quickly to spare as many of their kinsmen in Rwanda as they could. World coffee prices had collapsed in the last few years of the 1980s, gutting Rwanda's economy (the cultivation of coffee and tea being its primary revenue-generating activity), creating a rift in the Hutu leadership and causing further friction between Hutus and Tutsis in the endless struggle for what few opportunities the country had to offer. After a decade of economic growth, the Hutu elite could not obscure the reality that Rwanda was falling into a major economic slump.

The government's answer was to blame the Tutsis and further deprive them of what little share they had of the nation's wealth. Ominously, the Rwandan government's army had begun to equip and train militias and paramilitary organizations known as *interahamwe* ("those who stand together"). Properly organized and motivated, their primary purpose would be to kill Tutsis.

The invasion of October 1990 initially caught the Rwandan government forces by surprise. The Rwandan military was a minimally capable force, poorly led and numbering about six thousand, one thousand of which were gendarmerie. But quickly buttressed by French and Belgian forces (sent by former colonial governments not prepared to lose their investment in Habyarimana), as well as troops from Zaire, the government troops rallied. The terrain in the northeast of the country, where the RPF chose to invade, was disadvantageous to foot-mobile infantry forces coming up against lightly armored vehicles and truck-mounted heavy weapons. The terrain readily allowed for cross-country movement by wheeled vehicles that could easily outrun and disperse lightly armed infantry, leaving them no place to hide.

After initial successes, the RPF suffered a number of serious setbacks. Most devastating was the loss of key leaders who had developed a style of leading from the front. Before forty-eight hours had passed, the Rwandan Patriotic Army's high command was dead.

Caught off guard in open, rolling hills by the faster, heavier firepower of reinforced government forces, the RPA paid a heavy price. Years of hard-earned military leadership experience quickly bled into the savanna of the northeast. One by one, the leaders fell. Without their stalwarts to rally them, the rank-and-file soldiers went to ground. Instead of seeking combat with the enemy, the RPA had taken to hiding out in small packets of demoralized soldiers, unable and unwilling to support each other in the face of enemy attacks. When they did fight, tactics were disastrous. Actions were uncoordinated; discipline was lacking.

Absent in far-off Fort Leavenworth, Kansas, at the U.S. Army's Command and General Staff College was Maj. Paul Kagame. He had been assigned from his post as the intelligence chief of the Ugandan army to attend the prestigious school, which selects only the upper half of the American officer corps for resident study. Having arrived only that summer, he was barely three months into the first term when he was suddenly called home. In later years, he would say that he had in fact taken the most crucial part of the year's coursework: tactics.

Arriving back in Kampala, he changed uniforms and made his way to the front where he assumed command of the RPF. But he had arrived too late to reorganize an attack. His forces were broken and demoralized, their opposition strong. Kagame inherited an incoherent army. The RPF had tried to mount a conventional campaign, but out-manned and out-gunned, and reduced to fighting in uncoordinated defensive pockets, Kagame's forces suffered heavily.

To make matters worse, the invasion had incited the Kigali government to redouble its efforts against its indigenous Tutsis, blaming them for the invasion and portraying them as agents of the RPF. Old antagonisms were inflamed; the ranks of the *interahamwe* expanded. The embittered Kagame was forced to retreat, abandoning any near-term plans to overthrow the Hutu government, even as hundreds of Rwandan Tutsis were being rounded up and slaughtered.

Kagame needed time. He had to consolidate his forces, develop his subordinates, husband his human resources, train his army, build up ammunition and supplies, raise morale, and instill discipline. The last would be crucial. It would also be a natural extension of Kagame's own personality. In Uganda he had been known as the chief disciplinarian, the "Pontius Pilate," as he was called, of the Ugandan army. He had fought through harsh times before, and he knew that above all else it took discipline to make an army.

He also needed terrain where he could be free to develop his forces while protecting them from a better-armed and more mobile army. Not wanting to return to Uganda, from whose army he and many of his troops had deserted and where he was unlikely to find the conditions he needed to reconstitute an effective force, Kagame headed for the Volcano Mountains. Moving back across the Rwandan border into Uganda, turning west and climbing through the thick vegetation to heights of more than twelve thousand feet, the new commander drove his troops toward the roof of the continent. Even in equatorial Africa, such altitudes brought freezing cold weather. For Tutsis clothed only in the light garments suited to the lower altitudes of Uganda and Rwanda, the experience was brutal. Unaccustomed to the rigors of the mountains and the cold, poorly equipped for the steep slopes and frigid temperatures, they suffered intensely. Trench foot and frostbite compounded injuries. Some died from the exposure; the survivors found it hard to bury them in the frozen ground. Morale flagged and desertion grew.

But Kagame had found the base of operations he wanted. Astride the Rwandan border in the northwest, the Volcano Mountains gave him all the protection he needed to retrain his army. Moreover, it gave him the opportunity to foray into enemy territory to test his forces and to maintain the initiative for continued struggle. Slowly, he was developing an effective guerrilla force, weaning his troops away from the conventional tactics that had almost ruined them in the poorly chosen terrain of northeast Rwanda. He taught them to move at night, to dig foxholes and trench lines in order to defend themselves, to lay in interlocking fields of fire, and to combine fire-power and maneuver in order to overwhelm a less mobile, less rugged, and less disciplined force. He obtained hand-held radios and taught his commanders how to communicate in the open succinctly and cryptically, allowing for disparate forces to coordinate their movements and to come together swiftly at the right place and time.

By the spring of 1991, Kagame had effectively regrouped his shattered army. Combat-capable forces numbered only in the hundreds, but what he had were well trained and disciplined. Leaders had been taught to plan, coordinate, and synchronize their combat elements. Kagame had taught his commanders that if the plan was good, the soldiers trained, and discipline ensured, they did not have to needlessly expose themselves to enemy fire. He was building for the long term, and that meant developing leaders who would last, who could rise to the occasion when conditions demanded, and who could make decisions on the spot and adapt their specific tactics, so long as they continued to serve the purpose of the larger mission. Moreover, he began to draw more recruits, rebuilding his forces so that when they did come down from the mountains to stay, they could fight and defeat the larger forces of the Rwandan government.

Kagame decided to mount only small-scale operations during the remainder of that year, sending small bands back into Rwanda to stage hit-and-run attacks. At the same time, he needed to send a signal, both for internal and international consumption, that the RPF was capable of larger operations as well. He needed a tactical victory. He chose as his target Ruhengeri, one of the larger cities in

Rwanda about eight miles across the border. Well garrisoned by government troops, it sat astride a major crossroads leading to other key cities, including Kigali, the capital. The specific target was the Ruhengeri prison, where a large number of political prisoners were detained. An effective attack here would not only embarrass the government, it would leave open a number of avenues for further movement deeper into Rwanda while at the same time freeing sympathetic prisoners who might join Kagame's ranks. On the other hand, should the attack go sour, the mountains were not that far away and a quick retreat should preserve the force before it became decisively engaged.

Moving at night over several approach routes, the RPA forces totaled more than a thousand. Although large in numbers, they had not yet been tested in a coordinated military operation. Moreover, they were half-starved from the privations of their hidden life in the mountains. Nonetheless, Kagame felt they were ready.

As the RPA approached the town, local guides helped to move Kagame's forces into position. At dawn, they attacked with small arms, automatic weapons, and rocket-propelled grenades, combining their effects for maximum shock. A base of fire was laid down while maneuvering forces rushed the stronghold. Government forces were caught unprepared and quickly overrun. They broke within minutes, the survivors fleeing for their lives, abandoning weapons and ammunition, as well as the prison they were to defend. Hundreds of the released prisoners were eager to join Kagame's forces.

In one fell swoop, the RPA had demonstrated its ability to mass large numbers of forces, synchronize night movement over difficult and unfamiliar terrain, apply combined-arms fire and maneuver, and completely shatter a substantial government force. Having swelled his ranks, improved their morale, and indicated his intention to continue the fight to retake Rwanda for the Tutsis in the diaspora, Kagame withdrew back into the mountains, where he would continue to build throughout 1991 and into 1992.

The Peace Gambit

The emerging Paul Kagame had now shown the world that rare combination: the military leader who understood both warfare and politics. He knew that he could not hope to retake Rwanda without a political component to his equation. A high school graduate who had spent his young adult years in the savagery of the Luwero triangle, he had a knack for thinking his way through tough problems. He knew that his cause was hopeless without international support. He also knew that finding such support was not going to be easy. The Tutsis had been on the run since 1959. France had found it in its interest to support the Hutus, through whom they maintained their influence in central Africa. Belgium would be no help. And the rest of the European powers couldn't care less about the turmoil, other than as an opportunity to sell guns and mines. The United States was too distant, and too wedded to Mobutu in Zaire, the linchpin of American policy toward central Africa, and Mobutu was no friend of the Tutsis.

The international peacekeeping community was the only place that he could garner the slightest support. And that would come only if he had a voice, a way of being heard as both a victim of violence (in the image of the Tutsi diaspora) and a force to keep in check lest violence spread. Ironically, it was by simultaneously playing the peace card and the war drum that Kagame was heard and his cause given a chance. But that very same precarious balance would put his fellow Tutsis in Rwanda at grave risk.

On its surface, the peace process looked hopeful. In February 1991, the Organization of African Unity, the United Nations High Commissioner for Refugees, and the governments of Rwanda, Burundi, Uganda, Tanzania, and Zaire signed the Dar es Salaam accords, providing for the voluntary repatriation of refugees. In March, Rwanda and the RPF signed the more comprehensive N'sele cease-fire agreement. In July of '92, the two opponents agreed to the deployment of a Neutral Military Observers Group to the areas between the Rwandan army (the FAR) and the RPF.

But as the peace accords advanced, so did the preparations for war, and in Rwanda itself, the preparations for genocide. In the spring of 1992, Rwandan government forces concluded a $6 million arms deal with Egypt, underwritten by France, obtaining large quantities of small arms, mortars, rockets, grenades, and mines. In October, the FAR signed a similar arms deal with South Africa, upping the ante by another $6 million. For their part, the RPF continued small-scale operations out of its mountain stronghold throughout 1992, extending its influence a short way into Rwanda. By early 1993, RPF forces controlled a small strip of territory reaching from Ruhengari to Byumba and farther to the northeast along the Ugandan border. All the while, hate media controlled by the government in Rwanda stirred up the masses (read Hutus) to hate their enemies (read Tutsis). Increasingly, vulgar and ugly radio broadcasts were reaching out throughout the nation, inspiring revulsion for the minority population, linking them in the minds of the listeners to the external threat from the RPF, and describing the Tutsis as less than human vermin (e.g., "cockroaches") to be exterminated. At the same time, the organization and the preparation of the *interahamwe* grew. When the killing of Rwandan Tutsis began anew in January 1993, Kagame struck.

It had been more than two years since he had taken his shattered force into the Volcano Mountains and prepared them to fight an insurgency rather than a conventional war. During that time he rebuilt his forces, trained his leaders, added a strong dose of discipline, and obtained the arms and ammunition necessary to take the field once more as a conventional force. Emphasizing the benefits of speed in warfare, Kagame commenced on 8 February to move his battalion-size formations, overwhelming the more static government units directly in his path. Pushing out from his base in the north along the Byumba-Kigali axis, he progressed steadily toward the capital city, closing within a few kilometers of Kigali in a matter of days.

It was too much for the international community. France was alarmed that its proxy was losing. Paris rushed forces to help defend the capital city. The UN peace process lay in shambles, with the news threatening to explode on the world's front pages. The United States intervened with both carrot and stick. Promising to underwrite the peace process, the administration pressured Kagame to stop. But American diplomats also pressured Uganda, seeking to cut Kagame's only base of support and deny him a rear area should the fighting take a turn for the worse. In the face of the promises and the pressure, the RPF agreed to stop its attack. On 22 February 1993, the Rwandan government and the RPF announced a cease-fire. Reluctantly, the RPA withdrew.

The next year saw a hodgepodge of political and military maneuvering by all sides, the least effectual of which were any legitimate attempts to forward the peace process. The United Nations variously created a number of specific missions to observe and report (and, ostensibly, ensure) compliance with internationally sanctioned agreements between the warring parties. The key outcomes of all of this noise were the Arusha Accords signed on 4 August 1993 and the dispatch of a UN military force known as UNAMIR (for "UN Assistance Mission for Rwanda"). As it turned out, the former was a sham and the latter a disgrace.

The Arusha Accords allowed for President Habyarimana to share power with the Hutu opposition and the RPF. The intent was to establish a broad-based transitional government that would co-govern for a period of almost two years, after which elections would be held. The RPF eventually was to be integrated with the Rwandan army.

None of this ever happened. The Rwandan government instead continued to put in place an elaborate propaganda machine and an extensive militia organization that would facilitate future genocide. The one tactical outcome that turned out to be key was the arrangement for the RPF to place a six-hundred-man infantry battalion into Kigali. The leadership and men for this force were all handpicked, and in December 1993 they moved into place among the strength of their enemies. Kagame was looking ahead.

In the meantime, UNAMIR built itself on existing UN structures and reached a peak strength of twenty-five hundred by early 1994. Command fell to a Canadian, Maj. Gen. Romeo Dellaire, who had previously commanded the United Nations Observer Mission Uganda/Rwanda. The latter's mission was to monitor the Ugandan-

Rwandan border from the Ugandan side and assist in the reduction of arms trafficking and violence.

Although Dellaire accurately assessed the foreboding moves being taken by the Rwandan government and developed a number of operational plans to deal with what he saw as the coming confrontations, he never gained any support for the actions he advocated. When the killing began in the spring, UNAMIR did little more than quickly get the bulk of its forces out of the country. The few hundred that remained went to ground in their heavily sandbagged headquarters in Kigali, within sight and hearing of the murderous events that filled nearly a hundred days.

By April 1994, the coiled springs of the contending factions in Rwanda were wound to the breaking point. Something was bound to snap, and it was clear that the indifference of the rest of the world, indeed in some cases its complicity, would do nothing to keep the worst from happening. The trigger was pulled on the night of 6 April in the form of two missiles fired at President Habyarimana's plane as it approached the Kigali mission from another fruitless round of talks in Arusha. With the president were his own army chief of staff and the president of Burundi. All three and the crew went to a mangled death, the harbinger of things to come. That very night, the killings began in earnest, an indication that the assassinations (for all his brutality, Habyarimana was seen as too "moderate") and their aftermath were well planned. Radio Mille Collines found pleasure in letting the Tutsis and their sympathizers know what was coming: "You cockroaches must know you are made of flesh. We won't let you kill. We will kill you." With dispatch and efficiency, the *interahamwe*, joined by the army and the Presidential Guard, set up roadblocks throughout the country and went to work checking off names from their preprinted lists. Even before midnight, it was already too late to flee.

By morning, UN forces received a clear signal that it would be in their best interest to stand aside. Government forces seized ten Belgian soldiers assigned to guard Prime Minister Agatha Uwilingiyiman, who was hacked to death that day with a machete as she tried to make her way to the U.S. embassy. In a drawn-out affair, the

Belgians had their noses cut off, then their hands, then their legs, and then their genitals. The UNAMIR leaders got the message.

So did the "observer" battalion Kagame had placed in the middle of Kigali, under the able command of Lt. Col. Charles Kayanga. Unlike the UN forces, when they went to ground, they did so to fight. Seizing the Parliament building, a key strong point on dominant terrain in the middle of the city, Kayanga outposted the high ground in the immediate vicinity and established a defensive line in the middle of the main Rwandan government forces. Though cut off from the rest of the world, he was determined to hold on until Kagame reached him.

All around them, the country went mad. Hutus young and old rose up to join in the killing. Neighbors and colleagues were attacked without remorse. Priests killed their parishioners, and students their teachers. Local authorities pretended to extend safety, only to herd desperate Tutsis together in churches, schoolyards, and soccer stadiums for more efficient slaughter. In Kibye, a beautiful resort town in the west, more than five thousand Tutsis were herded onto the playing field of the local soccer stadium while their countrymen machine-gunned and grenaded them from the bleachers. As they lay wounded, their neighbors came among them and finished the job with machetes and bludgeons. By design, everyone was to be bloodied, both the killed and the killers. There could be no exceptions. A Hutu wife must kill her Tutsi husband if she were to live. It was the same for her children, who were Tutsi by convention. If a Hutu husband wanted to spare his children (and himself), he had to kill his Tutsi wife. Not to kill a Tutsi was to sign your own death warrant.

Philip Gourevitch, writing in the *New Yorker* in December of 1995, captures the mood:

> Throughout Rwanda, mass rape and looting accompanied the slaughter. Militia bands, fortified with potent banana beer and assorted drugs, were bused from massacre to massacre. Hutu prisoners were organized into work details to clear cadavers. Radio announcers reminded listeners to take special care to disembowel pregnant victims. Tutsi belongings were parceled

out in advance; the radio, the couch, the goat, the opportunity to rape a young girl. A councilwoman in one Kigali neighborhood was reported to have offered fifty francs apiece (about thirty cents at the time) for severed heads, a process known as "selling cabbages."

Although the world pretended not to notice, Paul Kagame had a clear picture. His decision was swift; on 7 April he launched his forces against the Rwandan government.

Winner Take All

Kagame understood what was at risk when he began his attack. Although his earlier foray into Rwanda in 1993 had demonstrated to him the ineffectiveness of the Rwandan government forces, he could not know how the array of forces might align against him. The United States had discouraged his earlier foray in 1993. The UN had never demonstrated any interest in supporting his ambitions to return to Rwanda. The French had openly supported his enemy, training and supplying the government's forces over the years. Save for Uganda, which could always close the back door on him and leave him without a line of communications to bring in ammunition and supplies, no African nation had shown support for the RPF. And the FAR was a larger and better-armed and -supplied force. Although he had roughed it up handily in 1993, the FAR had expanded and was spread out across the country. Government forces had proven formidable before on terrain where foot-mobile infantry could be run to ground by armored, mechanized forces. If they caught the RPF in the open again, things could go badly.

Kagame weighed all of the unknowns these variables presented against the certainty of what would happen if he did not attack. His countrymen would be annihilated. He attacked.

Most sources assess the RPF with having about twelve thousand troops at the beginning of April 1994. But as the invading columns cut deeper into Rwanda and as Tutsi survivors fled from the genocide, many of them young men or boys fast and agile enough to get away from the roadblocks, ranks swelled to as many as twenty-three thousand. The FAR is assessed to have fielded about twenty thousand soldiers, although various methods of counting tabulate the numbers as high as forty thousand. Government army forces were closer to the smaller number, but in the weeks leading up to the genocide, the government had augmented the army with other armed elements. The Rwandan gendarmerie was expanded to between four thousand and six thousand. Moreover, the *interahamwe*, which had received some military training over the preceding three years, was further organized and trained during late 1993 and early 1994. Armed with anything from clubs and machetes to hunting rifles to modern assault weapons and grenades, their totals reached between twenty and thirty thousand, loosely arrayed in structures that alternately had them working with the FAR, local officials, or responding directly to exhortations of Hutu extremist radio.

United Nations forces, although not likely to fight, were making noises that indicated they might enter into the strategic equation. Major General Dallaire, the UNAMIR commander, argued with his higher headquarters that with as few as five thousand soldiers and the freedom to operate flexibly, he could stop the genocide. But the UN's response was timid. The reality was that Dallaire could barely hold what forces he did have in place. Indeed, within six days of the onset of the war, the Belgian battalion, sobered by the slaughter of their soldiers and sickened by UNAMIR's weakness, abruptly withdrew. A week later, on 21 April, not only did the United Nations not give Dellaire the capability he was calling for, but the Security Council voted to slash his strength by 90 percent. The remaining 270 blue-bereted soldiers hunkered down behind their sandbagged headquarters while the UN dithered for the rest of the spring, shocked by the horror unfolding in Rwanda, but either unwilling or unable to actually do something about it. Even the simplest objectives, such as destruction of the broadcast means of the extremist radio stations, were ignored.

These developments fed into the aims of the Hutu political leaders. Government forces were free to set about their major purpose: killing Tutsis and their Hutu sympathizers. The retreat of the Belgians, along with other departing UN forces, strengthened the Hutus' hand. France was the only outside power that remained keenly interested in what was happening, and the French were decidedly pro-FAR. The French military had supported the FAR earlier in the civil war, trained their forces, and provided them with arms. Although all French forces had been withdrawn in December 1993, key French military advisers remained in Kigali throughout, most notable in their comings and goings on the night of the president's assassination. If the French were inclined to intercede on the ground, it would most likely be on the side of the Hutus. But if things went well for the government, most likely the French would stand aside, restricting their support to those areas less obvious to outside observers.

By the spring of 1994, the FAR had concentrated its best forces in and around Kigali. The battalion-size Presidential Guard, the commando, the paracommando, and reconnaissance battalions were all in place to cover the capital and the nearby airport. An artillery battalion and an air contingent of seventeen helicopters and a few fixed-wing aircraft supported them. Heavy weapons consisted of almost thirty reconnaissance vehicles and nine 105-millimeter howitzers, as well as mortars and rocket launchers.

Kagame knew that the Kigali-based enemy force would have to be either defeated or unseated, but his near-term objective was to stop the Tutsi genocide. The RPF "peacekeeping" battalion inside Kigali needed no further instructions to go to ground and fight. This hard-core six-hundred-man force would hold their position inside the capital city, tying down government forces while deceiving them that Kigali was Kagame's immediate objective. It was not.

On the night of 6 April as he learned of the president's assassination, Kagame called in his chief subordinate leaders. He knew something was afoot and correctly deduced that whatever was about to unfold had long been planned by the Hutu-dominated government. In the early hours of 7 April, he ordered four of his battalions to move to assembly areas throughout northern Rwanda in Tutsi-dominated territory. Although he did not yet know for sure what his eventual orders would be, he realized that by the time his units gathered the picture would become clearer, enabling him to develop his own plans and issue appropriate orders.

Even by the time the battalions moved into their respective assembly areas, the situation in Rwanda had deteriorated. The genocide was in full swing in no time at all, and reports of the butchery were reaching Kagame by word of mouth, often from survivors who had fled from massacre sites where entire families had been wiped out. The RPF commander also learned that seven government battalions were blocking the road forty miles north of Kigali at Byumba.

Kagame's immediate objective was to save as many of his fellow Tutsis as possible. But he also wanted to capture as much territory as he could, split the government forces while keeping them on the defensive, and, remembering the bitter experiences of the 1990 fighting, avoid direct combat whenever possible. Kagame therefore bypassed Byumba where a substantial enemy force waited for him and moved to the east around them before cutting south to Kigali. A second column cut even wider to the east, brushing up against the Tanzanian border before cutting south to the Burundi border and then turning back to the northwest toward Kigali. In the meantime, he feinted toward the west, further throwing FAR forces off balance.

Armed with Eastern European–manufactured automatic weapons, light mortars, and rocket-propelled grenades, the RPA pushed out on foot. Its tactics were to avoid frontal assaults and use the cover of darkness to encircle enemy forces, always leaving FAR elements a single avenue of escape. The tough years in the mountains had taught Kagame's forces the importance of discipline and the techniques of infiltration. They could move silently and swiftly, avoiding contact until they had placed themselves in positions of maximum advantage. When the government forces realized they were surrounded, they invariably fled down the open escape route, not realizing a way out had been deliberately left open. Then, without exposing themselves, the RPF would attack from the flanks and rear, inflicting heavy casualties on the government forces while losing few of their own.

Government morale plummeted. The RPA was using maneuvers

at the operational level to maximum advantage. Government forces were constantly on the defensive, withdrawing from one position to another, doing a bad job of consolidating defensive lines, constantly being outflanked, launching the odd counterattack that went nowhere, then having to retreat once again, only to be caught in ambush once again from the flank and rear. Any advantages they might have found in their armor, helicopters, and one airborne battalion were rendered useless under this style of fighting.

A major deficiency of the government forces was its defunct command and control system. The head of their army had been killed along with President Habyarimana when his plane had been shot down on 6 April. Hutu hardliners had then advanced their own candidate, overruling the army's own choice for succession, who proceeded to assume that Kagame would put his main effort against the capital city, which they were confident they could hold by blocking the approach roads. But Kagame did not stick to the roads. When he slipped by FAR elements in the dark, focused on his objectives of gaining territory and saving Tutsis, government forces were not only surprised, they were unable to get the information back to higher headquarters. Reports back to Kigali were lost in the zeal by Hutu extremists, now dominating the military forces as well as the *interahamwe,* to concentrate on their main objective: execution of the genocide. For the government in Kigali, political objectives were detracting from consolidating the military effort. For the RPF, however, the military and political objectives were reinforcing. Kagame's forces moved forward in all directions at once. Their mobility, discipline, and ability to communicate succinctly by shortband radio kept all efforts focused on the end state: retake Rwanda.

In Kigali, the lone battalion continued to hold out against repeated assaults by government forces. Kagame had invested enough forces to tie down the FAR and keep them from reinforcing other parts of Rwanda. The hard years of training in their mountain base had allowed the RPA to become masters of infiltration. Small, armed bands slipped undetected through government lines, linking up with the isolated RPA unit, bringing in supplies and reinforcements. Gradually, FAR elements lost the will to attack against the parliament building stronghold, only to be beaten back again and again, harassed by RPA units pressing in on them from the rear. While the RPA battalion continued to hold in and around the parliament building, it was increasingly gaining in strength from intermittently opened lines of communication with the few forces Kagame had been able to spare for the capital. Because of their timid response, government forces in Kigali surrendered the tactical initiative to the rebels, much as they had surrendered the operational initiative in the rest of the country.

As early as mid-April, RPA elements were able to close within range of the Kigali international airport, their small-arms and rocket fire closing the runway from incoming and departing aircraft. The government had been denied an important strategic advantage. All resupply for the government, troops, ammunition, and so forth were now denied the quickest route of entry. Diplomats, arms traders, financiers, and government officials could not readily come in and go out. The Hutu government and its benefactors were cut off from each other. Any contact with the outer world would have to rely on overland routes, and those wound through the terrifying killing grounds where no one wanted to go. Moreover, Kagame was increasingly gaining control over much of the country. The government was becoming isolated and afraid, knowing full well what they had unleashed and what might be done about it.

On 22 May, rebel forces captured the heavily defended airport. On the same day, Kanombe Barracks, the main FAR stronghold in the capital, fell. Kagame had concentrated forces around the city, pressing down from the north and from the east. But instead of driving home his attack into the city proper, Kagame dropped off sufficient forces to contain the FAR elements within Kigali while pushing on to the northwest toward Gisenyi on Lake Kivu and due south toward Butare, close to the Burundi border.

The one place he did not head was into the southwest, the region dominated by the Nyungwe Forest. This natural forest preserve is both the biggest (almost 1,000 square kilometers) and one of the last virgin forests at altitude in Africa. It rises in tiers from seventeen hundred to three thousand meters amid thick equatorial forest interspersed with jagged peaks. Save for one road that links Butare to Cyangugu at the southern tip of Lake Kivu, the terrain is virtually impassable. Kagame was not about to lose time trekking through tough jungle. Nor was he about to concentrate his forces on a single road where they might be forced to fight on unfavorable terms. But by leaving this one region open, he allowed the government one remaining hope: intervention from abroad.

Throughout the spring of 1994, Paris had become increasingly concerned about the way things were going in Rwanda. African hands were quick to attribute the mass murders to outrage at the assassination of Habyarimana and the desire of the Hutus to defend themselves against RPF, or Tutsi, invasion. The French press, on the other hand, was wont to charge French involvement in the planning and execution of the killing. The government was getting the worst of both ends: the charge of complicity in genocide and the loss of influence in central Africa.

The solution for Paris was French intercession under a humanitarian banner. Despite opposition by African leaders (such as Nelson Mandela) outside the Francophone bloc, studied noncommittal statements by UNAMIR, and explicit rejection of the idea by the RPF, France began preparations for an intervention. On 16 and again on 18 June, French arms shipments arrived in Goma and were quickly shuttled across the border into Rwanda. On the twenty-second, the Security Council at the United Nations, further soiling its record on Rwanda, endorsed the "impartial" French deployment.

The following day the first French troops flew into Goma, the lead elements of Operation Turquoise. But Kagame's forces were coming up out of central Rwanda at that time, and getting through to Kigali was difficult. Reinforced by continued airlift into Goma, French forces cut south and within a week had occupied nearly a quarter of the country, sweeping across southwest Rwanda to stop the RPA advance. Abruptly, they arbitrarily redefined their mission, trading the humanitarian label for the establishment of a "safe zone." "Safe for whom?" was Kagame's immediate question. The French military, in significant strength, was now holding open an exit corridor for Hutus, who were fleeing on foot in the hundreds of thousands. Mixed among them were the provincial officials who had organized the genocide, the *interahamwe* elements who had executed it, and Hutu power national leaders who were beginning to read the tea leaves of Kagame's offensive. Indeed, even former French President Giscard d'Estaing accused the French command of protecting some of those who had carried out the massacres.

The French military had arrived in their usual manner: full of themselves, armed to the teeth, and derisive of local forces that might stand in their way. They had poured into Zaire just across the border from Rwanda, with a mixture of artillery and armor, along with twenty military aircraft that immediately made it the most imposing air force in central Africa. They also came in with a force of rented Senegalese troops, to give themselves a multilateral air. Despite their humanitarian claims, it was their view that the RPA was the enemy, an invading, rebel army that was toppling the French-aligned official national government.

Kagame instantly understood the threat. Once again he had to face a major choice between caution and boldness. He immediately quickened his efforts to take Rwanda, French troops or no French troops, although once again he would do his best to avoid direct frontal assault. As the RPA closed on Butare in the south, the French general in Goma sent him a signal to back off. Instead, Kagame had his troops encircle the town under cover of darkness. By morning, he discovered the French had pulled out, moving west toward the town of Gikongoro on the road into the Nyngwe Forest. And they had with them approximately twenty-five vehicles, several of them lightly armored, bristling with heavy weapons. Finding courage in the light of morning, the French forces moved back toward Butare.

The RPA was ready for them. Unbeknownst to the French, they had blocked the route and beside the stretch of road behind it had moved into place a two-company-long ambush. The lead vehicle was stopped and the commander of the French column, who claimed he was proceeding into Butare to evacuate some Catholic nuns and the orphans in their charge, was informed he would have to submit to a vehicle-by-vehicle inspection. The French refused and trained their machine guns on the exposed rebels at the roadblock. At that moment, RPG-laden rebel soldiers emerged from hiding and pointed their weapons at the vehicles. For a second both sides stood eyeball to eyeball, poised to open fire. Then the French blinked.

They yielded to the inspection, which subsequently revealed some government soldiers, who were quickly dispatched by the RPA. Although the French fired some of their weapons into the air, they refrained from aiming at RPA forces.

Here and elsewhere, the French forces came to realize that the RPA would fight, and that indeed they might be good at it. Moreover, French units began to see that events that had unfolded in Rwanda were a great deal more complex than they had originally imagined. But although they never did engage the RPF in combat, they held on to their bastion in southwest Rwanda, secured safe passage for the Hutu genocide forces to cross over into the refugee camps, and enabled the slaughter of the Tutsis to continue for an extra month. Although they are credited for having saved ten thousand Tutsis in western Rwanda, their interference allowed countless thousands more to be slaughtered in the so-called safe zone.

For his part, Paul Kagame took Kigali on 4 July. On 13 July he pushed into Ruhengari, the town where he had originally tested his mountain-based force and secured his first tactical victory in 1991, and on 18 July, following an intense artillery battle, took Giseny and secured his northwest border with Zaire. The same day, the RPF declared a unilateral cease-fire and declared a "government of national unity" that included both Hutus and Tutsis. Millions of Hutus had fled into refugee camps over the border into Tanzania, Zaire, and Burundi. In their midst were the Hutu extremists who had organized the genocide and who would continue to plot to return and finish the job.

Postscript

When Cable News Network broadcast the images of the dead and dying in the mass refugee camp in Goma in July, the world finally motivated itself to act. Organized and led by the U.S. military efforts, relief efforts began flowing by the end of the month, even as the predominantly Hutu refugees continued to flood out of Rwanda. Surviving Tutsis emerged from hiding, at first tentatively, and trickled back toward their homes. The airport at Kigali, occupied by U.S. forces formed around the U.S. Army's Lion Brigade

(Airborne), expanded an air-bridge from one to two flights a day to fifty to sixty within a few weeks. A labor force was organized with returning Rwandans to unload and move the tons of supplies coming in. The power grid was restored and the water supply system in the capital was repaired. Countless mines strewn around the city and its approaches were identified and removed, but not before scores of returning Rwandese stumbled over them, suffering fatal or maiming wounds. Gradually UN officials took over the coordination of relief operations with the new government in Kigali.

By the end of August, more than a hundred international non-government organizations had arrived in Rwanda. At Goma, where the worst of the postwar suffering had at last brought public attention to the crisis in central Africa, a massive humanitarian operation involving more than 100 Non-Governmental Organizations (NGOs) and hundreds of U.S. soldiers lowered the death rate from six thousand a day to four hundred.

The new Rwandan government cautiously moved to a number of hideaways in the vicinity of the airport, and then, as it became incumbent upon it to receive and negotiate with world government and non-government organizations, into the one decent building still standing a few hundred yards from the main terminal. Paul Kagame did not declare himself president, allowing instead moderate Hutus to serve as both president and prime minister in order to better unite a divided country. He assumed the roles of vice president and minister of defense, two positions that gave him enough power to determine policy while avoiding the limelight. No matter what he called himself, however, it was clear to all that he remained the leader of the army and the country.

Whether Rwanda was a country at all was problematic. Only slowly did the vestiges of nationhood return. Relatively few Hutus returned to Rwanda during the rest of 1994 and through 1995. But conditions in the camps were so bleak, and Kagame's exhortations to return and become countrymen once again (promising to arrest and prosecute only those who were in the hierarchy of the genocide) so compelling, that many decided to take their chances and return home.

Hutu extremists, however, stilled such inclinations. The refugee

camps had become their power bases, a source of funds, suste-
nance, recruitment, and political power. As rank-and-file Hutus
tried to move out of the camps, they were assaulted. Many had their
Achilles tendons severed as a signal that walking away was not to be
condoned. Many were killed, and families were brutalized. A whole
people organized and unleashed to wreak terror became in turn
the terrorized by the very people who led them. The exodus
stopped.

For months and years to come, dozens of relief agencies poured
in supplies to the camps. Hutu leaders garnered the lion's share.
Host countries prospered from the presence of the refugees. And
so did the scores of contractors and agencies. The refugee camps offered lucrative rewards to those who purported to help their inhabitants, some legitimately, some less so. Refugee camps became not
only a political and military power source, but also an economic
boon to those who could exert power over them.

Kagame struggled to rebuild his country, restore civic order, create a viable economy, and institute a system of justice. He was handicapped in his efforts by the fact that most of the elites who had
done all of that prior to the spring of 1994 were dead or gone. He
had no oil to sell to the outside world, no natural resources to mar-
ket, and no tourism to attract money. What he did have was a
haunted population who had seen the worst of human nature. They
feared they might see it again.

By 1996, Kagame determined he could no longer tolerate the
refugee camps. By force of arms he broke them up, both those that
remained on Rwandan soil (allegedly administered by international, neutral organizations) and those in eastern Zaire. Hundreds
of thousands of Hutus returned to Rwanda, mingling with Tutsis
from the diaspora who were coming in from all over the world to
settle beside Tutsis that had survived the genocide. Tens of thousands of Hutus were arrested for crimes against humanity. Very few
have been brought to trial.

Zaire reacted to the camp raids by seeking out Tutsis and slaugh-
tering them, glad to bring Hutu militants into its army. Rwanda responded by supporting a rebellion against Mobutu, seeing him top-
pled from power in 1997. His successor, Kabila, proved no better,

and although he owed his office to Rwandan support, by 1998 he found it in his interest to turn on Kagame and gain popular support by killing Tutsis.

The cycle of violence continues. War begets war, killing begets killing. Paul Kagame, master of guerrilla and conventional warfare, maneuverist par excellence, and as accomplished a strategist as the world has seen in recent decades, continues to manage the survival of his people, both Hutu and Tutsi. In the summer of 1998, a two-pronged Rwandan-supported attack on Kinshasa, the capital of the Congo (the restored name for Zaire), came within a few days of toppling Kabila. Following his death by assassination two years later, the Congo grew even more unstable. But the Congo is wealthy in natural resources, and its dissolution potentially destabilizing to its neighbors and interested (read "profiting") Western powers. The entry of several African nations on the side of Kabila beat back the RPA-supported columns. Once again, the peace gambit is being played.

Where it all ends remains a chapter not yet written. In the meantime, one can only watch and wonder what lessons the Rwandan experience offers for modern war, as well as modern political reality. Perhaps they are ones not many care to learn.

Face of the Future: The Russian Assault on Grozny

An airborne battalion will settle the problem in a week.
—Russian defense minister Pavel Grachev [1]

Grozny, Chechnya, 1 January 1995: A terrific explosion shattered the quiet, cold, smoke-hazed afternoon. Artillery fire impacted in the distance, the reverberations of the 152mm shells and 120mm rockets from the Grad launchers shaking the ground. A Russian tank, its turret lying upside down near its tracks, smoldered in the desolate square near the city's railroad station. Chechen fighters scurried between the charred vehicles as nervous television crews scanned the battlefield with their camcorders. The scattered bodies of Russian soldiers—many burned and disfigured beyond recognition—lay everywhere.

In the opening days of January 1995, the city of Grozny in the rebel province of Chechnya became the bloody meat grinder of the Russian army. That once proud organization—the heir of the great Kutusov who beat Napoleon, and the invincible Marshal Zhukov, whose armies defeated Hitler—had been beaten and humbled by a people scorned in Moscow as "bandits" and "terrorists." The results of this tragic conflict would cripple the Russian army and shake the foundations of Pres. Boris Yeltsin's regime. For military professionals, the battle of Grozny is a stark precursor of war in the next century, a war fueled by a toxic mixture of corruption, ethnic hatred, and failed states.

The Russian government launched the Chechen war for myriad complex reasons, not the least of which was to preserve the "territorial integrity" of the Russian federation. Chechnya was a vital test of Yeltsin's authority and political will to hold together a polyglot of eighty-nine ethnic republics and regions. For twenty-one months, from December 1994 to August 1996, Chechnya would also test the Russian army's will to fight in the harshest conditions imaginable. Although the war was fought all over Chechnya, and the Chechens raided Russia itself, the fight centered on the important industrial city of Grozny.

Background to the War

At six thousand square miles, Chechnya, little larger than Connecticut, is bordered in the west by the Ingush Republic, in the south by the independent state of Georgia, in the east and northeast by Dagestan, and by the North Ossetian Republic to the northwest. Northern Chechnya is predominantly fertile plain and is crossed by the Terek and Sunzha Rivers. Southern Chechnya contains wooded hills that rise to the high slopes of the Caucasus Mountains.

The Chechens are a fiercely independent Muslim mountain people with a distinctive language that is neither Slavic, Turkish, nor Persian. Primarily herdsman and farmers, the Chechens have a long and bloody history of conflict with Russia that dates back to the eighteenth century. Annexed by czarist Russia in 1859 after bitter fighting, Chechnya never fully assimilated into Russian culture or political control. For Chechens, resistance to Russian oppression and occupation is the stuff of legends and the mainstay of Chechen tradition. In 1832, Sergei Lermontov, one of the great nineteenth-century Russian poets, said of the Chechens: "Their god is freedom, their law is war."

When Yeltsin took power from Mikhail Gorbachev in 1991, dissident leaders in Chechnya took advantage of the turmoil in the central government to declare independence from Moscow. The rebels elected Gen. Dzhokhar Dudayev—a former bomber pilot and Soviet air force general—by a 90 percent vote. Yeltsin refused to rec-

ognize the validity of the Chechen election. On 7 November 1991 Yeltsin declared a state of emergency in the Chechen-Ingush Republic. In response, the Chechens rallied behind Dudayev and thirty thousand protesters demonstrated in Grozny. To inflame the crowds, Dudayev declared an Islamic holy war on Russia.

The newly elected Chechen parliament immediately endowed Dudayev with special emergency powers. When Russian troops were airlifted to the Grozny airport in the hopes that a small military force could overawe the rebels, Chechen national guardsmen surrounded them at the airport. Unwilling to take drastic action, the Russian Parliament voted to rescind the state of emergency and a bloody incident was averted. Yeltsin was humiliated and forced to back down. After tense negotiations the Russian troops were evacuated from Grozny.

In exchange for the freedom of the Russian troops in Chechnya, Defense Minister Pavel Grachev turned over weapons and ammunition stored in Russian army depots and garrisons in Chechnya. Chechen forces amassed a considerable arsenal that included 260 airplanes, forty-two tanks, forty-eight armored vehicles, forty-four lightly armored vehicles, 942 automobiles, 139 artillery pieces, eighty-nine heavy antitank weapons, and 37,795 firearms.[2] Most ominously for the Russian army, they also procured thousands of rocket-propelled grenade launchers (RPGs)—lightweight, handheld antitank rocket launchers that would play havoc with Russian armor in the close confines of Grozny. As a result, Chechnya soon became a main supplier of arms for the Bosnian Muslims. Many of Dudayev's supporters, as well as a few Russians, benefited financially from the arms trade.

The Chechen crisis continued to boil as Yeltsin shouted threats that the territorial integrity of the Russian federation was indivisible. The Chechens retorted with shrill cries for independence. Matters came to a head on 26 November 1994 when forces made up primarily of "volunteers" recruited from the Russian army failed to overthrow Dudayev in a direct assault on Grozny. An unknown number of Russian servicemen were killed in the attack and Chechens loyal to Dudayev captured twenty-one. On the twenty-ninth, after the Chechens refused to negotiate the return of the captured Russian soldiers, Yeltsin issued a forty-eight-hour deadline for all Chechen forces to surrender their weapons.

The Chechens had never been disarmed in their history, and it was preposterous to believe that they would do so on Russian orders—let alone in forty-eight hours. Dudayev contemptuously ignored the ultimatum, prompting Defense Minister Grachev to propose direct Russian military intervention. Yeltsin, who had even less regard for the Chechens than Grachev, agreed and ordered the "full force" option to commence in December 1994.

Preparation for Combat

In 1994, the Republic of Chechnya boasted a population of more than one million, of whom four hundred thousand, many of them ethnic Russians, resided in Grozny. Although most of Chechnya's population lives in the densely populated cities, the high, snow-covered Caucasus Mountains are the historical refuge and spiritual home of the Chechen people. The Russians knew that the first phase of their conquest of Chechnya must include the capture of Grozny, the capital and the industrial and economic heart of the republic, followed by the capture of the major cities and villages in the plains. Once Russian forces controlled the urban areas, they would move into the mountains to finish the job.

Preparations for war in Chechnya—at least on paper—had been going on in the Russian army for some time. In September 1994, the North Caucasus Military District held a series of war games based on the premise that Chechen resistance would be weak. In November, Grachev put Gen. Lt. Anatoly Kvashnin in charge of the planning effort. Kvashnin assumed that a stand-up fight between Russian and Chechen forces was highly unlikely. He believed that Dudayev's forces were merely bandits and Mafia types that would fall to opposition forces within Chechnya in a matter of days or weeks once the Chechens saw the Russian army on the move against them. Defense Minister Grachev agreed with this view and certified to Yeltsin that the North Caucasus Military District was "ready for combat."

In spite of Grachev's optimistic reports, several Russian generals were opposed to an invasion of Chechnya. Eleven Russian generals, including the ground forces commander, Gen. Col. V. Semenov, appealed to the State Duma that Russian forces were not prepared to attack and subdue the rebellious province. They objected on the grounds that the army had not conducted a single division-level maneuver since 1992, that the ground forces were woefully undermanned, and that military equipment and morale were in sad shape. Yeltsin ignored these protests and most of the generals involved in the protest were asked to resign.

Once the opposition had been silenced, the Russians attacked Chechnya on 1 December 1994. The air force launched the first blow, destroying the weak Chechen air force on the ground without the loss of a single Russian aircraft to Chechen air defenses. This attack was followed up by more Russian demands. The Chechens responded with proud defiance. General Dudayev, unconcerned by the destruction of his fledgling air force, convinced that the weight of history was on the side of the Chechen people, wrote: "We can see how the Soviet empire is collapsing, the Russian empire is next."[3] Dudayev sent a congratulatory letter to the Russian air force general who commanded the attack, telling him that the action would now be decided on the ground. The Russians did not take Dudayev's promise seriously. They should have.

The Approach March

In the first week of December the Russian forces concentrated at Vladikavkaz, Beslan, and Mozdok. The forces were part of the newly reorganized immediate reaction force of the North Caucasus Military District and consisted of "an airborne and motorized rifle division, sub-units of two airborne assault divisions, several infantry brigades, two motorized rifle regiments, two battalions of naval infantry as well as MVD [Ministry of Internal Affairs] troops and border guards from all over Russia."[4] With the expectation that the Chechens would capitulate once they were faced with the Russian army, the plan called for a rapid advance converging on Grozny to block the city from reinforcement. As quickly as possible the army was to transfer authority for establishing a new government to the

MVD units. On 11 December—the first anniversary of the new Russian constitution—the Russian army moved into Chechnya, invading from the north, east, and west. The next day, Federation Council Speaker Shumeyko announced that Russian forces would not fight the local population and that Grozny would not be stormed. Accordingly, and due to the large number of Russians living in Chechnya, the army's "rules of engagement" at this time were to shoot only if fired upon.

As the Russians rolled forward, Chechen resistance slowed the invaders on every route, except in the north, where Chechen forces opposing Dudayev moved in advance of the Russian column. Along the other routes, mobs of unarmed civilian protesters—mostly women and children—blocked the roads and slowed the advance. The 76th Airborne Division and the 21st Separate Airborne Brigade, for example, were halted by residents of the settlement of Verkhniye Achaluki, who lay down in the road and would not let the convoy through. In other areas, Chechen snipers fired at vehicle fuel tanks and tires, avoiding direct fire at Russian soldiers.

But passive Chechen resistance soon transformed into active fighting as Russian commanders tried to bypass roadblocks or remove people from blocking the streets. The 19th Motorized Infantry Division's convoy, advancing and encountering opposition from civilians and Chechen snipers, had several vehicles set on fire and destroyed. A convoy consisting of the 106th Airborne Division and the 56th Separate Airborne Brigade was attacked by multiple-launch rocket fire—a clear indication that the Chechens were well armed and knew how to fight—killing six Russian soldiers and wounding thirteen.

The poor state of Russian discipline and training only increased these delays. The lack of veteran soldiers and poor maintenance slowed the columns as much as the armed Chechen guerrilla attacks. All the lessons learned in the bloody convoy battles in Afghanistan seemed to have been forgotten. Russian convoy operations were so flawed that a few days into the advance, General Babichev, commander of the western group of forces, refused to move any farther into Chechnya, citing his unwillingness to shoot mothers and children. In some areas, Russian troops fraternized openly with the civilian population. Elsewhere, violent robberies and murders were committed by drunken Russian troops.

As problems with the advance mounted, Gen. Eduard Vorobyov, the first deputy commander of Russia's ground forces, was sent to Chechnya to assess the situation. He arrived at the huge army base of Mozdok, on the northwest border of Chechnya in Ingushetia, on 19 December. Mozdok was the central headquarters for the Russian army for the attack on Chechnya. Rumors flew that he was there to take command. Vorobyov reviewed the state of the army and quickly concluded that the assault on Grozny, and the entire invasion, faced disaster.[5] Reporting to Moscow that whoever had ordered the operation should be "investigated for criminal irresponsibility,"[6] Vorobyov resigned on the twenty-second rather than take command of an unpopular invasion that showed clear signs of imminent failure.

By then, few Russians held the illusion that their advance to Grozny would be merely a peaceful drive in the country. General Kvashnin, who later became chief of the Russian General Staff, expressed surprise at the organization and weaponry of the Chechen resistance, noting that "by December 21st 1994 a grouping of Dudayev's armed formations was concentrated in 40–45 strongholds with engineering equipment including roadblocks, minefields, positions for firing from tanks, infantry combat vehicles, and artillery."[7] Short hit-and-run battles by Chechens, who fought and acted like regular soldiers rather than bandits, continued to delay the advance.

Moving slowly against scattered opposition, the three columns, totaling forty thousand men, reached Grozny by the twenty-sixth and took positions along the northern approaches. The Russians were in poor shape for battle and morale was low. Instead of being welcomed as liberators, they were advancing as invaders against women and children, snipers, and roadblocks. It had taken fifteen days to travel less than 120 kilometers. Grachev and his officers at their comfortable headquarters in Mozdok were shocked at the poor showing. "We never thought that on our own territory, anyone, hiding behind women and children, would shoot their own citizens in army uniform in the back."[8] As the columns advanced toward Grozny they met increasing resistance and it became clear that the Chechens would fight for their capital. Every turn in the road became an ambush against an enemy who would fire at the column and then fade away rather than engage in open combat. By that time the initial plan to seal off Grozny was impractical. The Grozny television tower was not destroyed until the nineteenth, and telephone communications were not cut until the twenty-first. These delays threw the original timetable into the gutter.

Frustrated and facing the promise of a protracted guerrilla war, Grachev decided that a show of force might cower the Chechens into submission. Based on this false hope, he ordered a rapid assault to seize Grozny and capture Dudayev during a party in Mozdok in honor of his birthday. The Russian plan to seize Grozny called for four "strike groups" to advance on the enemy's capital simultaneously: Group Sever (north), composed of the VIII Volgograd Corps, commanded by Gen. Lev Rohklin; the division-size Group Zapad (west), commanded by Gen. Maj. V. Petruk; Group Vostok (east), commanded by General Stas'ko; and a Spetsnaz group. Their orders were to advance to the center of the city, join forces, and destroy all enemy positions.[9] General Kvashnin described the intent of the plan as follows: "The operational concept at this stage provided for the assault detachments attacking from the northern, western, and eastern salients, entering the city and in collaboration with the MVD and FCS [Federal Counterintelligence Service] special subunits, seizing the 'presidential palace,' the government, television, and radio buildings, the railroad station, and other important establishments in the city center, and blocking the northern part of the city center and the 'presidential palace' from the north."[10]

Although commanders were instructed to minimize civilian casualties, especially among the ethnic Russians in Grozny, the plan called for an artillery and air bombardment. The real battle for Grozny was about to begin.

The Chechen fighters supporting Dudayev, in marked contrast to the invaders, faced the impending struggle confidently. With ample Russian weaponry and ammunition, their spirits buoyed by folk stories of heroes who defied Russia's armies and fought against terrible odds, they were mentally and spiritually prepared to fight.[11] "One thing I can tell you," said Adi Ismailov, a determined thirty-five-year-old fighter, "whatever the cost, whatever our fate, even if we are driven into the mountains, we will not forgive them a single drop of Chechen blood."[12] Although Chechen politics are highly fractured, most Chechens rose up to oppose the Russians—not for vague political reasons, nor for Dudayev, but to defend their families and homeland from a historic oppressor.[13]

Although the Chechens lacked a formal standing army, many Chechen fighters had served in the Russian army. Enough former officers were present to form makeshift staffs, and most Chechen males were familiar with the use of small arms. Observers with previous experience in Afghanistan and Beirut were struck by Chechen discipline, noting an absence of the accidental shootings and celebratory firing that characterized most tribal militias. Charismatic leaders like former Soviet colonel Aslan Maskhadov, chief of staff of the Chechen army, and Shamil Basayev, a celebrated terrorist and guerrilla leader, provided dynamic and inspirational frontline leadership. Only six thousand Chechen fighters would contest the Russian advance on Grozny, facing an equal number of Russian combat troops attacking with tanks, artillery, and armored personnel carriers.

The struggle now clearly centered on Grozny, the administrative and spiritual center of the Chechen forces. The city was a formidable obstacle in itself, encompassing hundreds of square kilometers of sprawling urban expanse. By 25 December, Grozny was blockaded by Russian troops in all directions except the south, which had been "deliberately left clear to provide a way out" but also served as a route from which Dudayev constantly received reinforcements.[14] To defend the city, Maskhadov created three defense lines: an inner one with a radius of 1–1.5 kilometers around the presidential palace; a middle ring to a distance of up to 1 kilometer from the inner ring; and an outer ring up to 5 kilometers from the city center. Taking the measure of their opponents, the Chechens did not set up obvious antitank traps and obstacles, which they knew would be blasted away at point-blank range by tank fire. Instead, they allowed the Russian columns to penetrate deep into the city, where they could be attacked at close range by small teams.

Chechen resistance was focused in the area near the presidential palace, where Maskhadov kept his headquarters. The buildings there were strongly built, consisting of many stone and reinforced concrete structures. The Chechens prepared the lower and upper floors of the buildings for defense and created firing platforms and openings for rifles, machine guns, and antitank weapons. Almost every rooftop had a 12.7mm antiaircraft machine gun, courtesy of Grachev's 1992 deal, which included surrendering the Russian army's weapons. Prepared positions were created for direct artillery and tank fire along the main streets.

The middle defense line was based on strongholds at highway entrances, in the residential areas, and at the bridges crossing the Sunzha River. Chechen fighters also established strong points in the chemical plant, the oilfields, and at the Lenin and Sheripov oil refineries. The Chechens planned to set the chemical plant and oil refineries on fire if necessary. The outer defense line consisted of strongholds on the Grozny–Mozdok and Dolinskiy–Katayama–Tashkala freeways, and in strongholds east and south of the city.

The Assault Begins

The attack began around noon on New Year's Eve. Group Sever moved forward as scheduled with the 131st "Maikop" Motorized Rifle Brigade (MRB) and a battalion of the 81st Motorized Rifle Regiment (MRR).[15] They advanced along Mayakovskiy Street without encountering organized resistance, successfully reaching the railroad station. Another battalion of the 81st MRR headed for the presidential palace. The lead BMP (a thinly armored infantry fighting vehicle) managed to drive right up to the presidential palace in the center of Grozny without a shot being fired. Puzzled at the empty streets and deserted square in front of the presidential palace, the battalion commander stopped the column and radioed for instructions. With his lead vehicles bunched up in the square, the column stretched along the entire route of march back to its start point. Inside their vehicles, many of the Russian conscripts were sleeping, exhausted after days of hard driving and hurry-up-and-wait operations.

The eastern group, Group Zapad, advanced three or four blocks, but was quickly stopped by several salvos and fire from small arms and grenade launchers. Group Vostok, for unknown reasons, moved only a few kilometers from its "forming up" position and halted. Elite Spetsnaz units were landed by helicopter in the mountains to support the mechanized drive, but soon became lost, wandering around for three days before surrendering to the Chechen fighters. With all but one of the Russian columns blocked, Group Sever found itself in the center of Grozny without support.

As the 81st MRR battalion idled in front of the presidential palace, the Chechens made their move. Using rudimentary but effective tactics, they destroyed the lead vehicles, blocking the route, then the rear vehicles. And finally, at their leisure, they smashed the entire column. The Russian soldiers panicked. "The Russian infantry wouldn't get out of their BMPs to fight," explained a Chechen fighter, "so their tanks had no infantry support. We just stood on the balconies and dropped grenades on them as they drove by underneath."[16]

A free-for-all ensued as BMPs and tanks tried to flee the killing zone. In the pandemonium many Russians abandoned their vehicles and fled on foot. This resulted in "a crazy game of hide and seek, with Russian soldiers hiding in apartments, bunkers and even toilets, and the Chechens hunting them with swords, knives and pistols."[17] The commander of the 81st MRR was killed and more than half the regiment's men were killed or wounded. The commander of the 131st MRB was also killed. Only scattered survivors escaped.

The Chechen hunter-killer teams went on a spree of destruction, virtually unopposed. The typical Chechen team consisted of three men: an RPG gunner whose mission was to destroy armored vehicles; a light machine gunner to drive the vehicle commanders and drivers under armor, which highly restricted their visibility; and a rifleman/sniper to provide security. Teams went from vehicle to vehicle, blasting BMPs and T-72 tanks with volleys of RPGs. A Russian private named Sergeyev, a BMP gunner in the Maikop brigade, described the horror of the debacle:

On December 31, they ordered us into our BMPs, and we set off. We did not know where we were going, but the next morn-

ing we found ourselves by the railway station in Grozny . . .
then all hell broke loose. There were 260 of us there. Our
commander was killed right away. We lost a lot of officers. We
did not know what to do. Our armor was burning. We gathered some wounded and tried to take them out, but the tank
transporting them was destroyed too. I escaped and tried to
hide in the basement of a bakery, but the wall collapsed. . . . I
don't know how many Russian soldiers died in that slaughter.[18]

Group Zapad, whose mission was to back up Group Sever, failed
to move to Sever's aid, even when the sounds of gunfire clearly indicated that Sever was in serious trouble. The 131st MRB lost twenty
out of twenty-six tanks, 102 of 120 infantry fighting vehicles, and all
six Tungas self-propelled antiaircraft vehicles. Only ten men and
one officer survived.

On 1 January, two airborne battalions from the 106th and 76th
Airborne Divisions were told to break through to the railroad station to rescue the survivors of the 131st MRB and 81st MRR. By 1740
the airborne troops reached the Grozny-Tovarnaya station, engaging the guerrillas about a kilometer from the station. But, as General Kvashnin reported, "It soon became known that the units
which the airborne troops were coming to assist had already left the
region of the railroad station."[19] In fact, those units had disinte-
grated, their commanders dead and the survivors scattered ran-
domly about the city center. International television reporters arrived on the scene and captured the carnage with their cameras.
Dozens of smoldering Russian armored vehicles and bunches of
dead Russian soldiers littered the streets of central and southwest
ern Grozny. Meanwhile, in the background, the sounds of battle
continued in the northwest and east.

General Kvashnin blamed the disaster on "the lack of resolve of
some commanders and the inadequate moral and psychological
preparation of the personnel." As a result, many leaders were replaced the next day, including General Major Petruk, commander
of the ill-fated Group Zapad, for his failure to come to Group
Sever's aid.[20] Others blamed Grachev, Kvashnin, and the Mozdok officers who had ordered the ill-fated attack. One officer placed the

failure of the New Year's Eve assault squarely on the Russian high command and particularly on General Kvashnin: "Those who fought in Grozny believe that Kvashnin and Shevtsov are mostly to blame for the faulty organization of the operation. When the troops entered the city, they had to protect themselves. What these generals created in Grozny is what the troops describe as a 'meat combine.' There are mountains of wrecked equipment in Grozny."[21]

In spite of this setback, the Russians regrouped. Russian leaders realized that fighting in cities is much more than small units clearing rooms, and much more than driving tanks down broad avenues into prepared ambushes. The first few weeks of the Chechen war saw failures by virtually every arm of the Russian armed forces.[22] The initial Russian assault also proved that lightly armed, untrained troops could not succeed against a determined enemy in complex urban terrain. Roof-to-roof, house-to-house, cellar-to-cellar city fighting against a determined foe is grisly business. The Russians knew that trained, disciplined, and rehearsed combined-arms forces were needed—but the Russian army did not have any.

From 2–5 January, Generals Rohklin's and Babichev's forces were reinforced with tanks, motorized infantry, naval infantry, artillery, and Spetsnaz units. On the sixth they attacked Grozny again, this time in vengeance and with little regard for the civilian population. Lacking well-trained, cohesive, combined-arms units, the Russians resorted to sheer firepower. General Rohklin introduced a new tactic called the "carousel of fire" that consisted of having a T-72 tank move into range of a building or block controlled by the Chechens and fire all twenty 125mm rounds in its automatic loader as fast as possible. The two other tanks in the three-tank platoon would move forward in turn and do the same while the first tank reloaded. The rate of fire was staggering and would continue without interruption until the Chechens were killed or fled.[23]

The Russians abandoned all restraint and every available gun was thrown into the battle to smash Grozny, which quickly degenerated into one of "no quarter asked, none given."[24] Led by new commanders, the Russians began to take the city block by block, pounding the enemy into submission with heavy firepower. These heavy-handed tactics alienated the civilian population and prompted many Chechens to join Dudayev's fighters. The heavy bombardment by artillery and aircraft quickly reduced more than half the buildings in Grozny to rubble, forcing many of the surviving residents to either flee for safety or cower for weeks in dark, cold basements.

Recognizing the Russian firepower advantage, the Chechens used "hugging tactics" to force the Russians into close combat, a stand-up fight the Chechens were well equipped to wage. The ambush was the standard technique, often organized into three tiers in basements, on the ground floor, and on rooftops. Each group had a different task in the ambush and had to be dug out in deadly, close combat.

Although the Chechens controlled most streets and buildings, the Russian Air Force had complete control of the air. Indiscriminate bombing of suspected enemy centers of resistance became commonplace. After the air force hammered Grozny's television tower and a few important buildings from the air, it switched to attacks on civilians. Chechen forces managed to shoot down two Russian helicopters—executing their crews—but the Chechen air defense capability was rudimentary and ineffective. Based only a few minutes' flying time away in North Ossetia, Russian Su-25 fighter-bombers plastered Grozny with impunity. As a result, the battle for Grozny began to look like a medieval siege conducted with modern weapons.

"We have stood for two months against this onslaught," Aslan Maskhadov said proudly. "The world has never seen anything like this. If you compare the size of our army and theirs, you'd never believe we could do it."[25] All the while, Russian casualties mounted. The Russian supply system, already strained to the limit, proved incapable of providing ammunition, food, and clean water. The lack of supplies, particularly clean drinking water, added to the drain on Russian combat capabilities.

The Russian army eventually adapted, regrouped, and fought on—a historic characteristic of Russian armies that should not be forgotten. When Russian forces finally surrounded the center of the city, those Chechens trapped inside waged a desperate battle, refusing to give up the fight. Massive Russian firepower eventually took its toll on the surrounded Chechen defenders. At one point in

the battle of Grozny a reporter counted four thousand artillery det-
onations per hour.[26]

In the end, Russian firepower blasted the city to rubble and
forced the Chechen militia to flee to the countryside. The presidential palace was never stormed; after a relentless bombardment,
special air-delivered munitions were used that penetrated to the
basements of buildings and exploded, driving out the die-hard defenders there. The Russian army finally took control of the charred,
bombed remains of Grozny in mid-February 1995. Sporadic out-
breaks of shootings, beatings, rapes, and other crimes against the
remaining civilian population followed.[27] Yet even after the Russian
flag finally waved over the smoking rubble of the presidential
palace, the killing continued. On 21 March the Russian army
launched a major offensive to capture all the cities and towns in the
open plain south of Grozny. At the same time, Russian forces advanced throughout Chechnya and into the mountains.

By April 1995, many of Chechnya's key cities were under Russian
control. But a hatred for all things Russian, fueled by the army's un-
restricted use of firepower, united the Chechens in a frenzy of defiance. Unable to oppose the Russian juggernaut in the cities or with
conventional forces, the Chechens girded themselves to fight a long
guerrilla war. One reporter close to a Chechen fighting group put
it this way: "The Chechens are prepared to make a very, very long
war. They have time, they know that there aren't enough Russians
to control everything . . . it may not be a well-organized guerrilla
campaign, but nearly every village will oppose the Russians."[28] As a
result of the ill-conceived New Year's Eve assault and the constant
drain of casualties with no end in sight, Yeltsin fired Defense Minister Grachev and replaced him with Gen. Col. Anatoly Kulikov.

The Aftermath

In a 27 February 1995 interview, Gen. Alexander Lebed remarked
that the assault on Grozny was "launched by either dilettantes or
madmen."[29] Although the Russian army captured the broken ruins
of the city of Grozny and several other villages, it could not stop the
fighting or break the Chechens. In June 1995, after the fall of

Grozny, Shamil Basayev seized two thousand hostages in the Russian town of Budennovsk. Spetsnaz units attempted to storm the hospital that Basayev was holding and a hundred of the hostages were killed in the battle. The botched rescue effort ended in the negotiated release of Basayev and his men and a victory for the Chechen cause. The war continued.

In January 1996 the Chechens seized more hostages in neighboring Dagestan, then moved them to the village of Pervomaiskoye just outside Chechnya. Again the rebels escaped, but many of the hostages were killed in the fighting. The Chechens even launched raids on Grozny in March 1996. The Russians, using a precision-guided bomb dropped from a Russian fighter that homed in on Dudayev's cellular phone, gained a victory of sorts when they killed the Chechen leader on 21 April in a gully near the village of Gekhi-Chu. Later that same month, Chechen gunmen ambushed a Russian army convoy in the village of Khurikau in Ingushetia, a restive region bordering Chechnya, killing a Russian general and five soldiers. The violence continued.

Despite Dudayev's death, the war in Chechnya ground on and Russian morale sagged ever lower. Colonel Maskhadov planned a climactic counterstroke. On 6 August 1996, three days before Yeltsin's inauguration for a second term as president, fifteen hundred Chechen fighters infiltrated Grozny and retook key positions in the city in a matter of hours. The Russians garrisoned the city with twelve thousand troops supported with tanks and artillery. By midday every Russian unit in the city was under fire and pinned down as more Chechens moved into the city. Russian units radioed frantically for support and ammunition resupply. Relief columns, composed of tanks and BMPs and using the same flawed tactics they had more than a year earlier, tried to fight their way to the isolated Russian units but were ambushed and destroyed by Chechen hunter-killer teams. Russian helicopters and artillery pummeled the city, but air-to-ground coordination was poor. Russian bodies lay everywhere and thick black smoke from burning tanks and buildings filled the sky. It was the New Year's Eve debacle all over again.

With little fighting spirit left, the Russians, in spite of their superior numbers and firepower, fought a losing battle with the

Chechens. General Lebed, appointed by Yeltsin as Security Council chief two days after the inauguration, went to Chechnya and, faced with the collapse of the Russian army in Grozny, met with Maskhadov to broker a cease-fire. The settlement negotiated in August 1996 led to the complete withdrawal of Russian security forces from Chechnya.

Despite Russia's history of fighting in cities, lessons learned in the unspeakably tough battles of Stalingrad, Budapest, and Berlin during World War II, the Russians had few units prepared for urban combat. In fact, only their marine battalions were well trained in city fighting.[30] The haste with which the initial attack on Grozny was planned and executed, coupled with the shoddy state of the units sent in to do the fighting, the poor tactics employed, and the lack of fighting spirit, resulted in a Russian nightmare.

The casualty figures in this twenty-one-month war speak to the scale of the horrific fighting. During the fighting for Chechnya, Russian casualties were 2,805 killed in action, 10,319 wounded, and 393 missing. The Russian forces claimed to have killed 13,000 Chechen fighters, and civilian casualties numbered approximately 30,000. The Russians also lost 250 tanks and armored personnel carriers, twenty-four aircraft, and three helicopters. The Chechens lost ninety-nine tanks and armored personnel carriers, 108 artillery and mortar systems, 219 aircraft, and two helicopters.[31]

The battle for Grozny was the worst defeat at the hands of an irregular force in Russian military history. The fighting in the city clearly required the use of "infantry with armored support, a tactic clearly described in Soviet Army manuals."[32] Of the six thousand combat troops that initially went into Grozny on New Year's Eve 1994, virtually all became casualties, precipitating a national trauma that continues today. In the August 1996 siege of Grozny, the Russian army lost nearly 500 killed, 1,407 wounded, and 182 missing.[33] The once-proud Russian army, a bear that had made the world tremble since 1945, was bloodied and beaten by an army of Chechen wolves seemingly more suited to thirteenth-century clan warfare than to high-tech war on the eve of the twenty-first century.

Chechnya continues to simmer, independent in all but name, its ultimate fate uncertain. Given the fault line that now runs between Russia and its former Muslim territories, the fight for Grozny is the face of the future, a precursor to many more rounds of ethnic struggle in an increasingly fractured world.

Postscript

What are the lessons of Grozny? Some emerge clearly, such as the absolute necessity of cohesive, well-trained combined-arms teams psychologically prepared for city fighting. The obvious lesson is that hastily assembled and ill-prepared conscripts cannot take a city held by determined fanatics defending their homes. Urban combat requires quality forces—forces with the edge in organization, training, technology, and the will to prevail in close combat.

The presence of large civilian populations in cities poses daunting problems for commanders at all levels. An enemy force that seeks refuge among the civilian population bears the responsibility for civilian casualties under international law. Nevertheless, the prospect of heavy losses to civilians, especially in the CNN age, will torment military and political leaders at every step. The first and best solution is to encourage civilians to leave. If they do not, either because the defenders will not permit it or because the population is hostile, then senior leaders will have hard, difficult decisions to make.

It is possible to limit civilian casualties by restricting the use of airpower, fire support, and heavy weapons to avoid collateral damage. Restrictive rules of engagement like those used by Russian units in the advance on Grozny will also serve that end. But the inevitable consequence of such decisions will be higher friendly casualties because the enemy will have to be dug out room by room and block by block, without the advantages of combined arms. Troop losses will also be necessarily high because combat is at close range, medical evacuation is difficult at best, and the numbers of troops needed to clear a large urban area are enormous. Commanders thus will face a true Hobson's choice: accept the deaths of civilians to limit friendly casualties or accept high losses to prevent the death of innocents.

The battle for Grozny also highlighted the effectiveness of asymmetrical warfare in urban settings. Russian artillery and tanks could not employ their standoff ranges in the close confines of Grozny's streets and alleyways. Indirect fires were less effective and air strikes almost useless against the small teams of tank killers that stalked the urban landscape. Expensive precision-guided weapons proved largely irrelevant due to the absence of discrete, high-value targets whose loss might cripple the defense of the city. High-tech information warfare systems, such as radio direction finding and voice intercept units, had little impact against a force that relied, like Muhammad Farrah Aideed's Somali militiamen, on runners and landlines. In twenty-first-century urban battles, the American military's great high-tech advantages will be largely negated and its vulnerabilities, most significantly a low tolerance for casualties, will be exposed.

Perhaps the most defining image of Grozny is the sight of the burned-out armored vehicles, disfigured corpses, and rubbled buildings that surrounded the city center. City fighting is always—*always*—brutal, deadly, and unforgiving—a face-to-face form of combat that imposes the greatest imaginable strain on leaders and soldiers alike. The psychological trauma of this kind of fighting is perhaps the greatest that can face a modern army, when death waits in the next room or around the next corner, and the soldier's reward for success is another chance, just down the hall, to roll the dice one more time. If combat in cities cannot be avoided, then Western armies must face the challenge with a sense of urgency if they are to have any reasonable prospect of success.

Much can be done at the individual and small-unit level to increase the soldier's chances of survival. Lightweight body armor that can stop small-arms fire, for example, is critically needed, as are protective pads to minimize rubble trauma. Miniaturized night-vision gear with thermal as well as infrared capability, aiming devices like the LPL30 laser pointer, hands-off individual communications systems, and truly portable, bunker-busting/antitank systems are just some of the innovations that make the difference in city fighting.

At squad and platoon level, techniques for clearing rooms and buildings are sound, but the use of combined arms in urban areas at higher levels has been neglected. Few leaders today have a grasp of the fundamentals for employing tanks, engineers, infantry, and artillery inside an urban grid. The three-dimensional nature of urban combat, its insatiable demands on casualty evacuation and resupply, the extreme decentralization forced on combat units because of intervening urban structures (which block line-of-sight radio communications), and the absence of situational awareness in extremely restricted terrain, all demand a different psychological and tactical approach.

To fight and win in large cities, the experiences of the Russian army in Grozny teach us that the individual soldier must believe that he can both survive and win. Here is not the place to fight on a shoestring; enough infantry must be on hand to rotate units so that the same troops are not required to assault buildings again and again. Where feasible, direct fire from tanks and artillery, supplemented by engineer demolitions, should be used in place of direct infantry assault. Infantrymen must dismount and work ahead of and to the flanks of armored vehicles, while tank units should be broken down to provide direct support for maneuvering infantry formations. Highly trained countersniper teams will be invaluable. Staffs should plan for high expenditures of ammunition, and ensure rapid, timely casualty evacuation. Here, more than anywhere else, civil affairs and psychological operations can play key roles in assisting commanders with civilian populations. Tactical commanders must fight forward where they can see and sense the tempo of battle, and maintain the confidence and aggressiveness of assaulting infantry.

These lessons only scratch the surface of combat in cities, a unique form of warfare that demands serious study and attention by our military establishment. The U.S. Army and Marine Corps carry their own painful memories of city fighting in places like Aachen, Manila, Seoul, and Hue. As so often in the past, they will face the challenge of urban warfare again. When they do, Grozny will still have a story to tell and lessons to teach.

Notes

1. Russian defense minister Pavel Grachev, December 1994, quoted in Christopher Pancio, *Conflicts in the Caucasus, Russia's War in Chechnya* (London: Research Institute for the Study of Conflict and Terrorism, July 1995), 14.

2. John B. Donlop, *Russia Confronts Chechnya, Roots of a Separatist Conflict* (Cambridge: Cambridge University Press, 1998), 1.

3. FBIS Daily Report, "Kvashnin Describes Chechnya Operation," *Krasnya Zvezda,* 2 Mar. 1995, 3.

4. Carl van Dyke, "From Kabul to Grozny," *Journal of Slavic Military Studies* 9 (Dec. 1996), 698.

5. Carlotta Gall and Thomas de Waal, *Chechnya: Calamity in the Caucasus* (New York: New York University Press, 1998), 179.

6. Ibid., 180.

7. FBIS Daily Report, "Kvashnin," 2.

8. Grachev, cited in Gall and de Waal, *Chechnya,* 8.

9. Spetsnaz are Russian Federal Force Special Forces units.

10. FBIS Daily Report, "Kvashnin," 5.

11. Chechen leader Sheikh Mansur Ushurma led an uprising that reached from north Dagestan to the Kuban and lasted from 1785 to 1789. In 1785, Sheikh Mansur's forces destroyed an entire Russian czarist army. He was finally captured and died in prison in 1793. Additional Chechen wars of revolt against czarist rule broke out in the 1830s, 1877–88, and again in 1922. The name of the capital of Chechnya, which means "menacing" in Russian, was the result of a fort built by Russian General Yermolov, governor of Georgia and the Caucasus (1816–26), who subdued the Chechens with terror and military might.

12. Ian MacWilliam, "Russian Forces Face Long Haul," *Newsday,* 22 Jan. 1995, A17.

13. There are reported to be more than 150 Chechen clans.

14. General Pavel Grachev, "We Must Proceed from the Fact that This Was a Special Operation," *Krasnaya Zvezda,* 2 Mar. 1995, 2.

15. The Maikop Brigade gets its name from the capital of Adygheya, another autonomous republic in the foothills of the Greater Caucasus. The soldiers of Group Sever were virtual

strangers to each other as the 131st Maikop Brigade was hastily filled with new recruits; some were not even issued ammunition for fear that they might shoot friendly civilians.

16. Anatol Lieven, "The Meaning of the Chechen War," unpublished manuscript, U.S. Army War College Library, Carlisle Barracks, Pa., spring 1996, 7.

17. Gall and de Waal, *Chechnya,* 9.

18. Yuri Zarakhovich, "Just Look at What They Have Done to Us," *Time,* 16 Jan. 1995, 46.

19. FBIS Daily Report, "Kvashnin," 8.19. Ibid., 8.

20. Ibid.

21. Mariya Dementyeva: "The Lessons of the Last Phase of the Chechen Operation," *Segodnya,* 15 February, 1995.

22. Anatol Lieven, *Chechnya: Tombstone of Russian Power* (New Haven, Conn.: Yale University Press, 1998), 112.

23. Capt. Second Rank Andrey Antipov: "Not a Matter of a Decoration. If Only There Were a Motherland," *Voin for Rossiyskaya Gazeta,* 6 Sep. 1995, 3.

24. Charles Blandly, David Isby, David Markov, and Steven Zaloga, "The Chechen Conflict: A Microcosm of the Russian Army's Past, Present and Future," *Jane's Intelligence Review,* Special Report no. 1, 1994, 8.

25. Ken Fireman, "It's Not Over Yet; Chechens Say They Will Keep on Fighting," *Newsday,* 12 Feb. 1995, A15.

26. Blandly et al., "Chechen Conflict," 17.

27. Lieven, *Chechnya,* 111.

28. Lee Hockstaer, "Not All Quiet on the Chechen Front," *Washington Post,* 6 May 1995.

29. Alexander Lebed, John Kohan, Yuri Zarakhovich, "For Better, For Worse: Awaiting His Nation's Call,*" Time,* 27 Feb. 1995, 26.

30. "The first days of the fighting for control of Grozny required a buildup of the grouping. The 165th Regiment of Marines of the Pacific Fleet and an infantry battalion from each of the Northern and Baltic Fleets were sent in, and they gave an exceptionally good account of themselves" (Grachev, "We Must Proceed from the Fact that This Was a Special Operation," *Krasnaya Zveda,* 2 Mar. 1995, 14).

31. Marine Corps Intelligence Activity, "Russia's War in Chechnya: Urban Warfare Lessons Learned 1994–1996." The MCIA is a field activity of Headquarters, Marine Corps, under the direction of the Marine Corps Director of Intelligence (DIRINT), Quantico, Va.

32. Blandly et al., "Chechen Conflict," 20.

33. Gall and De Waal, *Chechnya*, 350.

In and Out of Africa: Noncombatant Evacuation Operations in Liberia

You plan for the worst case, and you go in fast, you use speed, shock, stealth, to limit the potential for a firefight, to get in and out before the bad guys have time to get organized.
—Col. Matthew Broderick, USMC

The only thing in Liberia worse than the fighting was the cease-fires. You expected people to get blown away during the long, bloody months of active fighting. That was always a given, to the tune of 150,000 dead (some whispered 300,000) over six and one-half years of civil war. Death came only too easily in Liberia. Just as in unhappy Somalia, killing sometimes became an end in itself. By August 1995, the factions du jour, led by Charles Taylor and his former ally Roosevelt Johnson, had long since put paid to madman Samuel K. Doe. Now these brutal inheritors and their armed retainers squared off to dispute control of Liberia's battered capital, Monrovia. Nobody really expected the truce to last. The optimists gave peace a chance. Pessimists stocked up on ammunition.

Words replaced bullets for a few months as Taylor and Johnson joined a self-appointed six-man ruling council. As with previous cease-fires, the half-million inhabitants of Monrovia relaxed their guard a little. Innocents, women and children, came out of their hovels. They emerged into the blasted streets and tried to restart an approximation of normal life. Markets reopened. Schools resumed classes. Maybe this time would be different.

It was not. In late March 1996, Taylor and Johnson argued

openly, splitting the ruling council. Taylor and his followers tried to arrest Johnson, who escaped to rally his own well-armed associates, representing the Krahn ethnic group. That started the fun, sparking a running gun battle near the capitol building that soon spread throughout Monrovia. Gleeful teenage gunmen and ragtag soldiers of all varieties grabbed their automatic rifles, swigged their liquor, and took to the streets. Technically, the cease-fire was still in effect. This would have been news to the dead.

So it went in Monrovia, starting on 5 April 1996. Dull explosions thumped and rumbled. Bullets flew. Shells shattered cement-block buildings; their crumpled facades slid into the twisted, narrow streets. Within hours, rubble and corpses dotted deserted boulevards. Dried blood smeared walls and stained sidewalks. The sting of spent gunpowder and drifting smoke of a hundred fires hung in the thick, humid air, a miasma of suffering hanging over the seaside city like a pall. The U.S. embassy at Mamba Point stood just west of the smoldering Greystone slum-cum-refugee camp. That put it smack in the path of the growing storm. The Americans began to feel the backlash as Liberia's long civil war reignited.

On foot and from the back of speeding pickup trucks, rampaging factional fighters intermittently sprayed the low walls surrounding the U.S. legation buildings. Machine-gun rounds stitched the roofs of various buildings. Rocket-propelled grenades (RPGs) sailed overhead, launched by youths eager to see the streaking things hit walls and explode. Some of this incoming fire seemed accidental. Some did not.

Out along the six-acre American facility's long, urban perimeter, Sgt. Luis Sanchez and four other young marine security guards held the line, assisted by a few dozen contracted Liberian sentries. Later, Sanchez tried to describe his thinking as the trouble grew worse: "We had to take things very, very seriously. For a while, things got a little scary." *Scary*—a good word, and the unarmed embassy staff felt it more than a little.

An escalation to more scary, indeed to terminally scary, seemed like a mere matter of time. The fighting grew in intensity and scale. As long as opponents were killing each other, with careless crossfire and stray rounds in abundance, the situation was bad enough. It only got worse. Lightly armed Nigerian peacekeeping troops of the Economic Community of West African States Cease-Fire Monitoring Group (ECOMOG) might have intervened. Instead, fearing certain and significant casualties, they stood aside, well out of the line of fire, hoping for somebody else to keep the peace. United Nations observers objected to the rampaging war parties and, for their trouble, watched their offices stripped by rifle-toting looters as besotted crowds roared their approval. After two days of this, foreign aid workers and diplomats knew what came next on the menu of mayhem.

The U.S. embassy staff knew, too. Sooner or later, a certain number of jokers would elect to take a few cracks at the damned Americans. Some of the hostiles wanted American blood. Some wanted American loot. Some just wanted to fire up the Yankee compound for the hell of it. With more than two hundred people crowding into the embassy grounds, including more than a hundred from other countries, Ambassador William B. Milam called for help—military reinforcements—in no uncertain terms. If a chance remained to save the people trapped at the embassy, let alone hold the facility at all, American forces needed to act soon, very soon.

Within a day or so, within a few dozen hours—in fact, whenever the heavily armed gangs felt like it—they looked certain to overrun the U.S. embassy. Both Taylor and Roosevelt backers had their reasons. When they came, these numerous bold rebels would quickly finish off the handful of marines and Liberian rent-a-cops. The sequel promised to be equally quick and ugly. Militias seemed sure to slaughter the other Americans, plus all the other foreigners unlucky enough or stupid enough to overstay their welcome in the charnel house known as Monrovia.

You might say that intemperate U.S. policies preordained these unhappy circumstances, and you would be right. But none of the beleaguered American diplomatic staff or their outgunned defenders had the stomach for that sort of esoteric debate. The key question revolved around basic survival, life or death. The Apaches were swarming at the gates. Where was the cavalry?

That was a figure of speech, of course. With an embassy going down in Africa, the American armed forces needed a fast response.

What to use? Well, there was no shooting a cruise missile or dropping a smart bomb on this one. For better or worse, the encircled Americans needed ground reinforcements, then rescue. With a stout outfit employed, Uncle Sam's finest could certainly hold the embassy. Two U.S. infantry battalions, following some initial teams of bold special operators, were about to get an unexpected trip to the worst place in the world.

The State Department station in Monrovia had been to this party twice before, in 1990–91 and again in 1992. In the first case, a small contingent of marines kept the rebels at bay while helicopters and air force transport planes flew into Liberia and extracted their endangered fellow citizens and a good number of third-country nationals, a classic noncombatant evacuation operation (NEO). The 1992 version was an air force show run through Freetown in neighboring Sierra Leone. Both of these featured "permissive" environments, a Department of Defense way of saying that the locals did not interfere. This time, the situation rated as "nonpermissive," the prevailing euphemism for landing smack in the middle of a raging civil war. This time, speed counted.

A "No-Huddle" Offense

Ideally, running an NEO in coastal Liberia neatly matched the capabilities of a navy/marine amphibious readiness group. The marines and their navy "gator" comrades routinely trained for this type of mission. The usual landing force consisted of a Marine Expedition Unit (Special Operations Capable), a MEU (SOC). Built around a marine infantry battalion with a few tanks, engineers, and other key attachments, the MEU also included a capable helicopter squadron and a service-support group with fifteen days' worth of supplies, plus a colonel and staff with adequate communications to run operations across hostile shores. Best of all, a MEU (SOC) was trained to execute NEOs, along with twenty-one other likely amphibious warfare tasks. They knew their business. Unfortunately, the nearest MEU (SOC) was floating in the Adriatic Sea, backing up U.S. troops ashore in Bosnia. Good as they were, the 22d MEU remained a week or more away by sea.

It was the perfect answer, but too late. Screwing around increased the chance that by the time American troops got there, they would find a smoking hole at Mamba Point, plus a rack of dead bodies to boot. Someone had to go immediately.

That led to the next best answer, and it came in piecemeal, hustled out of Europe. On the big maps in the Pentagon, the country of Liberia fell under the purview of U.S. European Command (USEUCOM). Long accustomed to waiting for World War III in the Fulda Gap, the operations officers at USEUCOM headquarters in Stuttgart, Germany, did, of course, realize that the Cold War was history. Quite sensibly and predictably, following the Gulf War excursion and its lingering aftermath, the USEUCOM crowd and their North Atlantic Treaty Organization (NATO) allies transferred their attentions to the bleeding wound of Bosnia. By the spring of 1996, the American 1st Armored Division was on the ground, up to its turret rings in angry Serbs, Croats, and Muslims. Bosnia was the main event. The folks in Brussels looked at violent Africa as the geographic, economic, and military subbasement of their sprawling theater. They were only too happy that they had pawned off the eastern third, horrible Somalia and its equally awful neighbors, on the U.S. Central Command.

More than four decades of staring down the Soviet bear had made USEUCOM powerful enough, even in its reduced state seven years after the Berlin Wall came down. The command controlled the U.S. Navy's Sixth Fleet, the Seventh Army, and three numbered air forces: the Third, Sixteenth, and Seventeenth. If some miscreant launched a panzer onslaught or a massive bomber raid, USEUCOM guaranteed a powerful riposte. That said, the theater's forces were (surprise!) woefully short of basic infantry. Aside from the 22d MEU sailing south as fast as its inelegant gray amphibs could churn water, and its half-dozen mechanized battalions committed to Bosnia or stripped to assist in that endeavor, USEUCOM found the cupboard pretty bare. To deal with the horror show in Monrovia, the European Command turned to the special operations forces (SOF) of Special Operations Command, Europe (SOCEUR), plus the theater's lone airborne battalion, the 3/325th Airborne Battalion Combat Team (3/325 ABCT, the Blue Falcons) in Vicenza, Italy.

Even that slim force was not all there. Working for Brig. Gen. Michael A. Canavan of SOCEUR, the Blue Falcons had one reinforced rifle company in Croatia, recovering the remains of Commerce Secretary Ron Brown and thirty-four others killed when his airplane slammed into a mountain. Another 3/325 company waited in Hungary, standing by as a quick-reaction force (QRF) if anything blew down in Bosnia. This left available the rump of the 3/325 ABCT, Lt. Col. Mike Scaparrotti commanding, with his twenty-five-man tactical command post and Company C, reinforced with additional crew-served weapons, for a total of 220 paratroopers. The Blue Falcons joined other SOCEUR elements: a small command group, a SEAL platoon, two small companies or so of Green Berets from the 1st Battalion, 10th Special Forces Group (Airborne), and a clutch of five SOF helicopters, although only four of them actually proved airworthy. It was not a large force, but it had one big virtue: It could go *now*.

Canavan organized for the Liberia mission on the fly. He learned of the Monrovia NEO on the runway on 7 April, after returning from the discouraging search in the Croatian mountains. After flying to Stuttgart for some sketchy planning at USEUCOM headquarters, the general took off again within hours, flying toward Sierra Leone in Africa. Napoleon Bonaparte once observed that "the strength of an army, like the momentum in mechanics, is estimated by the weight multiplied by the velocity." Bringing his small SOCEUR teams in one by one, but very quickly, Canavan substituted speed for numbers.

Launched south beginning on 7 April, Canavan's Joint Task Force Assured Response (JTF-AR) formed up en route. Thanks to numerous missions in Bosnia, the Blue Falcon riflemen knew their SOCEUR counterparts well. Hastily assembled, JTF-AR hit the ground in Monrovia less than forty-eight hours after being told to go. They got there in time.

Factional fighting throughout the capital escalated even as Canavan's JTF-AR readied for action. As in the 1992 iteration, an air force airlift terminal element, supplemented by SOCEUR staffers and State Department experts, set up a "safe haven" reception base in Dakar, Senegal. Another SOCEUR team established a transfer site, an intermediate staging base (ISB) at the international airport in Freetown, Sierra Leone. Evacuees would leave embattled Monrovia via SOF helo, switch to air force MC-130H Combat Talon and C-130E Hercules transports in Freetown, then head to Dakar to await final movement back to America. The SOF helos, transports, and AC-130 Spectre gunships could park at ISB Freetown. Mike Scaparrotti's Blue Falcon paratroopers assembled there, too, to stand by as an overall QRF, ready to join the fight if things really went crazy after the first waves of special operators went in. Like the rest of the JTF gathering at the ISB, the 3/325 men would launch as necessary to get in and out of the wild Liberian capital. Of course, that was the challenge, wasn't it?

SOCEUR Goes In

Getting in went quickly enough for the first element. Skimming in over the sea from ISB Freetown, the lead MH-53J Pave Low flared up over the seventy-five-foot seaside cliff and plopped down. It was about 1600 on the warm afternoon of 9 April. Somehow, the big SOF helicopter squeezed into the embassy's basketball court, its single main rotor whacking away at overhanging tree branches. Things looked bad enough. The racket of firing, wriggling tracer trails, and drifting smoke filled the eastern horizon over Monrovia, right up to the wall of the U.S. compound.

Upon landing, the JTF-AR liaison team disembarked, looking to find the ambassador and his key staff. Simultaneously, a dozen-man SEAL platoon got out, heavily armed and carrying a full load of ammunition. Three guarded the tiny landing zone (LZ), cutting away offending tree limbs and beginning to marshal a crowd of cowed civilians anxious to leave. Meanwhile, the other nine SEALs moved tactically to the embassy's eastern boundary, overlooking United Nations Drive and the burning, rowdy Greystone quarter.

The SEALs attracted heavy but ineffective fire. Their leader, Lt. Cmdr. Steve Grzeszczak, reported Liberian teens "shooting RPGs all over the place." Sweating in the heat and humidity, the SEALs skillfully took up security positions without returning fire, though Grzeszczak said the Americans stopped now and then for some "concrete belly dancing." Working with Sergeant Sanchez and his four other marine guards, the small SEAL detachment fanned out to cover by fire all the major approaches into the six-acre embassy complex.

Behind this thinnest of thin screens, the air force Pave Low helicopter took off with twenty-six evacuees, outbound on a ninety-minute run to ISB Freetown. It finally returned in darkness, at 2010. Its passengers included Canavan himself, six more SEALs, plus the lead Special Forces (SF) team. Again it left laden with departing citizens, twenty-five to be exact. Two more similar flights occurred before daybreak.

Over that long first night, the SEALs and the newly arrived SF men kept watch. By the next morning, more arriving Green Berets allowed a better division of labor. A mix of forty-three army Special Forces officers and noncoms took the northern half, around the chancery building. The thirty-four SEALs handled the south, around Milam's ambassadorial residence, which just happened to be the old British embassy compound. Outside, the Krahn and their Liberian enemies continued to fight on, with more than a few shots whizzing into and over the embassy grounds.

The fun started soon enough on 10 April, just as all knew it would. The succession of big, wallowing American SOF aircraft attracted militia attention. After the first few sorties, two successive inbound MH-53Js watched volleys of RPGs whooshing skyward. Three rockets came way too close to the first chopper; the second swerved to avoid an RPG that passed within a hundred meters. Both flights waved off. With rueful memories of the helo scourging in Mogadishu in 1993, Canavan elected to switch to night flights to minimize exposure. Though armed, armored, and rigged with every sophisticated high technology navigation device known to man, the Pave Low birds were just too big and slow to play dodge 'em with Liberian RPG rounds. Losing an SOF bird crammed with civilians would unhinge everything.

Restricted largely to night flights for several days, the evacuation process ground slowly along. Endangered U.S. citizens and selected other foreigners departed from the embassy's single-ship LZ. By 20 April, 2,126 evacuees, including more than 436 Americans, had escaped the fighting. Each inbound chopper also brought in food and water for those waiting to leave, the JTF-AR troops, and the isolated embassy staff. All of this took ninety-eight helicopter sorties, one at a time, night after night. Monrovia burned on.

By day, SEALs, paratroopers, and Green Berets watched the sniper fire, street clashes, and looting in the Mamba Point neighborhood. By night, the embassy's beefed-up guard force witnessed Liberia's capital gushing flames and tracers. Both the Johnson and Taylor people claimed that they were not targeting the U.S. embassy. But as always, like in Port-au-Prince, Mogadishu, and all the other garden spots, incidents kept occurring. Bullets and RPGs routinely peppered the compound. Liberian gang leaders shrugged it off as the fortunes of war. To the young American men getting shot at, it sure looked intentional.

On 11 April, three youths scaled the embassy wall near the ambassador's residence. A female security guard tried to stop them, but they pushed her aside and slapped away her weapon. Intent on looting, the trio did not get far. Marine security guards led by Sergeant Sanchez and a SEAL reaction team responded to the incursion. The SEALs aggressively charged the interlopers. The Liberians dropped their stolen goods, raised their hands, and ran like hell. Alarmed by the penetration, which might have been a disaster had the Liberians nabbed Ambassador Milam, Canavan ordered beefed-up SF presence in the residential segment of the U.S. compound. He also brought forward a rifle platoon from Company C, 3/325 ABCT. Well, they had waited for days to respond to just these kinds of emergencies. Now they had their chance.

Nobody died in this episode, but all hands read the implications. Too much wall, too few sentinels—the bad guys were finding the weak spots. The next hostile intruders might be more heavily armed and less easily cowed. As Sanchez said, "It made for some long nights." Even with ample numbers of night-vision goggles and hand-held thermal sights, the paratroopers and SEALs could see only a dozen yards at best into the ravaged line of white structures that marked the lip of the Greystone ghetto, just across pocked, debris-strewn United Nations Drive. Ten blocks away, a block away, right behind that collapsed wall or inside a smoking car wreck, well, who really knew? Nobody wanted to find out.

One day, a SEAL sniper watched a Liberian male calmly shoulder an RPG launcher, leveled for what looked like a shot right into the chancery building. But the SEAL held his fire; something felt wrong. Sure enough, the local militiaman looked away and commenced to raise a sandwich with his other hand. The SEAL relaxed his trigger finger. Almost every American with a firearm remembered similar, if less dramatic, confrontations. Yes, it was a game of inches, all right.

The tumult in the streets did more than pin down and endanger the people at the embassy. Diplomatic staffers reported dozens of other Americans holed up across tortured Monrovia, cut off by the continued gun battling. The JTF-AR command post and ambassador's staff kept tabs by telephone on these pockets of Americans, as well as other worried foreigners. On 11 April, two MH-53Js extracted some U.S. contractors from a building near Spriggs Payne Airfield. The next day, another two-shipper clattered north to the ECOMOG barracks on Bushrod Island, where Blue Falcon riflemen guarded the LZ as hundreds queued up for flights to safety. Both of these quick diversions went off successfully.

Several other times, preemptive extractions or even hostage rescue efforts began—only to be called off as all involved elected to wait for gaps in the chaotic violence. To be honest, with only a few rather vulnerable helicopters, about 140 SOF troops (including headquarters personnel), and a single airborne rifle company to hold the embassy compound (no guarantees there, either), sending numerous pickup teams off into the Monrovia maelstrom sounded too risky. With insufficient boots on the ground to do much else, JTF-AR stood its ground and waited.

On the morning of 15 April more 3/325 troopers were ordered in from Freetown to take charge of securing the embassy compound. The command group, led by Scaparrotti and Cmd. Sgt. Maj. Joseph Picanco, linked up with their SOF counterparts while Capt. Mike Fenzel, the C Company commander, reconned the grounds with his officers and NCOs. Fenzel, a Tom Cruise look-alike and former captain of the Johns Hopkins University football team, was no stranger to danger. A veteran of the 75th Rangers, he had been decorated for valor in the Gulf War and flew into Bosnia with the lead U.S. units. Now he calmly conducted the relief in place, his troopers fanning out to thicken the embassy defense.

Daily, everyone in Liberia, no doubt including all enemies present and potential, tracked the movements of the 22d MEU as it sailed toward West Africa. The SOCEUR men and their attached 3/325 paratroopers had secured the embassy and moved a lot of scared bodies to safety. It had all gone off well, a tribute to speed and discipline. But the JTF-AR contingent remained heavily outnumbered and strung rather thin. To add to their woes, USEUCOM had pressing business for SOCEUR back in the Balkans. Once the marines arrived, SOCEUR and the Blue Falcons would pull out and head north. Although all of the American citizens had been flown out, the president had decided that the flag would continue to fly over the U.S. embassy in Monrovia, and that would take guns.

Battle Handoff

The MEU arrived in town on 20 April, its gray amphibs and escort warships standing visibly offshore. Prominent among the four vessels, the destroyer USS *Connelly* (DD-979) showed off its pair of 5-inch (127mm) naval guns—one fore, one aft. Not surprisingly, both the Johnson and Taylor factions suddenly decided "jaw, jaw" to be better than "war, war," and declared a cease-fire. Of course, as the marines soon learned, the only thing in Liberia worse than the fighting was the cease-fires.

Colonel Melvin W. Forbush brought the 22d MEU into Monrovia ready to fight. Like all marine expeditionary units, this one brought its own secure base in the form of three big amphibious warships, each carrying key pieces of Forbush's command. From the naval flagship USS *Guam* (LPH-9, landing platform helicopter, a small aircraft carrier), the MEU's aviation element staged as necessary to bring ashore marines, evacuate personnel if needed, and resupply the U.S. community, providing a guaranteed air bridge from sea to beach. About a third of the MEU's ground punch, the 2d Battalion, 2d Marine Regiment, also lived aboard the *Guam*. With its well deck full of landing craft and its wide, single-spot helo deck, USS *Portland* (LSD-37, landing ship dock) carried another third of 2/2 marines. Finally, with a two-aircraft helipad, a small hangar, and another big well deck, USS *Trenton* (LPD-14, landing platform dock) held the bulk of Marine Service Support Group 22, the MEU's logisticians, complete with thirty days' worth of beans, bullets, fuel, and spare parts. The *Trenton* also bore some of the MEU's attachments: SEALs, the Force Recon platoon, and amtracs. The destroyer *Connelly*, bristling with firepower, rounded out the flotilla.

But something was missing: namely, one of the newer ships in the navy's amphibious stable, the USS *Tortuga* (LSD-46, an updated version of the *Portland*). The *Tortuga* had experienced what sailors call a "casualty" in its boiler system and put in to Haifa, Israel, for repairs. As a result, Company E and about a third of the 2/2 Marines marked time on the eastern coast of the Mediterranean, out of the fight. Forbush and the rest of the 22d MEU pressed on without them.

At dawn on 20 April, rattling old CH-46E Sea Knights—the familiar, ancient "Frogs"—began landing one by one at the embassy's little basketball-court LZ. Along with Colonel Forbush's MEU headquarters team and a battalion-level team led by 2/2's commander, Lt. Col. W. E. Gaskin, the Frogs deposited Capt. Eric Mellinger and Company F, with about a hundred more marines from Weapons Company, including the 81mm mortar platoon and the heavy weapons platoon. The handoff with the SOCEUR contingent commenced right away. Forbush and his men had the ball by 1400 local.

Mellinger's rifle squads fanned out to replace army paratroopers around the embassy perimeter. The mortarmen took over the evacuation control center from the army Special Forces teams, assisted by navy medical corpsmen and others from the service support group. Finally, huge CH-53E Super Sea Stallions, sea service kin to the special operators' MH-53J Pave Lows, delivered six souped-up black dune buggies to the heavy weapons platoon. Coming in by sling ropes, dangling beneath the roaring heavy-lifters, the half-dozen Fast Attack Vehicles (FAVs) gave the marines mobile firepower. Two of them had M2HB .50-caliber machine guns, two more sported TOW missile tubes, and the other pair held MK-19 automatic grenade launchers. If the bad guys came over the walls now, the marine FAVs guaranteed an immediate wall of fire to stop them dead in all senses of the word. By sunset, some 276 marines and attached sailors secured the U.S. compound at Mamba Point. In the face of this significant increase of American capability in town, the factional cease-fire held. Nobody wanted to try these guys yet.

The MEU's arrival fundamentally altered the situation in Monrovia. With three times the riflemen of Company C, 3/325 ABCT, a quartet of CH-53Es, and a dozen elderly CH-46F helicopters, plus AH-1W Sea Cobra attack birds, tanks, armored cars, artillery, mortars, and the like, the 22d MEU had the weaponry to blow apart any Johnson or Taylor gangsters itching for a fight. Moreover, those amphibious ships allowed Mel Forbush the luxury of a safe staging base. Instead of an embattled islet in a sea of pain, the American embassy compound became an advanced position, a fulcrum to pivot even more combat strength into Monrovia if needed. Ambassador Milam and his staff relaxed and all talk of bugging out vanished. Instead, as Captain Mellinger noted, "The embassy staff seemed overjoyed that the marines are now here. There's a tradition with Marines being at embassies." The old cliché held up. The marines had landed, and the situation was well in hand.

So it seemed as the 2/2 Marines settled in. The Liberian militias opened formal negotiations, and U.S. Assistant Secretary of State for African Affairs George Moose announced plans to come to Monrovia to serve as an intermediary beginning on 30 April.

And why not? After all, here was one black African state with unquestionable links to the United States. Tracing back to its founding in 1847 by emancipated American blacks, Liberia consciously modeled itself on America. This explained a capital that commemorated James Monroe, the widespread use of common American surnames, the prevalence of Christianity, the American-style flag, and the legal and political traditions borrowed from the United States. When Pres. Abraham Lincoln occasionally talked about sending freed slaves "back to Africa," he meant to Liberia, the first free African republic.

Until the 1980 ascendancy of that lunatic Samuel K. Doe, the country avoided the usual pattern of dictatorial rule that plagued its fellow West African countries. But beginning with Charles Taylor's uprising at Christmastime in 1989, Liberia made up for all those quiet years with an orgy of blood and fire. The sputtering civil war pitted the tiny American-descended elite against indigenous ethnic groups. Longtime American political and economic interests, personified by the diplomats and businessmen who pursued them, naturally ended up in the crossfire. Hence, the NEOs of 1990–91, 1992, and now 1996 all formed part of a pattern. In stages, unwillingly, America was abandoning its ugly, violence-ridden West African offspring.

The MEU's presence stopped that trend, at least for the moment. Things in Monrovia settled back to as near calm as they ever did. Militiamen slung their arms; some even left them behind. The looting subsided. The shooting dwindled. Smoke cleared. And, once again, the city's inhabitants came out of hiding. Life picked up where it had left off two weeks before. Many desperately prayed that this time it would last. These prayers, too, were destined to go unheeded.

Easing tensions slowed the NEO to a trickle. Many U.S. expatriates decided to stay the course. The same families whose distant homes once conjured images of hostage dramas and bedeviled Ambassador Milam's staff now told the U.S. mission they intended to stay put. Only forty-nine more Americans departed, along with 260 more third-country nationals. The rest stood pat.

With the streets calm and the NEO mostly over, a lesser breed of fighting men might have let down their guard. But the marines knew better—especially the 0311s, those who held the specialty "riflemen." Nobody in Liberia relaxed, not yet. Bitter experiences in Beirut in 1982–84, Monrovia in 1990–91, Mogadishu in 1991 and again in 1992–94, and Cap Haitien in 1994 conjured up powerful memories. These Third World cities all featured ambushers and horrors by the gross. The opponents came when you slacked off. So the marines learned not to slack off—ever. You were not safe until you got back to Camp Lejeune.

Local patrols, battle drills, and emplacement improvement went on day and night. To keep the edge, Companies F and G swapped out on 27 April, the beginning of a weekly rotation between guarding the legation buildings and standing by as a sea-launched QRF. "Things are mostly quiet now," mused Colonel Forbush on 26 April. "But you never know for sure with this type of thing." Out in the dark, dank back alleys of Monrovia, somebody did know. On 30 April, they acted.

Nobody ever figured out exactly for whom the eight toughs worked, although the Krahns eventually took the blame. As usual, they wore no uniforms. Who did anymore? They might have been Johnson fighters. They might have been freelancers. It mattered little.

Shortly after 0830 local time on another warm tropical morning, the Liberians decided to shoot up a sandbagged perimeter post not far from the ambassador's home. Their first fusillade nicked an American sniper, Cpl. Jason S. Farrand, tumbling him out of his perch overlooking the marines' Post Number 7, on the north face of the ambassador's residence section. Marines on and around Post Number 7 chambered rounds and watched for further Liberian action. The enemy formed out on Seckou Toure Street. Somebody evidently wanted a showdown this morning.

Meanwhile, comrades brought sniper Farrand to a nearby medical site, where navy corpsmen debated about whether to send him out to the clean, well-staffed wards onboard the USS *Guam*. But Farrand wanted none of that. Before the amazed aidmen could restrain him, the corporal grabbed his bloody shirt and hustled out of the aid station. "I knew something was going to happen," he said, "and I couldn't live with myself if something happened to my team and I wasn't there."

Something was happening, all right. Corporal William A. Gardner and his fire team at rooftop Post Number 7 watched Liberians moving in a wedge, directly toward the marine position. The hostiles "flagged" their rifles, marine-speak for saying that they pointed the muzzles at the Americans. It was like a scene from a Western movie, the Earps strolling down the street toward the Clantons, drawn and ready, high noon come three hours early in Monrovia.

The Liberian point man calmly raised his shoulder arm and squeezed the trigger. *Crack!* The round missed Gardner and a marine squad automatic weapon (SAW) gunner by six inches, smacking into the plywood that held up his post's sandbagged roof. The marines all ducked, but that did it.

"Open up! Fire! Fire!" commanded Gardner, shooting his own M16A2.

Marine rifles barked their slow cadence of aimed fire, the same lethal rhythm that has spoken on a hundred battlefields, always with the same final result. The fire team's SAW gunner ripped off two hundred 5.56mm bullets. The big 7.62mm M60 machine gun, the ugly old "pig" of Vietnam fame, spat a belt of quarter-inch long slugs into the street. Every fifth round was a tracer. These hit the pavement and spun upward at crazy angles, red sparks arcing into the hot morning sky. Then the marines paused, eyes wide.

Four Liberians lay broken on the hot pavement, finished. Two more stumbled and moaned, winged and out of the fight. Leaving their dead comrades, the other two enemies fled.

One of the "dead" showed plenty of life, however. He rolled prone and took up a firing stance, clipping off another round at Post Number 7. Gardner ordered the M60 gunner to fire again. The pig hammered through another belt, flipping the Liberian over with multiple impacts. That ended it. The marines watched wraith-like figures emerge from the shadows, strip the bodies of weapons and shoes, and then scuttle away. Later, dogs crept out to feed on the corpses. None of it was pretty.

An hour later, more Liberians appeared at the next marine post, Number 8. Marine sentries counted forty or fifty of them across United Nations Drive, apparently conducting a house-to-house battle with some rival group. Tracers and ricochets cascaded upward and outward. Once again, for no known reason, the hostiles wheeled on the marines. They fired first, as high and outside as ever.

The marine fire team responded instantly, their methodical mix of M16A2 and SAW shots knocking down more Liberian gunmen. The enemy scattered, panicked. But a few kept blazing away, undeterred.

Enter Cpl. Jason Farrand, patched up and back in the fight. Restored to his high window, the marine sniper finished this dozen-man foray decisively. With a long, black Barrett M82A1A .50-caliber sniper rifle in hand, the master marksman coolly took aim. *Blam!* A

Liberian automatic rifleman pitched over, his leg ripped from its socket by the merciless .50-caliber slug. *Blam!* Another hostile fell back, his chest blown apart. Those two big bullets ended it, both for that incursion and the day.

Farrand found it hard to recall exactly what happened that day. "It's like I wasn't even there," he recounted much later. "My body was doing what the Corps taught me. After the last shot, I was amazed at what had happened."

As inhuman and awful as this sounds—and make no mistake, it is—the Barrett sniper rifle is certainly kin to the F-117A Nighthawk stealth jet. Those technophiles advocating fleets of slick, racing-black stealth fighters plinking two-thousand-pound bombs right down the old chimney had better remember what happens at the receiving end. It is all the same: evisceration, sucking chest wounds, torn-off limbs, death in Technicolor—screams and all. And unlike the soaring stealth jockey, a poor marine sniper like Jason Farrand has to live with the faces. That is because, day or night, a sniper *sees* his quarry. Thanks to a superb ten-power Unertl scope, a marine shooter does not miss a bit of it. It is very personal.

The marine encounters coincided with U.S. envoy Moose's entry into Monrovia. Evidently, nobody wanted to talk yet. Although the troublemakers studiously avoided the fields of fire around the U.S. embassy, they worked out on each other. The fighting kept Moose contained in the chancery building on Mamba Point. But with most Americans gone and the embassy well defended, the assistant secretary could afford to let the gun battles sputter out on their own. By nightfall, they did.

The marines' good shooting created an important political effect. Local parties decided to quit challenging the Americans. In fact, both the Johnson and Taylor factions eventually came to the peace table in Accra, Ghana. Roosevelt Johnson of the Krahns rode there in one of the 22d MEU's helicopters. Although there were other sparks of mayhem, Monrovia's latest round of civil war ended with a few bangs and a whimper. As Colonel Forbush expressed it, "We're finally getting back to as close to 'Monrovia-normal' as we can."

As tensions ebbed in Monrovia, a relief navy/marine team, cobbled together from forces just returned from their own six-month

MEU float, boarded USS *Ponce* (LPD-15, sister ship of the *Trenton*) and headed toward a late June 1996 changeover date. Meanwhile, with the appropriate chunk of the 22d MEU embarked, the USS *Trenton* broke station and headed off toward the Mediterranean Sea on 9 May, to join the rehabilitated USS *Tortuga* and various Spanish units for Exercise Matador 96. It was like the sideshow performer with all those plates spinning: *Guam* and *Portland* and their marines cruising off Monrovia, the embassy security team ashore, an NEO transit site in Freetown, the safe haven in Dakar, and now, some damned NATO exercise. You had to feel for Mel Forbush and his people. Somewhere, some staff geniuses thought Monrovia was not enough to keep the 22d MEU busy. So while the USS *Ponce* prepared to sail, the plates on the sticks spun on.

A plate fell off on 19 May 1996, when the Central African Republic imploded. The local excuse for an army mutinied over pay complaints, and the disgruntled soldiery turned on the helpless populace. When Ambassador Mosina H. Jordan called for help, staff experts in USEUCOM looked at the giant map boards, saw that Forbush and the 22d MEU were in the neighborhood, relatively speaking, and ordered the navy/marine team to get cracking and send succor to Bangui.

Well, this was interesting. The marines and their gator brothers were "nearby" in the same way that New Orleans, Louisiana, is nearby San Francisco, California (two thousand miles away). But with everyone else tied down in and around Bosnia, and nobody closer, the European Command brain trust had few options. Marines knew NEOs. Let them pull off another.

Led by Maj. Norman J. Robison and a few staff types, a marine rifle platoon moved by helicopter to Freetown, Liberia. There, the thirty-five-man detachment boarded a marine KC-130R Hercules transport and flew east toward Bangui. Simultaneously, a small navy/marine detachment moved to Yaoundé, Cameroon, to establish a safe haven. When Robison and his men landed on 21 May, frightened U.S. citizens left on the same Hercules that brought in the reinforcements. Over the next several days, some five hundred Americans and other endangered foreigners left for Cameroon courtesy of Marine transport planes.

Norm Robison and his platoon of marine grunts found that rebel soldiers often took shelter at the base of the embassy walls in Bangui. Opposing units refused to take the bait, fearful of provoking the well-armed marines. "Everyone knows there is no pointing weapons towards the embassy. There has been no problem with that here," Robison stated. A second marine platoon arrived soon after, serving to underscore America's intentions to protect its diplomatic staff and their installation. Although odd rounds continued to fly, some into the embassy grounds, none of the insurgents or their government foes chose to test the patience of the marine 0311s protecting the U.S. legation.

Moving with customary alacrity into a former African colony, an aggressive French paratrooper task force also deployed into Bangui. Patrolling in strength and more than willing to shoot recalcitrants, the tough French paras soon restored order throughout the city. French diplomats compelled both sides to the bargaining table. Taken aback by the will of France's *Force Action Rapide* and a few U.S. Marines, the military rebellion in the Central African Republic slowly subsided.

By 20 June 1996, the USS *Portland* and its marines departed what the navy had begun to call "Mamba Station," the waters off Monrovia. The USS *Guam* followed a week later with Col. Melvin Forbush and the remnant of the 22d MEU embarked. Following its rapid crossing of the Atlantic Ocean, the helo carrier USS *Ponce* began slowly turning ovals off Mamba Point, and Special-Purpose Marine Air-Ground Task Force (SPMAGTF) Liberia took over. For a few weeks, it, too, spread marines and sailors across Senegal, Sierra Leone, Liberia, Cameroon, and the Central African Republic, finishing up business at the NEO sites and embassies. This pickup team came home in August 1996, mission accomplished. Thanks to the 22d MEU's work, especially in convincing locals to stay well back from Uncle Sam's real estate, the follow-on force enjoyed a relatively uneventful time of it.

The marines in the 22d MEU had every right to feel satisfied with their efforts. Few other U.S. fighting forces could have carried out the simultaneous Monrovia/Bangui NEO and embassy security missions. As Col. Mel Forbush told an interviewer, "Doing two [NEOs] doesn't even come up in training. Who would ever think of something like this happening at the same time?" That was a question for America's enemies to ponder.

The Marines' Monrovia firefight and "911" call to Bangui somewhat overshadowed the only notable flaw in the MEU concept. Most of the time there are only three or four amphibious groups at sea. Since it is impossible to anticipate all of the crises about to blow, they often find themselves out of place, in the wrong sea or sometimes even the wrong ocean. Tied to the torpid pace of amphibious shipping, a MEU may be a week away from the objective area.

Enter America's other rapid-deployment fighting forces. The great thing about being a superpower is that there is plenty of useful capability. Special operators and airborne riflemen, though lightly armed, can move out very quickly. If speed matters, they become the force of choice, at least until the nearest batch of marines and gators appear out past the horizon. Had SOCEUR not gone in so swiftly, there might not have been an embassy left for the marines to secure.

This helps explain the present fascination with all things "joint," as each service and each type of unit brings different strengths and weaknesses to the fray. Not surprisingly, each component sees and fights its own kinds of battles, part of the overall team effort, but very much unique in every sense. This certainly held true in West Africa in 1996.

Special Forces, paratroopers, and the navy/marine amphibious team each saw a different view of Liberia in 1996. For SOCEUR's special operators, Operation Assured Response looked like a preemptive hostage rescue, an NEO on a massive scale. Saving Americans took priority.

For the Blue Falcon paratroopers from Vicenza, their QRF mission changed into an embassy security task. The SOF had cleared the decks of endangered civilians, with some airborne help. As the Special Forces troops finished up their NEO, it fell to a company or so of 3/325 ABCT soldiers to hold the line, to keep Ambassador Milam in business, and to preserve the American footprint in Monrovia. They prepared the way for the 22d MEU.

Finally, the marines came in batting cleanup, not their usual spot in the order, but one for which they proved well suited in this case. The marines used their wide range of air, sea, and land combat power to secure the U.S. legation, finish off the NEO, and reply to unexpected trouble in the Central African Republic. In the process, they confronted Liberian factional fighters and thereby encouraged them to choose the peace of the brave over the peace of the grave.

For those looking for boldness, for mission-type orders in action, for nonlinear maneuver on a transcontinental scale, the Liberian operation bears consideration. Here stands true operational art: mixing a few elite air, sea, and ground components with the will to act. Joint Task Force Assured Response saved thousands of lives, preserved the embassy in America's oldest African ally, and held the fort in the Central African Republic to boot. Despite a lot of shooting, not a single American died. And those involved made it look a lot easier than it was. But don't be fooled. In Liberia, after all, ceasefires never come easy.

About the Editor

COLONEL RICHARD D. HOOKER JR., USA, is currently assigned to the Army Staff. A former enlisted paratrooper, he is a West Point graduate and commanded a parachute infantry battalion in the 82d Airborne Division. He saw combat in Grenada and Somalia, and served in Rwanda, Bosnia, Kosovo, and the Sinai. A former White House Fellow, Colonel Hooker served on the National Security Council Staff, as Aide de Camp to the Secretary of the Army and as Special Assistant to the Chairman of the Joint Chiefs of Staff. He taught at West Point and holds M.A. and Ph.D. degrees in International Relations from the University of Virginia and an M.S. in National Security Studies from the National War College. Colonel Hooker has published twenty-six articles on national security topics and is the editor and coauthor of *Maneuver Warfare: An Anthology*.

About the Authors

COLONEL JOHN F. ANTAL, USA (Retired), served as the III Corps G3 Operations Officer and commanded the 16th Cavalry Regiment at Fort Knox, Kentucky, before retiring in 2003. A former Special Assistant to the Chairman of the Joint Chiefs of Staff, Colonel Antal holds a Master of Military Arts and Sciences degree, commanded a tank battalion in the 2d Infantry Division, and is a graduate of the Army War College. A West Point graduate and prolific writer, he served for many years in Korea and is the author of numerous articles and books, including *Armor Attacks*, *Infantry Combat Team*, and *Proud Legions*, a novel about a future Korean War.

COLONEL DANIEL P. BOLGER, USA, is the Chief of Staff of the 2d Infantry Division in Korea and commanded its 2d Brigade. Colonel Bolger earned a Ph.D. in History from the University of Chicago, taught at West Point, and commanded an infantry battalion in the 101st Airborne Division (Air Assault). An Army War College graduate, he has also served as a Special Assistant to the Army Chief of Staff. Colonel Bolger is the author of *Americans at War*, *The Battle for Hunger Hill*, *Savage Peace*, *Death Ground*, and *Feast of Bones*, a novel about the Russian experience in Afghanistan. He was selected for promotion to Brigadier General in 2003.

MAJOR MICHAEL R. FENZEL, USA, is second-in-command of a parachute infantry battalion in the 173d Airborne Brigade and fought in Iraq in 2003. He graduated from the Naval College of Command and Staff and recently served as a White House Fellow assigned to the National Security Council Staff. A graduate of The Johns Hopkins University and the Naval College of Command and Staff, he holds a graduate degree in National Security Studies from the John F. Kennedy School of Government at Harvard. Major Fenzel is a former platoon leader in the 75th Ranger Regiment and was decorated for valor in the Gulf War while serving with the 24th Infantry Division. He later commanded two parachute infantry companies, served with the first U.S. combat unit to enter Bosnia, and led the embassy security force during the evacuation of U.S. citizens from Liberia in 1996.

COLONEL H. R. MCMASTER, USA, is chief of the Commander's Advisory Group at U.S. Central Command and will soon assume command of the 3d Armored Cavalry Regiment. Previously, he commanded the 1st Squadron, 4th Cavalry in the 1st Infantry Division. A USMA graduate, he commanded Eagle Troop, 2d Armored Cavalry Regiment in the 1991 Gulf War, where he was decorated for valor. Colonel McMaster holds a Ph.D. in History from the University of North Carolina at Chapel Hill, taught at West Point, and completed a War College National Security Fellowship at the Hoover Institution, Stanford University. He is the author of many articles and the bestselling *Dereliction of Duty: Lyndon Johnson, Robert McNamara, the Joint Chiefs of Staff and the Lies that Led to Vietnam.*

LIEUTENANT COLONEL ROBERT R. LEONHARD, USA, retired in 2002 and is an author and consultant to the Department of Defense. An infantry officer, he served as Professor of Military Science at West Virginia University. A graduate of the Command and General Staff College and the School for Advanced Military Studies at Fort Leavenworth, he served in combat during the Gulf War with the 3d Armored Division and later with the 1st Cavalry Division. Lieutenant Colonel Leonhard is the author of numerous articles on military subjects and several books, including *Art of Maneuver* and *Principles of War for the Information Age.*

COLONEL PETER R. MANSOOR, USA, was commissioned from West Point and commands a tank brigade in the 1st Armored Division, which fought in Iraq. An Army War College graduate, he previously served as the Division G3 and Division Cavalry Squadron commander in the 4th Infantry Division. A veteran of the 11th Armored Cavalry Regiment, he served on the Joint Staff, taught history at West Point, and holds a Ph.D. from The Ohio State University. Colonel Mansoor is the author of *The GI Offensive in Europe: The Triumph of American Infantry Divisions 1941–1945.*

COLONEL JAMES R. MCDONOUGH, USA, (Retired), commanded an airborne brigade and a mechanized infantry battalion, and served as Commander, Joint Task Force Bravo, during the Rwandan Refugee Crisis. A former War College Fellow and Director of the School of Advanced Military Studies at Fort Leavenworth, he is a West Point graduate of the Class of 1969 and later taught at the Academy, after earning a graduate degree in Political Science from the Massachusetts Institute of Technology. Colonel McDonough was wounded and decorated for valor in Vietnam, and is the author of *The Defense of Hill 78* and *Limits of Glory*, a novel about Waterloo. *Platoon Leader*, an account of his experiences as a young officer in Vietnam, is considered the classic study of small-unit combat in that conflict and is still in print. After retiring from the Army, he served in the White House with the Executive Office of the President. He is currently the head of the Office of Drug Control Policy for the State of Florida.

COLONEL DANA J. H. PITTARD, USA, is a 1981 West Point graduate and commands a tank brigade in the 1st Infantry Division after previously commanding a tank battalion in the 2d Infantry Division. An Army War College Fellow at Harvard and graduate of the School of Advanced Military Studies, he holds a Master of Military Arts and Sciences degree. Colonel Pittard served as Military Aide to the President, and commanded a troop in the 11th Armored Cavalry Squadron and tank companies in the Berlin Brigade and 1st Armored Division, where he was decorated for valor in the Gulf War.

LIEUTENANT COLONEL JOHN K. TIEN, USA, will assume command of a tank battalion in the 1st Infantry Division in 2004 after service as Deputy Commander and Regimental Executive Officer in the 11th Armored Cavalry Regiment. An armor officer and graduate of the Army Command and General Staff College, he is a Rhodes Scholar and former White House Fellow. Lieutenant Colonel Tien was First Captain at the U.S. Military Academy, and earned a graduate degree in Politics, Philosophy, and Economics at the University of Oxford. He served in combat with the 1st Armored Division in the Gulf War, and commanded two tank companies in the 1st Cavalry Division.

355